RONALD ROLHEISER

The Holy Longing

The Search for a
Christian Spirituality

DOUBLEDAY

New York   London   Toronto   Sydney   Auckland

PUBLISHED BY DOUBLEDAY
a division of Random House, Inc.
1540 Broadway, New York, New York 10036

Doubleday, and the portrayal of an anchor with a dolphin are trademarks of
Doubleday, a division of Random House, Inc.

Library of Congress Cataloging-in-Publication Data

Rolheiser, Ronald.
The holy longing: the search for a Christian spirituality /
Ronald Rolheiser. — 1st ed. in the U.S.A.
    p.   cm.
1. Spirituality—Catholic Church. I. Title.
BX2350.65.R65   1999
248—dc21   98-46109
                CIP

ISBN 0-385-49418-1
Copyright © 1999 by Ronald Rolheiser
All Rights Reserved
First published in the United Kingdom in November 1998
Printed in the United States of America
August 1999
First Edition in the United States of America

10 9 8 7

For Henri Nouwen, 1932–1996, our generation's Kierkegaard. By sharing his own struggles, he mentored us all, helping us to pray while not knowing how to pray, to rest while feeling restless, to be at peace while tempted, to feel safe while still anxious, to be surrounded by a cloud of light while still in darkness, and to love while still in doubt.

Contents

Preface

This is a book for you if you are struggling spiritually.

Teilhard de Chardin, who was both scientist and mystic, used to ask why so many sincere, good persons did not believe in God. His answer was sympathetic, not judgmental. He felt that they must not have heard of God in the correct way. His religious writings are an attempt to make faith in God more palatable for those who, for whatever reason, are struggling with it.

This book, in its own modest way, tries to do something similar, namely, to be a guide-book of sorts for those who have not been exposed to Christian spirituality in a way that makes it palatable.

And many good, sincere persons struggle today with their faith and with their churches. Lots of things contribute to this: the pluralism of an age which is rich in everything, except clarity; the individualism of a culture which makes family and community life difficult at every level; an anti-church sentiment within both popular culture and the intellectual world; an ever-growing antagonism between those who see religion in terms of private prayer and piety and those who see it as the quest for justice; and a seeming tiredness right within the Christian churches themselves. It is not an easy time to be a Christian, especially if you are also trying to pass your faith on to your own children.

Hopefully this book will, in the midst of all this, help make the things of faith a little clearer, a little more acceptable, and a whole lot more hopeful. The hope too is that a bit of God's sympathy and consolation might seep through and touch you as you struggle with faith and church in a very complex time.

A comment is in order too regarding the language and the style of the book: I have tried to use as simple a language as possible. First, because the spiritual writer who most influenced our generation, Henri Nouwen, used to re-write his books over and over again to try to make them simpler. That, it seems to me, is the ideal. Jesus spoke the common language of the people of his time and was understood at family tables and not just in academic classrooms. Second, I belong to a religious congregation, the Missionary Oblates of Mary Immaculate, whose charisma it is to serve the poor. The poor have many faces and there are many kinds of poverty. To serve the poor also means to try to make the word of God and God's consolation available in a language that is accessible to everyone and not just to those who have the privilege of advanced academic training. Hence, as much as I know and value the critical importance of the more technical language of the academy of professional theologians, this book will try, as did the founder of the Oblates, to speak the dialect, the patois, of the poor. Hopefully it will find itself at home in the living rooms, workplace, and conversations of ordinary people for it is meant, like Jesus' table-fellowship, to be religious talk, done over wine, beer, and food.

Finally, a few grateful acknowledgments: I want to thank the Oblates of Mary Immaculate for freeing me up from other ministry in order that I might write this book. Most especially, I want to thank Zygmunt Musielski OMI and the community (clerics and lay) living or working at the Oblate house on Indian Trail in Toronto for giving me the ideal space out of which to write this book—a family, a roof, an altar, a well-laden table, a fireplace, two skylights, and some exceptionally pleasant and faith-filled fellowship. I thank too my family, that amorphous clan of siblings and nieces and nephews who rejoice in my small virtues, smile at my many faults, and put up with seasons of neglect when ministry calls me away from them.

To Eric Major, formerly of Hodder and Stoughton in London and now at Doubleday in New York, a huge thanks for suggesting this book and to Annabel Robson, my capable editor, a big thank you for all the work she continues to do for me.

—Ron Rolheiser
Toronto, Canada
June 1, 1998

PART ONE

The Situation

Tell a wise person, or else keep silent,
Because the massman will mock it right away.
I praise what is truly alive,
what longs to be burned to death.

In the calm water of the love-nights,
where you were begotten, where you have begotten,
a strange feeling comes over you
when you see the silent candle burning.

Now you are no longer caught
in the obsession with darkness,
and a desire for higher love-making
sweeps you upward.

Distance does not make you falter,
now, arriving in magic, flying,
and finally, insane for the light,
you are the butterfly and you are gone.

And so long as you haven't experienced
this: to die and so to grow,
you are only a troubled guest
on the dark earth.
    —JOHANN WOLFGANG VON GOETHE, "The Holy Longing"[1]

1

What Is Spirituality?

"We are fired into life with a madness that comes from the gods and which would have us believe that we can have a great love, perpetuate our own seed, and contemplate the divine."[2]

Desire, Our Fundamental Dis-Ease

It is no easy task to walk this earth and find peace. Inside of us, it would seem, something is at odds with the very rhythm of things and we are forever restless, dissatisfied, frustrated, and aching. We are so overcharged with desire that it is hard to come to simple rest. Desire is always stronger than satisfaction.

Put more simply, there is within us a fundamental dis-ease, an unquenchable fire that renders us incapable, in this life, of ever coming to full peace. This desire lies at the center of our lives, in the marrow of our bones, and in the deep recesses of the soul. We are not easeful human beings who occasionally get restless, serene persons who once in a while are obsessed by desire. The reverse is true. We are driven persons, forever obsessed, congenitally dis-eased, living lives, as Thoreau once suggested, of quiet desperation, only occasionally experiencing peace. Desire is the straw that stirs the drink.

At the heart of all great literature, poetry, art, philosophy, psychology, and religion lies the naming and analyzing of this desire. Thus, the diary of Anne Frank haunts us, as do the journals of Thérèse of Lisieux and Etty Hillesum. Desire intrigues us, stirs the soul. We love stories about desire—tales of love, sex, wanderlust, haunting nostalgia, boundless ambition, and tragic loss. Many of the great secular thinkers of our time have made this fire, this force that so haunts us, the centerpiece of their thinking.

Sigmund Freud, for example, talks about a fire without a focus that burns at the center of our lives and pushes us out in a relentless and unquenchable pursuit of pleasure. For Freud, everyone is hopelessly overcharged for life. Karl Jung talks about deep, unalterable, archetypal energies which structure our very souls and imperialistically demand our every attention. Energy, Jung warns, is not friendly. Every time we are too restless to sleep at night we understand something of what he is saying. Doris Lessing speaks of a certain voltage within us, a thousand volts of energy for love, sex, hatred, art, politics. James Hillman speaks of a blue fire within us and of being so haunted and obsessed by daimons from beyond that neither nature nor nurture, but daimons, restless demanding spirits from beyond, are really the determinative factors in our behavior. Both women's and men's groups are constantly speaking of a certain wild energy that we need to access and understand more fully. Thus, women's groups talk about the importance of running with wolves and men's groups speak of wild men's journeys and of having fire in the belly. New Age gurus chart the movement of the planets and ask us to get ourselves under the correct planets or we will have no peace.

Whatever the expression, everyone is ultimately talking about the same thing—an unquenchable fire, a restlessness, a longing, a disquiet, a hunger, a loneliness, a gnawing nostalgia, a wildness that cannot be tamed, a congenital all-embracing ache that lies at the center of human experience and is the ultimate force that drives everything else. This dis-ease is universal. Desire gives no exemptions.

It does however admit of different moods and faces. Sometimes it hits us as pain—dissatisfaction, frustration, and aching.

At other times its grip is not felt as painful at all, but as a deep energy, as something beautiful, as an inexorable pull, more important than anything else inside us, toward love, beauty, creativity, and a future beyond our limited present. Desire can show itself as aching pain or delicious hope.

Spirituality is, ultimately, about what we do with that desire. What we do with our longings, both in terms of handling the pain and the hope they bring us, that is our spirituality. Thus, when Plato says that we are on fire because our souls come from beyond and that beyond is, through the longing and hope that its fire creates in us, trying to draw us back toward itself, he is laying out the broad outlines for a spirituality. Likewise for Augustine, when he says: "You have made us for yourself, Lord, and our hearts are restless until they rest in you."[3] Spirituality is about what we do with our unrest. All of this, however, needs further explanation.

What Is Spirituality?

Few words are as misunderstood in the contemporary English language as is the word spirituality. First of all, in English, this is a relatively new word, at least in terms of signifying what it does today. That is not the case in the French language, where the word has a much longer and richer history. However, in English, it is only within the last thirty years that this word has become part of our common vocabulary. Thus, for example, if one went to an English library and checked the titles of books, he or she would find that, save for a few exceptions, the word spirituality appears in those titles only published within the last three decades. It is also only within these years that the concept of spirituality has become popular, both within church circles and within the population at large. Today bookstores, church and secular alike, literally teem with books on spirituality.

A generation ago, with some notable exceptions, this was not the case. The secular world then had virtually no interest in the area. This was also true for most of the churches. What we would call spirituality today existed, but it had a very different face. In the Christian churches it existed mainly within certain charismatic prayer groups and theologies of the Pentecostal churches, the social action of some Protestant churches, and the devotional life within the Roman Catholic Church. In secular bookstores you would have found very little in the area of spirituality, other than a section on the Bible and some books on the merits of positive thinking. In ecclesial bookstores, since this was considered an area distinct from strict, academic theology, you would have found very little as well, save for Roman Catholic bookstores where you would have found devotional literature and some books labeled ascetical theology.[4]

Today there are books on spirituality everywhere. However, despite the virtual explosion of literature in the area, in the Western world today, especially in the secular world, there are still some major misunderstandings about the concept. Chief among these is the idea that spirituality is, somehow, exotic, esoteric, and not something that issues forth from the bread and butter of ordinary life. Thus, for many people, the term spirituality conjures up images of something paranormal, mystical, churchy, holy, pious, otherworldly, New Age, something on the fringes and something optional. Rarely is spirituality understood as referring to something vital and nonnegotiable lying at the heart of our lives.

This is a tragic misunderstanding. Spirituality is not something on the fringes, an option for those with a particular bent. None of us has a choice. Everyone has to have a spirituality and everyone does have one, either a life-giving one or a destructive one. No one has the luxury of choosing here because all of us are precisely fired into life with a certain madness that comes from the gods and we have to do something with that. We do not wake up in this world calm and serene, having the luxury of choosing to act or not act. We wake up crying, on fire with desire, with madness. What we do with that madness is our spirituality.

Hence, spirituality is not about serenely picking or rationally choosing certain spiritual activities like going to church, praying or meditating, reading spiritual books, or setting off on some explicit spiritual quest. It is far more basic than that. Long before we do anything explicitly religious at all, we have to do something about the fire that burns within us. What we do with that fire, how we channel it, is our spirituality. Thus, we all have a spirituality whether we want one or not, whether we are religious or not. Spirituality is more about whether or not we can sleep at night than about whether or not we go to church. It is about being integrated or falling apart, about being within community or being lonely, about being in harmony with Mother Earth or being alienated from her. Irrespective of whether or not we let ourselves be consciously shaped by any explicit religious idea, we act in ways that leave us either healthy or unhealthy, loving or bitter. What shapes our actions is our spirituality.

And what shapes our actions is basically what shapes our desire. Desire makes us act and when we act what we do will either lead to a greater integration or disintegration within our personalities, minds, and bodies—and to the strengthening or deterioration of our relationship to God, others, and the cosmic world. The habits and disciplines[5] we use to shape our desire form the basis for a spirituality, regardless of whether these have an explicit religious dimension to them or even whether they are consciously expressed at all.

Spirituality concerns what we do with desire. It takes its root in the eros inside of us and it is all about how we shape and discipline that eros. John of the Cross, the great Spanish mystic, begins his famous treatment of the soul's journey with the words: "One dark night, fired by love's urgent longings."[6] For him, it is urgent longings, eros, that are the starting point of the spiritual life and, in his view, spirituality, essentially defined, is how we handle that eros.

Thus, to offer a striking example of how spirituality is about how one handles his or her eros, let us compare the lives of three famous women: Mother Teresa, Janis Joplin, and Princess Diana.

We begin with Mother Teresa. Few of us would, I suspect,

consider Mother Teresa an erotic woman. We think of her rather as a spiritual woman. Yet she was a very erotic woman, though not necessarily in the narrow Freudian sense of that word. She was erotic because she was a dynamo of energy. She may have looked frail and meek, but just ask anyone who ever stood in her way whether that impression is correct. She was a human bulldozer, an erotically driven woman. She was, however, a very disciplined woman, dedicated to God and the poor. Everyone considered her a saint. Why?

A saint is someone who can, precisely, channel powerful eros in a creative, life-giving way. Søren Kierkegaard once defined a saint as someone who *can will the one thing.* Nobody disputes that Mother Teresa did just that, willed the one thing—God and the poor. She had a powerful energy, but it was a very disciplined one. Her fiery eros was poured out for God and the poor. That—total dedication of everything to God and poor—was her signature, her spirituality. It made her what she was.

Looking at Janis Joplin, the rock star who died from an overdose of life at age twenty-seven, few would consider her a very spiritual woman. Yet she was one. People think of her as the opposite of Mother Teresa, erotic, but not spiritual. Yet Janis Joplin was not so different from Mother Teresa, at least not in raw makeup and character. She was also an exceptional woman, a person of fiery eros, a great lover, a person with a rare energy. Unlike Mother Teresa, however, Janis Joplin could not will the one thing. She willed many things. Her great energy went out in all directions and eventually created an excess and a tiredness that led to an early death. But those activities—a total giving over to creativity, performance, drugs, booze, sex, coupled with the neglect of normal rest—were her spirituality. This was her signature. It was how she channeled her eros. In her case, as is tragically often the case in gifted artists, the end result, at least in this life, was not a healthy integration but a dissipation. She, at a point, simply lost the things that normally glue a human person together and broke apart under too much pressure.

Looking at Joplin's life, and at our own lives, there is an interesting reflection to be made on Kierkegaard's definition of being a saint—*someone who can will the one thing.* Most of us are quite like Mother Teresa in that we want to will God and the poor. We do will them. The problem is we will everything else as well. Thus, we want to be a saint, but we also want to feel every sensation experienced by sinners; we want to be innocent and pure, but we also want to be experienced and taste all of life; we want to serve the poor and have a simple lifestyle, but we also want all the comforts of the rich; we want to have the depth afforded by solitude, but we also do not want to miss anything; we want to pray, but we also want to watch television, read, talk to friends, and go out. Small wonder life is often a trying enterprise and we are often tired and pathologically overextended.

Medieval philosophy had a dictum that said: Every choice is a renunciation. Indeed. Every choice is a thousand renunciations. To choose one thing is to turn one's back on many others. To marry one person is to not marry all the others, to have a baby means to give up certain other things; and to pray may mean to miss watching television or visiting with friends. This makes choosing hard. No wonder we struggle so much with commitment. It is not that we do not want certain things, it is just that we know that if we choose them we close off so many other things. It is not easy to be a saint, to will the one thing, to have the discipline of a Mother Teresa. The danger is that we end up more like Janis Joplin; good-hearted, highly energized, driven to try to drink in all of life, but in danger of falling apart and dying from lack of rest.

Janis Joplin is perhaps an extreme example. Most of us do not die from lack of rest at age twenty-seven. Most of us, I suspect, are a bit more like Princess Diana—half-Mother Teresa, half Janis Joplin.

Princess Diana is worth a reflection here, not just because her death stopped the world in a way that, up to now, few others ever have, but because is interesting to note that in looking at her, unlike either Mother Teresa or Janis Joplin, people do spontaneously put together the two elements of erotic and spiritual. Princess Diana is held up as a person who is both, erotic and spiritual. That is rare, given how spirituality is commonly understood. Usually we see a person as one or the other, but not as both, erotic and spiritual. Moreover, she deserves that designation for she does reflect, fairly clearly, both of these dimensions.

The erotic in her was obvious, though not always in the way many people first understand that term. On the surface, the judgment is easy: She was the most photographed woman in the world, widely admired for her physical beauty, who spent millions of dollars on clothing, and was clearly no celibate nun. She had affairs, vacationed with playboys on yachts in the Mediterranean, ate in the best restaurants in London, Paris and New York, and had a lifestyle that hardly fits the mode of the classic saint. But that itself is superficial, not necessarily indicative of a person with a powerful eros. Many people do those things and are quite ordinary. More important was her energy. Here she was a Mother Teresa and Janis Joplin, someone who obviously had a great fire, that madness the Greeks spoke of, within her. Partly this was an intangible thing, but partly it could be seen in her every move, in her every decision, and in every line of her face. It is not for nothing, nor simply because of her physical beauty or because of her causes, that people were drawn so powerfully toward her. Her energy, more so than her beauty or her causes, is what made her exceptional.

The spiritual part of her was also obvious, long before she became friends with Mother Teresa and took up seriously trying to help the poor. It was this dimension that her brother spoke of when he eulogized her—her causes, yes, but more important, something else inside of her, a depth, a moral ambiguity that never allowed her to be comfortable simply with being a jet-setter, a habitual effacement, an anxious desire to please, a person under a discipline, albeit often a conscriptive one, a person who, however imperfectly, willed what Kierkegaard spoke of, God and the poor, even if she still willed many other things too.

Spirituality is about how we channel our eros. In Princess Diana's attempts to do this, we see something most of us can identify with, a tremendous complexity, a painful struggle for choice and commitment, and an oh-so-human combination of sins and virtues. Spirituality is what we do with the spirit that is within us. So, for Princess Diana, her spirituality was both the commitment to the poor and the Mediterranean vacations . . . and all the pain and questions in between. Hers, as we can see, was a mixed road. She went neither fully the route of Mother Teresa nor of Janis Joplin. She chose some things that left her more integrated in body and soul and others which tore at her body and soul. Such is spirituality. It is about integration and disintegration, about making the choices that Princess Diana had to make and living with what that does to us.

Thus, we can define spirituality this way: Spirituality is about what we do with the fire inside of us, about how we channel our eros. And how we do channel it, the disciplines and habits we choose to live by, will either lead to a greater integration or disintegration within our bodies, minds, and souls, and to a greater integration or disintegration in the way we are related to God, others, and the cosmic world. We see this lived out one way in Mother Teresa, another in Janis Joplin, and still in a different manner in Princess Diana.

We can see from all of this that spirituality is about what we do with our spirits, our souls. And can we see too from all of this that a healthy spirit or a healthy soul must do dual jobs: It has to give us energy and fire, so that we do not lose our vitality, and all sense of the beauty and joy of living. Thus, the opposite of a spiritual person is not a person who rejects the idea of God and lives as a pagan. The opposite of being spiritual is to have no energy, is to have lost all zest for living—lying on a couch, watching football or sit-coms, taking beer intravenously! Its other task, and a very vital one it is, is to keep us glued together, integrated, so that we do not fall apart and die. Under this aspect, the opposite of a spiritual person would be someone who has lost his or her identity, namely, the person who at a certain point does not know who he or she is anymore. A healthy soul keeps us both energized and glued together.

However, to understand this more deeply, we need to look more closely at the soul, both at how it is a principle of fire and also, at the same time, the glue that binds our persons together.

The Two Functions of the Soul

What is a soul?[7] It would be interesting to record impressions of what comes to mind spontaneously when one hears the word soul. For many of us, I suspect, the word, to the extent that it conjures up anything at all, produces an image, a very vague one, of some white, semi-invisible, spiritual tissue paper that floats somewhere deep inside of us and which takes on stains when we sin and that will separate from the body at the moment of death and go off to be judged by God. Whatever the inadequacy of that picture, it is not without merit. We are after all trying to conceive of something inconceivable and we need to form some picture of it.

What is wrong with that conception, though, is that it separates the soul too much from the core of our persons, from our self-conscious identity. Our soul is not something that we have, it is more something we are. It is the very life-pulse within us, that which makes us alive. Thus, we speak of someone as dying precisely when the soul leaves the body. That is accurate. The soul is the life principle within a human person, as indeed it is the life-pulse within anything that is living. As such it has two functions:

First of all, it is the principle of energy. Life is energy. There is only one body that does not have any energy or tension within it, a dead one. The soul is what gives life. Inside it, lies the fire, the eros, the energy that drives us. Thus we are alive as long as there is a soul in our bodies and we die the second it leaves the body.

It is interesting that sometimes when we use the word soul,

and think we are using it metaphorically, we are actually using it in a strangely accurate way. Thus, for example, we speak of "soul music." What gives music a soul? This can be understood by examining its opposite. Imagine the music that you so often hear in airports, supermarkets, and elevators. It is simple filler, soulless. It does nothing to you. It does not stir your chromosomes. Certain other music does and that is why we, precisely, call it soul music. It is full of energy, eros, and all the things that eros carries—desire, disquiet, nostalgia, lust, appetite, and hope. Eros is soul and soul gives energy.

But the soul does more than merely give energy. It is also the adhesive that holds us together, the principle of integration and individuation within us. The soul not only makes us alive, it also makes us a one. At the physical level this is easy to see. Our bodies, considered biologically, are simply an aggregate of chemicals. However, as long as we are alive, have a soul within us, all of these chemicals work together to form a single organism, a body, within which all the separate chemicals and all the processes they produce work together to make a oneness, a single thing which is greater than the simple combination of all its parts. We call this a body and every body depends for its existence upon a soul. Thus, when we see somebody die, we see precisely that from the second of death onward we no longer have a body. In fact, we no longer even call it a body, but a corpse. At the second of death, all the chemicals begin to go their own way. Death and decomposition are precisely this. Chemicals which used to work together for a oneness and were, indeed, a oneness, now go their separate ways. For a time, after death, they still give the appearance of the body, but only because they are still lying contiguous to each other. That, soon enough, changes. Once the soul has left, the body too is no longer a body. Chemicals, going each in their own way, do not make life.

What is true biochemically, is also true psychologically. Here too the soul is the principle of oneness. In the heart and in the mind, the soul is also what keeps us together. Hence, when we use the expression, "to lose one's soul," we are not necessarily talking of eternal damnation. To lose one's soul is to become, in contemporary jargon, unglued. To lose one's soul is to fall apart. Hence, when I feel my inner world hopelessly crumpling, when I do not know who I am anymore, and when I am trying to rush off in all directions at the same time but do not know where I am going, then I am losing my soul. This, as much as the question of eternity, is what Jesus meant when he asked: "What does it profit a person to gain the whole world and suffer the loss of his or her own soul?"

A healthy soul, therefore, must do two things for us. First, it must put some fire in our veins, keep us energized, vibrant, living with zest, and full of hope as we sense that life is, ultimately, beautiful and worth living. Whenever this breaks down in us, something is wrong with our souls. When cynicism, despair, bitterness, or depression paralyze our energy, part of the soul is hurting. Second, a healthy soul has to keep us fixed together. It has to continually give us a sense of who we are, where we came from, where we are going, and what sense there is in all of this. When we stand looking at ourselves, confusedly, in a mirror and ask ourselves what sense, if any, there is to our lives, it is this other part of the soul, our principle of integration, that is limping.

In a manner of speaking, the soul has a principle of chaos and a principle of order within it and its health depends upon giving each its due. Too much order and you die of suffocation; too much chaos and you die of dissipation. Every healthy spirituality, therefore, will have to worship at two shrines: the shrines of the God of chaos and the God of order. One God will keep us energized, the other will keep us joined together. These two functions of the soul are always in a creative tension. That is why we experience such intense struggles sometimes inside of ourselves. Energy and integration, passion and chastity, fire and water, are forever fighting each other, each having its own legitimate concerns for our health. Small wonder that living is not a simple task.

This has immense practical implications for our lives. What is healthy for our souls and what is unhealthy for them? Thus, for example, is it healthy to see violence or sex on television or in the movies? Is this or that particular experience healthy or unhealthy for me right now? Given this background, we see that the question of what makes our souls healthy or unhealthy is very complex because, on any given day, we might need more integration rather than energy, or vice versa. To offer just one simple example: If I am feeling dissipated, unsure of who I am and what my life means, I am probably better off reading Jane Austen than Robert Waller, watching *Sense and Sensibility* rather than *The Bridges of Madison County,* and spending some time in solitude rather than socializing. Conversely, though, if I feel dead inside and cannot find any enthusiasm for living, I might want to reverse the menu. Some things help give us fire and certain things help us more patiently carry life's tensions. Both have their place in the spiritual life.

It is for this reason, that the elements of fire and water have always been so central in religious symbolism. Fire symbolizes energy, eros, passion. Water symbolizes a cooling down, a holding in containment, a womb of safety. Mythically, spirituality is often seen as an interplay between these elements, fire and water. Small wonder. In mythology the soul is forever in a forge, heated and shaped by fire and then cooled off by water.

Along these same lines, it is utterly fascinating to study, in various cultures, the different legends concerning the origins of the soul and all that is involved in its getting into our bodies.

In Japanese culture there is the idea a baby has come into the human community from very far away. Its soul is strange to this world and, therefore, it is of critical importance that, initially, the child be kept close, that the mother or primary care-giver must not ever leave the baby alone. This strange creature must be made to feel welcome. There is something, a fire, inside of this child that comes from elsewhere. Among the Norwegians there is a beautiful legend that, before a soul is put into the body, that soul is kissed by God and, during all of its life on earth, the soul retains a dark, but powerful, memory of that kiss and relates everything to it. And then there is the Jewish legend that says that just before God puts a soul into the body that soul is asked to forget its preternatural life. Hence, just as the soul enters the body, one of God's angels presses the baby's mouth shut, as a gesture that, during its earthly life, it is to be silent about its divine origins. The little crevice below each person's nose is the imprint of the angel's forefinger, sealing your lips—and that is why, when you are trying to remember something, during your ponderings, your own forefinger spontaneously rises and rests in that crevice.[8]

Beautiful legends truly honor the soul. They also intimate, as we have been suggesting, that there is a fire in the soul that comes from beyond and what the soul does in this life is very much driven by that fire.

One last thing, an important one, and this concerns the soul's omnipresence in all of nature. The ancients and the medievals believed that it is not just human beings that have a soul and a spirituality. In their view, every living thing, plant, insect, or animal, has one as well. They were right. Moreover, today, given our understanding of physics, we know that even the tiniest particles of the universe, with their positive and negative charges, have something akin to desire and thus too have their own kind of soul. It is important to realize this, not for romantic or mythical reasons, but because we are all of one piece with the rest of nature. To properly understand ourselves, and what spirituality means for us, we need to set ourselves into the widest possible context, the entire cosmic world.

Pierre Teilhard de Chardin*, who was both a scientist and a

---

* Pierre Teilhard de Chardin was a scientist, philosopher, theologian, and poet, who lived from 1882–1955. A world-renowned paleontologist, he was also a Jesuit priest. He spent most of his years doing paleontological research in China, writing a number of books in both the areas of science and religion. In terms of science, his most famous work is entitled, *The Phenomenon of Man* (New York: Harper and Row, 1955). Theologically, his major work is entitled, *The Divine Milieu* (New York: Harper and Row, 1960). Few persons, certainly within our theologian, once defined the human person as evolution become conscious of itself. That is insightful for we, as human beings, are not separate from nature, but merely that part of nature that can think, feel, and act self-consciously. Nature is all one piece, a certain continuum; some of it is self-conscious, some merely conscious, and some has only a very dark, analogous consciousness. But all of it, including ourselves, as humans, is driven by soul, spirit, desire, eros, yearning. Nature too is fired by a madness that comes from the gods. The difference is that, prior to the level of human self-consciousness and freedom, the force that drives nature is a dark, seemingly sightless, unconscious, sometimes brutal, relentless pressure. Nothing is ever really quiet, even at the most basic level of nature.

Oxygen unites with hydrogen and this combination is in turn driven outward to unite with still other elements and so on and on. All things in nature, just like all human beings, are fundamentally dis-eased and are driven outward. An illustration here:

A friend of mine relates how, after buying a house, he decided to get rid of an old bamboo plant in his driveway. He cut the plant down, took an ax to its roots, and, after destroying as much of it as he could, he poured bluestone, a plant poison, on what remained. Finally, he filled the hole where the plant had been with several feet of gravel that he tamped tightly and paved over with cement.

Two years later, the cement heaved as the bamboo plant began to slowly break through the pavement. Its life principle, that blind pressure to grow, was not thwarted by axes, poison, and cement.

We see this same incredible, seemingly sightless, spirit in all things. In everything, from the atom to the human person, there is the blind power to unite with other things and to grow. Nothing can stop this. If you put a two-inch band of solid steel around a growing watermelon it will, as it grows, burst the steel.

---

century, have brought together so unique and rich a combination of science, mysticism, and Christian faith.

Everything is driven outward. Rocks, plants, insects, and animals are just as erotic, and as relentlessly driven, as are human beings. There is, at some level, a stunning similarity between a bamboo plant pushing blindly upward through the pavement, a baby feeding, a young adolescent restlessly driven by hormones, the tangible restlessness of a singles' bar, and Mother Teresa kneeling consciously in prayer before her God. Desire is working in each case, sometimes blindly and sometimes consciously. St. Paul would say that, in each instance, the Holy Spirit is trying to pray through something or somebody. The law of gravity and the pull of emotional obsession is not so different.

Teilhard de Chardin once said that God speaks to every element in the language it can understand. Thus, God lures hydrogen through its attraction to oxygen. God draws everything else, including each of us, in the same way. There is, in the end, one force, one spirit, that works in all of the universe. The chemicals in our hands and those in our brains were forged in the same furnace that forged the stars. The same spirit that drives oxygen to unite with hydrogen makes a baby cry when it is hungry, sends the adolescent out in hormonal restlessness, and calls Mother Teresa to a church to pray. There is a discontent, another word for soul and spirit, in all things and what those things, or persons, do with that discontent is their spirituality.

We are part of a universe, that part that has become conscious of itself, wherein everything yearns for something beyond just itself. We have in us spirit, soul, and what we do with that soul is our spirituality.[9] At a very basic level, long before anything explicitly religious need be mentioned, it is true to say that if we do things which keep us energized and integrated, on fire and yet glued together, we have a healthy spirituality. Conversely, if our yearning drives us into actions which harden our insides or cause us to fall apart and die then we have an unhealthy spirituality. Spirituality is about what we do with that incurable desire, the madness that comes from the gods, within us.

Everyone has to have a spirituality. While this is clear as a fact, it is not so clearly understood, or accepted, today in Western culture. For all kinds of reasons, we struggle with the spiritual, and whether we have a Christian background or not, we all tend to struggle particularly with the ecclesial dimension of spirituality. It is to that, our struggles to both theoretically and existentially understand this, that we now turn.

The Current Struggle
with Christian Spirituality

What is madness
but nobility of soul
at odds with circumstance.

The day is on fire
and I know the purity of pure despair.
—THEODORE ROETHKE, "In a Dark Time"[1]

At Odds with Circumstance

In his autobiographical novel, *My First Loves,* Czechoslovakian novelist Ivan Klima struggles with some painful questions. He is a young man, full of sexual passion, moving among young men and women his own age who are less hesitant than he is. Klima is reticent, celibate, and not sure why. Certainly it is not for any religious reasons. So he wonders: Is it because I respect others more than my peers and am less willing to be irresponsible? Is it because I carry some high, quasi-religious, moral solitude that I'm rightly hesitant to compromise? Or, am I just uptight, timid, and lacking in nerve? Am I virtuous or sterile? He is not sure:

> Suppose I spent my whole life just waiting, waiting for the moment when at last I saw that starry face? It would turn its glance on me and say: "You've been incapable of accepting life, dear friend, so

you'd better come with me!" Or, on the other hand, it might say: "You've done well because you knew how to bear your solitude at a great height, because you were able to do without consolation in order not to do without hope!" What would it really say? At that moment I could not tell.[2]

His question is, ultimately, a spiritual one. It is also a difficult one. It is not easy to know the right disciplines by which to creatively channel our most powerful and intimate energies so the result is happiness and delight in life. No matter what we do, some questions will always haunt us: Am I being too hard or too easy on myself? Am I unhappy because I am missing out on life or am I unhappy because I'm selfish? Am I too timid and uptight or should I be more disciplined? What is real growth and what is simply my ego making its demands? Where do I find that fine line between discipline and enjoyment? Why do I always feel so guilty? What do I do when I have betrayed a trust?

These are perennial questions, ultimately about spirituality, which every generation has to answer for itself. However, they pose themselves quite differently from generation to generation.

In the past these questions usually posed themselves in an explicitly religious context. Thus, questions of meaning and morality were generally answered within a framework that included God, religion, and church. Past societies were more overtly religious than we. They simply had less trouble believing in God and in connecting basic human desire to the quest for God and to the obedience that God demands. In some ways, that gave them a religious advantage over us, but they had their own, serious, religious problems. They believed in God easily, but then struggled with superstition, slavery, sexism, unhealthy notions of fate and predestination, excessive fears of eternal punishment, and legalism. They also, at different times, burned witches, waged religious wars, slaughtered innocent people while thinking themselves on a crusade for Christ, forbade scientists to look through telescopes, and, further back still, sacrificed humans, mainly children, on altars. Every generation has struggled spiritually. There has been no golden age.

Neither is our time that golden age, spiritually. While we have gained some moral and religious ground in comparison to some of the aberrations of the past, our generation should not too harshly judge that past. Hindsight is an exact science. Nobody is above his or her age. Besides, we are not as free from the things previous generations struggled with as we would like ourselves to believe. Superstition, slavery, sexism, fatalism, legalism, religious and ideological wars, and child sacrifice are still among us. Their face is simply more subtle.[3]

Beyond that, we have our own struggles with spirituality. What are the spiritual demons of our own time? What is particularly peculiar to our religious, moral, and spiritual struggle? Where is it that we most struggle to channel creatively our erotic and spiritual energies?

While demons are always legion, three should be named as especially coloring the contemporary struggle for healthy spirituality.

What demons torment us? The struggles in spirituality that are more unique to our age might be named as follows: Naivete about the nature of spiritual energy, pathological busyness, distraction, and restlessness, and a critical problem with balance, leading to a bevy of divorces.

1. Naivete About the Nature of Spiritual Energy

All energy is imperialistic, especially erotic and creative energy. Energy is not friendly, it wants all of us, it can beat us up like the playground bully. Karl Jung once said this explicitly, but premodern cultures lived their whole lives in the face of that truth. They treated energy with a holy reverence. They had their reasons.[4]

The first of these was a religious one. The Bible tells us that "God is a jealous God!" More is contained in that statement than we spontaneously imagine. Energy is not just difficult to access, it is just as difficult to contain once it enters. Many is the obsessed lover, possessed artist, or unbalanced religious fanatic who gives testimony to that. It is hard to be on fire with love, creativity, or religiosity, but it is just as hard to contain that fire once it hits.

Former cultures, whatever their faults, understood the imperialistic nature of energy, especially of spiritual, erotic energy. For the most part, they feared energy, particularly sexual and religious energy. That fear expressed itself in all the various buffers they put up to protect themselves against its brute force. Energy, they felt, needed some mediation, like high-voltage power lines need transformers to cut down the voltage. Hence, they had a lot of taboos, fears, timidities, rituals, and prohibitions, especially sexual and religious ones. As well, it was generally advised and often forbidden to ask certain questions. Too much free thinking was considered dangerous, certain books were put on an index and pronounced condemned, and Galileo was forbidden to look through a telescope. The very desire of the human mind to think and to ask questions was feared.

We can judge all of this harshly, but not all of it was unhealthy. The premoderns understood, however flawed that understanding, not just what the Bible means when it says that we have a jealous God, but also what it means when it says: "No one can see God and live!" What this meant for them is that energy, especially creative energy which contains the sexual, must have some mediation, some filters, and some taboos surrounding it or it will destroy us. On its own, it is too raw, too demanding, too powerful. We need help not just in accessing it, but equally as much in containing it. Knowing this, they tried to do two things with energy, especially spiritual, sexual energy.

First, they would always try to understand that energy as coming from God and as ultimately directed back toward God. Hence, they surrounded religious and sexual energy, desire, with very high symbols. Where we use biological and psychological symbols, they used theological ones; for example, where we look at desire and speak of being horny or being obsessed, they spoke of "eternal longings" and "hunger for the bread of life." Desire was always understood against an infinite horizon. In this type of framework, very high symbolic hedges, we can understand why St. Augustine would sum up his whole life in one line: "You have made us for yourself, Lord, and our hearts are restless until they rest in you."

Second, to try to contain the imperialistic nature of spiritual and erotic energy, they placed around desire a lot of taboos, prohibitions, and strict laws. At its most basic level, long before any taboos and prohibitions were ever named and codified, the idea here was simply that, as a human being, you were meant to genuflect before a God, that is, to bow beneath and put your will beneath the holiness and will of God. Through genuflection, physical and intellectual, they felt, one properly respected energy. Of course, things did not stay at this unnamed level. Every kind of prescription, law, taboo, and restriction was eventually laid down and imposed. In the minds of those who formulated and enforced those restrictions, there was the idea that these taboos, by mediating sacred energy, in the end, protected people from themselves.

The premodern world understood that spirituality is about how we channel our eros and, for them, the path needed to channel it correctly was the path that directed that desire toward God, the path of genuflection. That path also often became the path of fear and the path of control through external taboos, prohibitions, and laws.

This had a mixed result, not all of it bad. On the one hand, they lived with a lot more fear, superstition, restriction, and timidity than we do. On the other hand, they had both a social stability and a psychological substantiality that we, for the most part, can only envy. Put more simply, we can look at how they handled their spiritual and erotic energies and consider them legalistic and uptight, but their families and communities held together better than do our own and they were less restless and slept more peacefully than we do because all those high symbols and restrictions, whatever their dysfunctions, taught them that they were immortal beings, created in God's image, whose every action, however private, was important. They did not have to give themselves their own meaning. Because of this, a real irony perhaps, they suffered less from both depression and inflation than we do.

Today, whatever our sophistication, we are naive about the nature of energy. Unlike Jung, we consider it friendly, as something we need not fear and as something we can manage all on our own, without the help of a God or of external rules and taboos. In fact, we tend to disdain any external force, religious or secular, that would in any way censor or restrict an absolute freedom to let energy flow through us. Obedience and genuflection are not very popular. We want to manage energy all on our own.

Partly this is a good and necessary step in human maturation and partly it is its opposite. The rejection of any external censor of our actions can be a sign of growing up and it can also be a sign of infantile grandiosity, the child in the high chair, demanding that the world revolve around him or her. In either case, we pay a price for demanding to manage all on our own, mostly in our incapacity to find that fine line between depression and inflation. What this means is that, all on our own, outside of the classical social and ecclesial taboos, we invariably fluctuate between being out of touch with the deep source of energy, depression, and not being able to properly contain it, inflation. We are rarely on an even keel, always either too low or too high, feeling dead inside or unable to act or sleep properly because we are too hyper and restless.

Mostly though, in this struggle, it is depression, feeling dead inside, that is the big problem. Generally speaking, today, in the Western world, most of us adults live in a certain chronic depression. How is this to be understood?

Depression, here, does not mean clinical depression but something wider. What is depression? It can be helpful sometimes to understand things by their opposites and that is the case here. Spontaneously we tend to think of the opposite of depression as being the life of the party, optimistic, upbeat, fun-loving. But that is not necessarily, nor indeed often, the case. An upbeat temperament, gritty optimism, and positive thinking are just as often symptoms of a masked depression, the schizophrenia of the clown, as of its opposite, a genuine joy in living. We often see that same pathos in the shallow optimism, forced joy, and artificial energy of the guru on positive thinking.

The opposite of depression is delight, being spontaneously surprised by the goodness and beauty of living. This is not something we can ever positively crank up and make happen in our lives. It is, as every saint and sage has told us, the by-product of something else. It is something that happens to us and which we can never, on our own, make happen to us. As C. S. Lewis suggests in the title of his autobiography, *Surprised by Joy,* delight has to catch us unaware, at a place where we are not rationalizing that we are happy. The famous prayer of Francis of Assisi, with its insistence that is only in giving that we receive, suggests the same thing.

This is what it would mean to not be depressed: Imagine yourself on some ordinary weekday, walking to your car, standing at a bus stop, cooking a meal, sitting at your desk, or doing anything else that is quite ordinary. Suddenly, for no tangible reason, you fill with a sense of the goodness and beauty and joy of just living. You feel your own life—your heart, your mind, your body, your sexuality, the people and things you are connected to—and you spontaneously fill with the exclamation: "God, it feels great to be alive!" That's delight, that's what it means not to be depressed.

But how often do we feel like that? For most adults, this experience is rare. We can go for years and, for all that time, be loving, dedicated, generous, positive, contributing, compulsive adults—good spouses, good parents, trusted employees, giving friends, prayerful, churchgoers—and never once during all those years enjoy a thimbleful of genuine delight. It happens all the time. Delight is rare for adults, though not for children. If you want to see what delight looks like, go by any school yard sometime when kids, little kids, kindergartners and first graders, come out for their recess break. They simply run around and shriek.

Now that's delight. This, the spontaneous response to the goodness and beauty of life, not the commercialized tapes of someone expounding the merits of positive thinking, is what nondepression sounds like. When you see a child in a high chair, just fed, shouting and throwing Jell-O and mashed potatoes around the room, you are party to delight—and you are also party to something that, outside of children, is exceedingly rare. In Western culture, the joyous shouting of children often irritates us because it interferes with our depression. That is why we have invented a term, hyperactivity, so that we can, in good conscience, sedate the spontaneous joy in many of our children.

We struggle with depression, with accessing properly our energies; but, as has already been said, we have the opposite problem too. We are also prone to inflation, to becoming so possessed by energy and so full of ourselves that we are unlikely candidates to ever be caught off guard by delight. Sometimes we are not depressed, but, sadly, at those times, we are generally so full of ourselves that we are a menace to our families, friends, communities, and ourselves. We have a problem both ways, accessing and containing energy.

Rare, in our culture, is the person who has found just the right balance between self-assertion and self-effacement, between egoism and altruism, between self-development and commitment, between creativity and sacrifice, between being too hard on herself or being too easy on herself, between being too high or too low, between clinging dependence and unhealthy independence, and between bending the knee in too infantile a fashion and uttering the self-destructing defiance of Lucifer: "I will not serve."

The balance we are all searching for lies in a proper relationship to energy, especially creative, erotic, spiritual energy—and these are one and the same thing. Spirituality is about finding the proper ways, disciplines, by which to both access that energy and contain it. Our age, in its struggle to grow up and to grow beyond what it considers the rather infantile and legalistic approach to this in the past, has naively begun to believe that we in fact understand this energy, that we can control it, and that we need little, if any, external help in coping with it.

This naivete is, to my mind, one of the major spiritual stumbling blocks of our time. In terms of understanding spiritual energy and its relationship to us we are not unlike an adolescent boy or girl whose body is bursting with hormonal energy and who feels that he or she is up to the task of creatively coping with that tension without any rules or guidance from elders. Such naivete is, as we know, both arrogant and dangerous. The fires that burn inside us are much more powerful than we naively assume. When we neglect them, thinking that these fires are domestic enough for us to control, we end up either depressed or inflated. Let me offer an example of how naivete about the power of erotic energy can depress us.

Some years ago, CBC television aired a drama about three middle-aged couples from Ontario who decided to take a summer camping holiday together. The holiday was meant to be a middle-aged fling of sorts, a reunion of old college friends who had spent the last twenty-five years raising children and paying mortgages and doing the kinds of civic and church things that come with that turf. Now after years of being tied down with commitments, their children more or less grown, they finally had some time again to spend with each other, traveling the country, and renewing old friendships.

So they each rented some kind of trailer home, packed it with food and drinks, left their respective houses to the precarious care of their young adult children, and set out for a month to enjoy the vacation they had never had.

It started well. For the first two days and nights there were high spirits, lots of laughter and banter, and the table conversations sounded something like this: "Isn't this great! Isn't it great to be together like this again! Isn't it great to have the freedom, the money, and the time to just enjoy ourselves and see our country in this way." Even the weather was great.

Things changed on the third night. Parked in a campground

near a resort, late in the evening as they sat around their campfire, they saw the campground fill with young people. A wild party ensued, loud rock music, booze and drugs of all kinds, and various couples having sex rather openly among the trees. Initially, huddled around their own fire, the three couples said the types of things any middle-aged couple might say in a similar situation: "What's the world coming to? Who raised these kids?"

What they did not realize is what seeing such primitive rawness was doing inside of them. From that moment on, basically until the end of their month-long trip, each of them went into a depression. The real enjoyment of the trip, the sense of freedom and delight, was gone and the bantering and humor of the first days gave way to a silence and feelings about their own marriages, bodies, sexual histories, kids, and lives in general that often had them bickering and unhappy.

What had happened here? They had had a firsthand experience of what Jung meant when he said, energy is not friendly. In this case, it was an experience of the negative effect of pornography. What is wrong with pornography is not that there is something wrong in seeing the sexual act. Sex is not dirty or sinful. What is wrong with pornography is that it overstimulates our archetypal erotic energies, leaving us no choice but to act out those energies (as a mythical god or goddess might, without restraints and limits) or to go into a depression, namely, to turn on the cooling mechanisms inside of us, restrain those energies, and then sizzle in inchoate frustration as they slowly cool.

Our culture is too naive about the power of energy. We see nothing wrong in exposing ourselves to it in all its rawness. We are right in one way, erotic energy is good, there is nothing wrong with Aphrodite and Eros having sex under a tree. What is problematic is that this is not an event meant to be watched. It is too raw. Love is meant to be made behind closed doors. Every society has had taboos about sex, about having it and about exhibiting it. The wisdom in the taboo against exhibition is not, first and foremost, about morality and sin. It is about protecting people's souls from the kind of unhappiness that our three Ontario couples experienced after they, precisely, saw Aphrodite and Eros under a tree.[5]

The truth of this concerns not just pornography and sexuality, but pertains to anything that is so raw as to overstimulate our energies. Energy is imperialistic, not with the tyranny of a bad dictator, but with the overpowering force of a divine agent. The energy inside us is simply too much and when we attempt to handle it without the proper reverence, safeguards, taboos, and mediation, we will soon find ourselves stripped of all joy and delight. Channeling eros correctly is not, first and foremost, about sin and morality, it is about whether or not, like those Ontario couples, we sit in delight or depression while eating our suppers at night.

Conversely, how can naivete about spiritual and erotic energy inflate us?

A clear example here is that of religious cults. What is wrong with a religious cult is not that those in it are insincere or that the energy it attempts to access and contain is not real. The reverse is more true. What is wrong is that a cult, by its very definition, tries to access the divine, the real divine, without the proper mediation and reverence; tantamount to somebody sticking a knife into a 220-volt electrical socket, the effect is real, but you are fried to death. That is precisely what happens in a religious cult, as can be seen in what happened to David Koresh and his followers in Waco and to the members of the Solar Temple cult in Switzerland and Canada. It is no mere accident that, so often, people in cults die and that they die by fire. Spiritual energy is fire, the hottest fire of all, and people who too naively play with that fire get burned.

David Koresh, leader of the Davidian Cult in Waco, Texas, stockpiling machine guns, sleeping as if by divine right with all the women in the compound, and promising that he, and he alone, could reveal the deepest secrets of God and life, is the prime analogate of inflation, of somebody dangerously possessed by energy and by what that has done to his own ego. That he went up in a ball of fire is no biblical surprise.

The Bible tells us that nobody can see God and live. When Moses asks to see God, God tells him to stand in a cleft by the rock and that he, God, will cover Moses' face as he passes and then Moses will get a look at God's back—but never his face![6] That is metaphorical language, warning us that divine energy (and all energy ultimately is divine) needs to be approached with caution, with bare feet.[7] For it to be life-giving for us, there must be a genuflection before it, a clear knowledge that it is separate from us, and a cautious, reverential accessing of it. The old moral and religious taboos, as well as the classical liturgical rituals, whatever their faults, tried to teach us this. As Annie Dillard puts it: "I often think of the set pieces of liturgy as certain words that people have successfully addressed to God without their getting killed."[8] David Koresh might be alive still had he understood that.

Spirituality is about properly handling the fires, those powerful energies, that flow through us. We struggle because we are naive and underestimate both the origins and the power of this fire. We think that energy is ours, and it is not. We think we can, all on our own, control it, and we cannot. There is a madness in us that comes from the god and unless we respect and relate it precisely to its divine source we will forever be either too restless or too depressed to ever fully enjoy life or we will be some miniversion of David Koresh, convinced that we are God.

2. Pathological Busyness, Distraction, and Restlessness

Jan Walgrave once commented that our age constitutes a virtual conspiracy against the interior life.[9] What he meant is not that there is somewhere a conscious conspiracy against proper values, the churches, and true spirituality, as paranoid conservatism likes to believe. What he meant was that, today, a number of historical circumstances are blindly flowing together and accidentally conspiring to produce a climate within which it is difficult not just to think about God or to pray, but simply to have any interior depth whatsoever. The air we breathe today is generally not conducive to interiority and depth.

Why? What factors are accidentally conspiring to cause this? In an earlier book, *The Shattered Lantern*,[10] I tried to name and analyze these. Thus, here, I will merely name them.

Among the many things that work against interiority today, three can be singled out as particularly cankerous: *narcissism, pragmatism,* and *unbridled restlessness.*[11]

Defined simply, narcissism means excessive self-preoccupation; pragmatism means excessive focus on work, achievement, and the practical concerns of life; and restlessness means an excessive greed for experience, an overeating, not in terms of food but in terms of trying to drink in too much of life. Narcissism accounts for our heartaches, pragmatism for our headaches, and restlessness for our insomnia. And constancy of all three together account for the fact that we are so habitually self-absorbed by heartaches, headaches, and greed for experience that we rarely find the time and space to be in touch with the deeper movements inside of and around us.

There is no limit to rich analysis on this: Thomas Merton once said that the biggest spiritual problem of our time is efficiency, work, pragmatism; by the time we keep the plant running there is little time and energy for anything else.[12] Neil Postman suggests that, as a culture, we are amusing ourselves to death, that is, distracting ourselves into a bland, witless superficiality.[13] Henri Nouwen has written eloquently on how our greed for experience and the restlessness, hostility, and fantasy it generates, block solitude, hospitality, and prayer in our lives.[14] They are right. What each of these authors, and countless others, are saying is that we, for every kind of reason, good and bad, are distracting ourselves into spiritual oblivion. It is not that we have anything against God, depth, and spirit, we would like these, it is just that we are habitually too preoccupied to have any of these show up on our radar screens. We are more busy than bad, more distracted than nonspiritual, and more interested in the movie theater, the sports stadium, and the shopping mall and the fantasy life they produce in us than we are in church. Pathological busyness, distraction, and restlessness are major blocks today within our spiritual lives.

3. A Critical Problem with Balance, Leading to a Bevy of Divorces

Good spirituality, as we saw, is a question of channeling our eros correctly. Among the things our own generation struggles with here is the question of balance. Maybe it is where history has landed us or maybe it is our incurable itch to overanalyze everything; whatever the reason, healthy balance, in anything, is not the strength of our age. Invariably we split things up and pit elements against each other. This is especially true spiritually.

One of the critical problems of our age is that we have created a bevy of divorces within spirituality, forcing ourselves and others to have to make unhealthily choices. We are forever creating illicit dichotomies, bad divorces, that force us to choose between two things when, in fact, both are needed for us to healthily channel our spiritual energies.

What are these bad divorces? Like biblical demons, they are legion, but *five* of these are particularly destructive in terms of spirituality today and need to be named and examined briefly:

a. The Divorce Between Religion and Eros

Among all the false choices facing us today, none are more harmful to us spiritually, whether we are in a church or not, than is the choice we often make, however unconsciously, between religion and eros. What is this false dichotomy? It can best be explained by using an example.

Some years ago, I was serving as counselor to a young nun who was struggling to make sense of her religious life. Her struggle was not easy. On the one hand, she had genuine faith. She believed in God and believed, moreover, that God had called her to be a nun, even though the vows of poverty, chastity, and obedience did not sit very well with her natural temperament. On the other hand, there was within her a gnawing restlessness and her erotic pulse for life made living in the convent hard to take.

Eventually she made a decision. She gave up trying to be a nun and this is the way she reasoned it. Her words, which I quote here, are the words of our culture, uttered consciously or unconsciously by millions of sincere women and men as they try to sort out their spiritual lives: "I've decided that I'm too full of life to ever be truly religious. I love life too much, am too sexual, too physical, too red-blooded, and too much rooted in this earth and what it offers to ever be really spiritual. I can't serve God and church, I've too much erotic and creative energy!"[15]

What she articulates here is the divorce in Western culture between religion and eros. Like all divorces it was painful, and as in all divorces, the property got divided up: Religion got to keep God and the secular got to keep sex. The secular got passion and the God got chastity. We, the children of that divorce, like all children in a broken home, find ourselves torn between the two, unconsciously longing for them to come back together again.

But, for now, we live in a broken situation. Religion, especially as it is lived out in the churches, is perceived as being antierotic, antisex, anticreative, antienjoyment, and anti-this-world. The God who underwrites the churches is then perceived as stoic, celibate, dull, cold, otherworldly, and threatened by sex and by human creativity. The secular world is seen as the champion of eros, sex, creativity, and enjoyment, but is seen as anti-God and antichurch. And we are torn; how does one pick between the two?

b. The Divorce Between Spirituality and Ecclesiology

A strange thing is happening in the Western world today. As the numbers of persons participating in our churches is dramatically decreasing, the numbers of persons interested in spirituality is proportionately increasing. We are witnessing a drastic decline in church life right in the midst of a spiritual renaissance. What is happening?

A divorce is taking place between spirituality and ecclesiology, between those who understand themselves to be on a spiritual quest and those inside our churches. Again, the simplest way to explain this is to give an example.

Several years ago, an American author, Sam Keen, published a book entitled *Hymns to an Unknown God*. Keen is no novice to organized religion since he holds both a master's degree and a doctorate in divinity. What he does in this book is to draw a distinction between spirituality (the spiritual quest) and religion (church life) so as to legitimate the former and denigrate the latter. He calls himself a "trustful agnostic," a "recovering Presbyterian," and wears a question mark rather than a cross around his neck. He understands himself as a searcher on a spiritual quest. But the path of spirituality, in his view, is not the path of organized religion. Every religion begins with the answers, he asserts, the spiritual quest begins with the opposite. It begins with the questions. For Sam Keen, within spirituality, unlike religion, you don't just surrender. You don't just obey.[16]

Moreover, in this view, in the spiritual quest you never, in this life, really arrive. For him, once a person settles into the practice of a religion, he or she can no longer claim to be on a spiritual quest. Spirituality has been traded in for religion.

In saying this, Keen speaks for our age, articulating something that millions of men and women in fact feel and believe. Typical today is the person who wants faith but not the church, the questions but not the answers, the religious but not the ecclesial, and the truth but not obedience. More and more typical too is the person who understands himself or herself as a "recovering Christian," as someone whose present quest for God has embittered him or her toward the church where there once was membership.

But this split is not just one-sided. The reverse, sadly, is just as true. We have more than enough churchgoers who want the

church but not faith, the answers but not the questions, the ecclesial but not the religious, and the obedience but not the truth.
The "recovering secularist" bears a striking similarity to his or
her alienated cousin, the "recovering Christian." The effect of
this divorce clearly cuts both ways.

c. THE DIVORCE BETWEEN PRIVATE MORALITY AND SOCIAL JUSTICE

Ernst Kaseman, the renowned Scripture scholar, once commented that what is wrong in the world and in the churches is
that the pious aren't liberal and the liberals aren't pious. He is
right and that, in caption, names another tragic divorce that has
taken place within spirituality and within Western culture in general—private and social morality are too rarely found within the
same person.

Too rare is the case where we see together in the same person, the same ideology, the same group, or the same church, an
equal passion for social justice and for private morality, for action as for contemplation, and for statecraft (politics) as for soul-
craft (mysticism). What this means is that the person who leads
the protest group usually does not lead the prayer group, the
person concerned with family values is usually not as concerned
with poverty in the inner cities, and the social, political agitator
generally lacks the interior depth, selflessness, and calm of the
mystic. The reverse is also true.

Spirituality, as we shall see, is equally about both—liberality
and piety, action and contemplation, private morality and social
justice, the concerns of feminism and Green Peace and the ten
commandments. Sadly today, and this is one of our major stumbling blocks to living a healthy spirituality, these are invariably
divorced from each other.

d. THE DIVORCE OF THE GIFTED CHILD AND THE GIVING ADULT

Spirituality is ultimately about self-transcendence, altruism, and
selflessness. Religion has always made this its centerpiece. To be
religiously mature was to be a person who freely gives his or her

life away. As Jesus put it: "No greater love has one than to lay down one's life for a friend."[17]

While that is obviously true, the way it has been preached has sometimes been problematic. What looks like selflessness can actually be self-serving and manipulative and what looks like a free gift can have strings attached. True selflessness is not so easy to define. We are all too familiar with the situation where one sacrifices for a friend but ends up being bitter about it and feeling used. One can carry someone else's cross and send him or her the bill.

In our search for self-transcendence we often cannot draw the distinction between self-donation and being a victim. When is something altruism and when is it simply being a doormat? When is a selfless act virtue and when is it a sign of weakness and timidity?

Nearly twenty years ago, Swiss analyst Alice Miller wrote a short essay that made a huge impact, "The Drama of the Gifted Child."[18] For Miller, the gifted child is not the child with the extraordinary intelligence quotient, Einstein's kid. Rather the gifted child is the person who, from the womb onward, is extraordinarily sensitive, the person who picks up, internalizes, and lives out the expectations of others. The gifted child is the pleaser, the person who does not want to disappoint others.

But, as Miller goes on to show, the persons who sacrifice themselves for others because they are afraid to disappoint eventually end up, in mid-life, bitter about it, feeling victimized, angry that they have always had to sacrifice their personal need to others' wishes. The gifted child ends up becoming the embittered adult. Selflessness can just as easily lead to anger as to joy.

Spirituality is about laying down one's life for one's friends. Today, tragically, there is a divorce between those who preach this, but without sensitivity to the drama of the gifted child, and those who, oversensitive to the pain of the victim, are unable to see that the most noble thing a human being can do is to die for something beyond himself or herself. Spiritually the gifted child is meant to become the gifted adult, the person who, like Jesus, can say: "Nobody takes my life from me, I give it freely."[19] Unfortunately, in today's cultural and religious climate, too few people can hold those two, the gifted child and the giving adult, together. Generally too society emphasizes with the former and the churches with the latter.

e. The Divorce by Contemporary Culture of Its Paternalistic, Christian Heritage

What is meant by this rather curious phrase? All me a parable: There is a myth called *The Sweetness of Life*.[20] It is a long, involved story, but there is a part that sheds light on our question:

Once upon a time there was a man who was a hunter, a great hunter who knew everything there was to know about the forest. He knew which berries were poisonous and which could be eaten; which herbs were good and which were not. He knew which birds could be hunted and he knew where they hid themselves. He knew all of this because his father had taught it to him and his father had been instructed by another father before him—and so on back through many generations. The great hunter came from a long line of noble and wise hunters.

One day the hunter's wife became pregnant and the hunter, intuitively, knew that the child would be his firstborn son. And so, each night, as his wife slept, the hunter, through a magic he had created, drew the spirit of his son out of his wife's womb and took him into the woods where he taught him all the secrets of the woods: which berries were poisonous, which herbs could be eaten, where all birds lived, and how they could be hunted. Then, before morning, through his magic, he would place the son back into the mother's womb. She, on her part, slept and did not know that each night her son left her womb to learn hunting with his father.

Finally, the day arrived for the son to be born. The women of the village gathered to sing songs of praise for the firstborn and the child was delivered. What a huge baby! And how precocious! He nursed for just one day. The next day, he refused milk and asked for meat. On the third day he began to walk. On the fourth day he ran and the next day, now all grown up, he joined his father for a hunt in the forest.

Father and son set out and, immediately upon crossing the clearing and entering the forest, they came upon the honeybird. Aware of the secrets of the woods they followed the honeybird, knowing it would lead them to honey. When they reached the tree within which the bees had stored a large cache of honey, the father climbed the tree and instructed his son: "I will hand the honeycombs down to you. Put them into the calabash, but do not eat any of the honey. Don't even lick your fingers for the honey is very bitter; it is not to be eaten!"

But the son, knowing all that the father had taught him, knew too that the honey was in fact very sweet and so instead of putting it into the calabash as the father had ordered he ate it, all of it, down to the last drop, licking his fingers clean when he had finished. When the father came down from the tree and saw what had happened, he became enraged. He glared in anger and disbelief at his son who stood defiantly before him . . .

Among many things, this is an image of the relationship between the Judeo-Christian tradition and the culture within the Western world today.

The culture is the son. It stands before its parent, the Judeo-Christian tradition, more than a little deviant. Using the very secrets that it learned from its father, it is telling him: "You handed bitterness to me when you should have been handing me sweetness. You lied to me! You are too full of false prohibitions, bitter taboos, and needless fears! You are supposed to be handing down the sweetness of life, but your commandments and taboos bring death and guilt instead of life and sweetness."

The Judeo-Christian tradition is the father, patriarchal, hierarchical, standing at the foot of the honey tree, feeling betrayed by the child who it itself taught the secrets of the woods—indeed, as René Girard says, it is not because we invented science that we stopped burning witches but rather when, because of the

Judeo-Christianity, we stopped burning witches that we invented science.[21]

And so we are caught up in another divorce. On the one side, we have the Judeo-Christian tradition which taught us the secrets of the woods and which now feels itself betrayed, sees its foundational commandments breached, and senses itself as harshly judged by its own children. On the other side, stands our culture, adolescent in its defiance, accusing that tradition, its parent, of dealing it death not life. Like any child, caught in a painful divorce, we stand between them, sense their incompatibility, and do not know to which we should give our hearts.

Toward a Christian Spirituality

Nobody doubts our generation's sincerity. In terms of spirituality, our struggle is not with sincerity, but with direction. Our hearts are good, but it is our minds and feet that do not know which way to go. Many roads beckon, many voices call, and we already know that there are many ways that one can fall off the narrow tightrope that Jesus once called the path to eternal life.

Each generation has its own dark night of the soul, its own peculiar temptation to despair, as it tries to find peace of soul and make peace with its God. Our own dark night of spirituality is very much shaped by our naivete about the nature of spiritual energy; by the conspiracy against depth and prayer caused by the narcissism, pragmatism, and unbridled restlessness of our age; and by our inability to hold together in tension a series of dualities.

How do we walk forward and at the same time be realistic and take into account all the unique pressures of our age? What vision and what disciplines do we need to creatively channel the erotic, spirit fire inside of us so that its end result is creative days and restful nights and an enduring peace with our God, each other, and within ourselves?

The chapters that follow try to answer, however inadequately, those questions. They will not try to offer answers from the widest humanistic and religious perspective possible, albeit that would be the ideal. Because one book cannot be the full perspective on anything, it is good sometimes to be humble. The effort here will surely be that. It will limit itself to one perspective rather than attempting to be comprehensive. It will try to formulate a spirituality from one perspective, a Christian one. In doing this, it wants to be the first to admit that there are invaluable insights, religious insights, that should be drawn from secular, humanistic thought and, even more obviously, from other world religions. God still speaks in many and diverse ways and no one person or one religion has a monopoly on truth.

But with that being said, I make no further apologia for choosing to weave these perspectives for discipleship into a specifically Christian framework. I write, not as a neutral analyst, but as someone within a confessing, worshiping, Christian, Catholic community. What follows is intended, first of all, to help others who find themselves within that same community. The hope, however, is that these perspectives can also help those who, for whatever reason, stand outside that community and wonder what it might have to offer.

And so, leaning on the words of Augustine, I begin with these words: "Let my reader travel on with me when she shares fully in my convictions; let her search with me when she shares my doubts; let him return to me when he recognizes that he is in error; let him call me back to the right path when he sees that I am in error. In this way let us advance along the road of charity toward Him [Her] of whom it is written."[22]

PART TWO

The Essential Outline
for a Christian Spirituality

Pray, fast, and give alms
— Jesus

The religious right thinks that to be religious you have to be extremist and fundamentalist . . . and the religious left agrees!
— Jim Wallis

It is time for both the left and the right to admit that they have run out of imagination, that the categories of liberal and conservative are dysfunctional, and that what is needed is a radicalism that leads beyond both the right and left. That radicalism that can be found in the gospel which is neither liberal nor conservative but fully compassionate.
— Jim Wallis

We need to be on fire again,
for our hope is no longer an easy hope.
We live in a culture of despair
within which Pentecost can no longer be taken for granted.
Hence we must take upon ourselves the burden of the times
and refuse to make the Holy Spirit a piece of private property
but a spirit that matters.
— Mary Jo Leddy

We have some bad habits that only God can cure!
— Los Angeles gang member to a church group

3

The Nonnegotiable Essentials

> *Lead, Kindly Light, amid the encircling gloom*
> *Lead Thou me on!*
> *The night is dark, and I am far from home—*
> *Lead Thou me on!*
> *Keep Thou my feet; I do not ask to see*
> *The distant scene—one step enough for me.*
> —JOHN HENRY NEWMAN, "The Pillar of Fire"

The State of the Question—An Overwhelming Pluralism

We live in a world that is rich in most everything, except clarity in the area of spirituality. It is not easy to know how we should live out what is essential within our lives of faith. Concretely, what should we be doing? To whom should we be listening? Even though we may have accepted a creed, been baptized into a church, and are familiar with the Bible, we are still constantly subjected to voices calling us in different directions. Daily we face a perplexing series of questions: Is this important or not? Is this something of substance or just a fad? Will this endure or will it pass away? Must I get involved in this or can I choose to ignore it? Is this church and is this teaching right or wrong? Is this something essential or merely accidental?

What is essential and nonnegotiable within Christian spirituality? What are the pillars upon which we should build our spiritual lives?

Before naming and examining these, it is useful first to have a brief look at our recent history in spirituality and where this has brought us. Where have we come from? What historical, spiritual baggage do we bring to the present situation?

1. Our History—Where Have We Come From?

Our history here has not been monolithic. As Christians we find ourselves standing in a rich, but confusing, spiritual pluralism with quite different backgrounds in spirituality. We have not always agreed on what is essential within the spiritual life and we have lived out our faith lives somewhat differently. Roman Catholicism, Protestantism, and secular society each have a separate history in the area of spirituality and each of us has arrived at the situation of today with our own unique baggage.

a. ROMAN CATHOLICISM

Until the last thirty years, Roman Catholic ecclesiology and spirituality were characterized by a number of clear, distinct emphases. You were considered a practicing Catholic if you went regularly to church, prayed privately, tried to live the commandments, were not publicly at odds with the church's teaching on marriage and sexuality, were contributing to the support of the church, and were not in some public way causing scandal.[1] This, however, was seen as the minimum high-jump bar. Doing these things merely made you a Catholic, but did not necessarily define you as a healthy one.

What helped define you as healthy was participation within certain spiritual practices, especially certain devotional and ascetical ones. Thus, you were not just a Catholic because you went to church and respected the church's laws on sex and marriage; you were also one because you did a number of other things: You were a Catholic because you did not eat meat on Fridays, fasted during Lent, gave money to the poor, prayed the rosary, supported the foreign missions, and participated in various other devotional practices. To be a Catholic meant attending benediction; praying the Stations of the Cross; saying litanies to the Blessed Virgin Mary, St. Joseph, and the Sacred Heart; going to church on first Fridays and first Saturdays; reading the lives of the saints and other devotional books, praying for the souls in purgatory; incorporating certain sacramentals, like icons, holy water, and blessed metals into your life; and going to various shrines like Lourdes and Fatima.

As well, for the last century, since Pope Leo XIII's social encyclical of 1870, the need to practice social justice has been growing as an important component within Catholic spirituality. It, or its absence, too helped define you as a Catholic. However, save for a few exceptions, this imperative never lodged itself as centrally within the heart of Roman Catholic spirituality as did the devotional and sacramental elements just named.

These spiritual practices (spirituality), as distinct from essential churchgoing (ecclesiology), were seen as nourishing and nurturing faith, as opposed to being the essence of the faith. Sometimes, of course, this perspective was lost and, for some people, these practices became the essence of their faith, but that was never the official teaching of Roman Catholicism nor, indeed, ever its central practice.

As well, these practices generally had a certain tone to them, namely, with some salient exceptions, they had within them the tonality of monasticism, asceticism, piety, and solitude. Monks and nuns, ascetics of all kinds, celibates, the pious, and introverts who loved silence, did well within Catholic spirituality. Paradoxically, so too did those who loved drinking alcohol, smoking tobacco, and partying.[2]

Granted this is a bit of a caricature, but, until quite recently, for a good number of centuries, Roman Catholic spirituality was characterized by these practices and this tonality.

b. PROTESTANTISM

And what was Protestantism doing during this time? For its part, Protestantism, agreed with Roman Catholicism's emphasis on churchgoing and the importance of private prayer and private morality. It too defined a practicing Christian essentially by these characteristics.

However, beyond agreement on these more essential practices, Protestantism differed from Roman Catholicism considerably in its practical spirituality. How did Protestants try to nurture and nourish their faith, apart from going to church on Sunday?

Protestantism took quite a different practical option in the area of spirituality. It distrusted—both healthily and in a paranoid way—Roman Catholic devotions and sacramentals. It placed instead the emphasis on the Bible—on reading it and on trying actively to guide your life with it. It also emphasized strongly works of private charity and, in some churches, there was a clear motif challenging its members to get involved in the struggle for justice. In some Protestant groups, to be a Christian and to nurture your faith as a Christian meant working against injustice of various kinds. Because of this, Protestant spirituality was the driving force behind many justice movements, from the freeing of slaves to the foundation of free, universal medical care.

As well, like Roman Catholicism, Protestant spirituality also had a certain tonality. It was biblical, nonmonastic, and (especially in some churches) emphasized the need for personal justification by God. Those who loved reading the Bible, those who wanted a pure, stoic Christianity (without devotion, piety, and ritual sacramentals), those who wanted a felt, personal experience of rebirth in Jesus, and those who wanted to lead social reform did well in Protestant spirituality. Paradoxically, so too did those who favored the ban of alcohol, tobacco, gambling, and excessive partying.

Again, admittedly, this is an oversimplification, but is still useful, as are most caricatures, in providing a certain horizon against which to understand something. In this case, it helps shed light on where we have come from in the past few centuries in terms of Protestant spirituality.

c. Secular Society

Simply put, secular society, insofar as one can extrapolate a general attitude from so amorphous a term, looked upon Christian spirituality with the eyes of the Enlightenment. Hence, for the main part, it looked upon Christian spirituality (and at theistic spirituality in general) with very suspicious eyes. For it, spirituality is at best a helpful poetry, and at worst, a harmful superstition.

Although that attitude is now changing, essentially it still dominates secular philosophy and shapes all of our political and judicial decisions. In this view, spirituality, insofar as it centers itself on an actual belief in God, if it belongs anywhere, belongs in the churches and in the privacy of people's homes, but it certainly has no place within the public domain, other than as objective material for historical study. Hence, it should have no place in politics, economics, or in the academic curriculum of a university. Theistic spirituality in general, and Christian spirituality in particular, is, for the secular mind, something highly privatized and esoteric, tolerable at the fringes of society but having nothing important to say at the center. Such was the view of the Enlightenment and such is still, basically, save for a few confederate pockets of cognitive deviance, the view of secular society.

However, the human spirit is incurably religious and, secular philosophy notwithstanding, it keeps doing religious things. Thus, in the Western world, even though the Enlightenment wrote off religion, its most fervent converts continued, and continue, to be zealously religious, albeit in covert forms.[3] Everyone worships at some shrine.

Thus, for example, ideologies of all kinds, from Marxism to secular feminism, substitute a normative theory of history for the Judeo-Christian story of salvation and propose this new story as the story of salvation; secular art turns creativity into a religion whose God is so jealous as to make the old demanding God of Judaism, Christianity, and Islam appear lax; secular moralists demand a doctrinal orthodoxy (political correctness) which religious fundamentalists can only envy; secular moral zealots continue to find no end of causes that call for religious martyrdom; positive thinking and pedagogues of excellence propose a new religious hope; the cults of physical health, replete with ever more demanding forms of asceticism, replace old spiritualities regarding the soul; ancient animism, the worship of nature, takes on new religious forms; myths and fairy tales replace the old Bible stories; new shrines (from Graceland to Lady Diana's tomb) continue to appear; and secular forms of canonization, of books and people, do what religious canonization formerly did. Religion is never at the margins. Everyone has a spirituality, including today's adult children of the Enlightenment.

The secular world too enters today's spiritual arena carrying plenty of religious baggage.

2. The Situation Today

Where has all of this left us? In a pluralism that is staggering both in its riches and its potential for confusion.

To walk into a spiritual bookstore today is to be nearly overwhelmed by variety and choice. The same holds true for the many moral and religious voices that daily bombard us. These voices tempt us toward every kind of spiritual practice, traditional or new. . . . *Attend a Bible study. —Go to a prayer meeting. —Become involved in a social-justice group. —Become a feminist. —Join a men's group—sign up for Promise Keepers. —Practice this kind of prayer. —Try that kind of meditation. — Face your addictions through a twelve-step program. —Develop your highest potentials through these steps. —Learn what Eastern religions can offer you. —Do an enneagram. —Make a marriage encounter. —Recover the fire in your belly. —Get in sync with the wolf inside you. —Do an Ignatian retreat. —Be born again. —Give your life to Jesus. —Be more in touch with nature.* We hear many spiritual voices today.

If, for example, you were to classify just the major schools of thought or the key movements within spirituality in the West today, you would end up with a fairly extensive list; each, in essence, a spirituality. In each, you have a certain notion of God, sometimes more implicit than expressed, and in each you have a certain path for discipleship spelled out. In each case too, a strong focus on one thing clearly shapes how everything else is understood. And so if you walked into a bookstore today that specializes in spirituality, you would find an extremely rich variety of books, each calling you to shape your discipleship in terms of a particular sensitivity. Thus, you would find books, spiritualities, centered upon . . .

Physical creation, nature (creation-centered theologians, parts of New Age, parts of Scientology); the *Lordship of Jesus and the word of God* (Charismatic groups, Pentecostal groups, evangelical groups, Promise Keepers); *women and other oppressed peoples* (feminism, liberation theology, social justice groups); *men and their struggles* (masculine spirituality); *injustice in the world and God's new order* (social justice groups); *private meditation and prayer* (various prayer and meditation groups); *our addictions and the means to be free of them* (twelve-step programs, literature of dysfunctional families and institutions); *the soul and its angels and demons* (Jungians, disciples of James Hillman, parts of New Age); *mythology, active imagination, and the recovery of anthropological ritual processes* (feminism, masculine spirituality, New Age, Hillmanians); *the pursuit of excellence and creative contact with what is highest inside of ourselves* (gurus of positive thinking, parts of Scientology, Shirley MacLaine). As well, you would find a bevy of books on *Eastern religions, grieving as a route to spiritual renewal, blessing as the route to adult generativity and spiritual renewal,* and *personality types, enneagrams, and archetypes.*

These are just the salient ingredients of the stew, and it is within this rich, confusing pluralism that each of us must sort out what is essential for ourselves.

3. Sorting Out—the Search for Substance and Balance

Among all these voices, which are the right ones? Among all these perspectives and theories, which have real spiritual substance and which are simply the stuff of fads? What is useful and what is harmful? More specifically, for us as Christians, what should be part of our Christian discipleship and what should we, in the name of Christ, ignore or reject?

Classically, within Christianity,[4] we have made a distinction that can be helpful to us as we try to find some order and balance in all of this. Christian theology has always taught that there is a hierarchy of truths, that not all truths are of the same importance, and that we must distinguish between truths that are essential and truths that are accidental.

Essential truths are those that are necessary for everyone, prescribed for everyone, and nonnegotiable for everyone. They cannot be ignored or bracketed on the basis of temperament, taste, situation, or lack of time. In the case of essential truths, like the ten commandments for instance, it is not a question of personal choice ("I feel like doing them or I don't"). They are nonnegotiable, universally prescribed.

Accidental truth, on the other hand, refers to real truth, but to truth that takes its importance only in relationship to more essential truth. Accidental truth can, for a variety of reasons, be ignored or bracketed. Thus, to give just one example, it can be true that the Blessed Virgin Mary appeared at a given shrine. However, even if it is true, that truth in no way has the same importance as does the central truth of God becoming incarnate in Christ. The truth of a Marian apparition is what classical theology calls an accidental truth. The truth it teaches is not universally prescribed, but is one that you can choose (on the basis of temperament, taste, background, culture, or time) to either respond to or not. Unlike the truth of the incarnation or of the ten commandments, there is a certain negotiability here, not about its being true, but about whether or not it is something to which we should attend.

On the basis of that distinction, between substance and accident, we can ask ourselves: In all the rich spiritual pluralism of today what is essential? What are the higher truths? What is universally prescribed for Christian discipleship? What are the nonnegotiables of the spiritual life?

The Essentials of a Christian Spirituality—The Four Nonnegotiable Pillars of the Spiritual Life

1. *In Caption*

Four essential pillars undergird any healthy Christian spirituality. These are universally prescribed spiritual challenges and are revealed by Christ as being the nonnegotiable elements within Christian discipleship. What are they?

At one point in his ministry, Jesus specifies three clear components to discipleship: prayer, fasting, and almsgiving.[5] For him, these were the pillars of the spiritual life. However, we must understand these prescriptions in the way Jesus meant them. For him, prayer meant not just private prayer, but also keeping the commandments and praying in common with others; fasting meant a wide asceticism that included within itself the asceticism demanded by living a life of joy; and almsgiving meant, among other things, justice as well as charity.

Looking at this, we see that Jesus was prescribing four things as an essential praxis for a healthy spiritual life: a) Private prayer and private morality; b) social justice; c) mellowness of heart and spirit; and d) community as a constitutive element of true worship.

For Jesus, these four elements comprise the essentials, the nonnegotiables, of Christian discipleship. These are not elements we may choose or not choose to incorporate within our spiritual lives. They comprise the essence of the spiritual life. They also supply its balance. Only when all four of these are present in our lives are we healthy, as Christians and as human beings. What specifically comprises each of these?

Before examining each in some detail, a certain digression is in order. Freud once said that if you want to understand something, look closely at it when it is broken. With that in mind, let us examine a series of stories within which the wholeness of spirituality, as Christ prescribed it, is broken. What does a fractured spirituality look like?

What follows are four stories, each of which lets us meet a Christian who, while very sincere, is somehow one-sided and lacking in balance because he or she is bracketing one or the other of the nonnegotiable pillars within Christian spirituality.

2. Some Stories of Imbalance

a. Private Prayer and Private Morality—but Lacking in Justice

Some years ago, I was listening to a national radio program, a phone-in show, and the topic was sparking a fierce debate: Should the churches be involved in politics? The studio guest was a Roman Catholic bishop who had a national reputation for his strong views on social justice. In his view of things, the churches should clearly be pushing governments, business corporations, and everyone else toward establishing a more just economic, political, and social order.

At one point an irate woman phoned in and posed this question to the bishop: "Your Excellency, what I can't understand is why the churches, and people like yourself, are forever wanting to preach about economics, poverty, universal health care, human rights, and things like that, which are really not the concern of religion. A few radicals and social-justice types get all bothered about these things and then try to foist them on everyone else. Why doesn't the church stay where it is supposed to stay, inside the church, and teach us about faith, prayer, and the ten commandments and the real things of religion? Why don't you leave politics and economics to the politicians and the economists? . . . who, incidentally, know something about it!"

The bishop's response, in effect, ran something like this: "I will answer your question, if first you answer mine. What would you do if you were a bishop and some very sincere woman phoned you and said to you: 'Our priest refuses to preach about faith, private prayer, and the private morality. He says they are just something that a small group of contemplative nuns, with their monastic hang-ups, are trying to foist on to the rest of the church. He says that prayer and the ten commandments (except those that deal with justice) are not important. God attaches no importance, he says, to our petty private little struggles with faith, prayer, and the commandments, especially those which deal with private morality. God is concerned with saving the world, with the bigger picture, and has no concern for our private little hang-ups.' What would you do in that situation?"

She never hesitated: "I would suspend that priest on the spot!"

"Well," countered the bishop, "what should I do when people tell me, 'our priest refuses to preach about what the gospel demands regarding social justice. He says it is just something that a small group of liberation theologians, with their leftist hang-ups, are trying to foist on to the rest of the church. He says that what Jesus says about justice for the poor is not important, as long as you are praying and keeping the commandments.' What should I do then? I ask this because the gospel's demand to help create justice for the poor is just as clear and nonnegotiable as is its call to pray and keep our private lives in order. Both, prayer and justice, are nonnegotiable."

This is an interesting exchange because it highlights clearly the faith imbalance that can occur in the life of a very sincere, faith-filled person, if she brackets something that is essential within the spiritual life. In this case, we have a woman who, while she probably went to church regularly, prayed, and had her private life essentially in order, does not have a balanced spirituality. A major component of Christian discipleship is lacking in her life. Hers is a one-sided faith. In this, however, as we shall see, she is not alone.

b. Social Justice—but Lacking in Private Prayer and Private Morality

As a young priest, while I was in graduate school in San Francisco, I helped pay for my studies by serving as chaplain at a hostel in an economically depressed section of the city. Through my work there, I met and got to be friends with David, a young social worker in the area. He was a Roman Catholic, though he attended church only occasionally, had basically no private prayer in his life, and no longer even tried to live the church's moral teachings regarding sex and marriage. These he flaunted openly and considered a medieval hang-up. He was, however, deeply committed to the church's social teachings, had a passion for justice, and was quite generous, at some cost to himself, in serving the poor.

One day, he asked me: "Do you really think that God gives a damn whether you say your morning and evening prayers, whether you hold a grudge against someone who's hurt you, whether you masturbate or not, or whether you share a bed with someone you aren't married to? Do you really believe God cares about these pettily little things? As Christians we are always so hung up on these little private things that we neglect the big picture—the fact that half the world goes to bed hungry every night and nobody gives a damn. Justice, not our pettily little prayer lives, is what is important, religiously and morally. Why are we forever hung up on what's insignificant?"

This young man, David, is, at one level, the religious antithesis of the woman who phoned in to the radio program and challenged the bishop. At another level, however, he is not all that different from her. He, like her, has a one-sided spirituality, having chosen to bracket a nonnegotiable part of Christian discipleship. His mistake was to answer his own question wrongly: Does God care about our private prayer, our private grudges, and our private morals? Very much so. God cares because we care and these things make a big difference to God because they, in fact, make a big difference for us.

However, if he and the woman whose story we heard earlier married their differences, they still might not have a whole spirituality—as we shall see from our next story.

c. PRIVATE PRAYER AND PRIVATE MORALITY AND SOCIAL JUSTICE—BUT LACKING MELLOWNESS OF HEART AND SPIRIT

In the summer of 1985, I attended a conference in Belgium on ecclesiology that had been organized by Christiane Brusselmans. It was held in a retreat house just outside Brugge.

The conference brought together persons from every continent and was organized in such a way that, in each discussion group, there was one participant from each continent. My role was to be the recorder for one of these groups. For the first day, everyone in the group told his or her story, sharing with the group each person's experience of church.

In the group within which I was the recording secretary, there was a young nun from Asia who was very much in the mode of Mother Teresa. She wore a traditional religious habit, had a deep life of prayer, went to Eucharist every day, and nobody could have had the slightest doubt concerning her private life. She had no private life in fact; her life was an open book, with someone from her community with her almost twenty-four hours a day. Hence, regarding private prayer and private morality, her life was extraordinary in its honesty.

But, unlike the woman who challenged the bishop on the radio phone-in show, she was no stranger to the church's social teachings. She was exemplary here as well. In sharing her story, she described how, at one point, she and her whole community had made a decision to try to be in solidarity with the poor in a more radical way. Hence, they had abandoned many of the comforts they had formerly enjoyed in terms of food, clothing, housing, running water, and other creature-comforts. Now she lived in a convent within which the nuns slept on straw mattresses, had only two sets of clothing each (a Sunday habit and a work habit), fasted regularly, avoided luxuries of all kinds, and, as a ministry, worked full-time with the poor. Her own particular ministry was to work with political prisoners. Hence, even more so than the young man in the previous story, she had made an option for the poor, to serve the cause of justice.

But that is not the end of what she would share with our group. Her story will take a strange twist.

Our conference was being held in a retreat center and the accommodation there, while comfortable, was not palatial. Hence no one was scandalized that we were living too high, even as we talked about poverty in other parts of the world. As well, the conference organizers were working us hard. We had work sessions morning, afternoon, and evening, and after four days, everyone was getting pretty tired. On the fifth day, at the noon meal, Christiane stood up and announced that we had been working too hard and deserved a break. Accordingly, she decreed a free afternoon. Our sole challenge for the rest of the day was to ride an air-conditioned bus into the beautiful city of Brugge, spend the afternoon shopping, taking strolls, having drinks, and at seven o'clock in the evening, meet at a fancy restaurant for a long, gourmet dinner. A general cheer went up . . . but not everyone, as we found out the next day, was equally as enthusiastic about this celebratory time.

We spent part of the next day doing some damage control. A number of the participants complained that it was wrong that we, while talking about the poor, should spend time and money so frivolously. The young nun, however, was strangely quiet.

The conference ended with a Eucharist, and just before the final prayer and blessing that would end the conference, there was an open microphone and an invitation was issued to anyone who felt that he or she had experienced some deep grace to come forward and share it with the group. Many people went forward, especially those from the more economically affluent parts of the world, who shared how much of a grace it was for them to meet, face to face, and share with their brothers and sisters from other parts of the world. Near the end of this, the young nun from Asia also approached the microphone. She shared something to this effect:

"I too had a grace-experience these past few days and I was converted in a way that I never dreamed I needed to be converted. My conversion began with the announcement of the free afternoon. From the second it was announced, something inside of me froze up and I was angry. I kept thinking, 'What an insult to the poor! This is a waste of time and money. We are here with the money and time of the poor, and what do we do with it? We walk around terraces, drink alcohol, and have a gourmet meal at the Holiday Inn!' I was angry and I only went along because I wanted to stay with the group and not impose my own will. But I was miserable all afternoon. We walked along, looked at shops with all kinds of luxury things in them, and then had a drink on a café terrace. I was so miserable that I didn't even refuse the drink I was offered. I drank my first gin and tonic. Well, everything culminated when we got to the Holiday Inn for the dinner. I walked into the restaurant, saw all the silver knives and forks and the linen serviettes, and I became nauseated and couldn't go through with it. So I went out and sat on the bus and waited while everyone else ate.

"But I had to sit there a long time. Many thoughts ran through my head, and at one stage, I asked myself the question: 'Would Jesus be in there eating and drinking and having a good time?' And I had the horrible realization that he would be! John the Baptist—with his leather belt and his grasshoppers!—would be with me on the bus, boycotting all this joy in the name of the poor. I realized that, in my mind, Jesus and John the Baptist were all mixed up, and I also realized that there was something wrong with me. There was something cold inside of me. I had become like the older brother of the prodigal son, doing all the right things, but having no celebration in my heart."

A most revealing story. Here is a young woman who is seemingly living out Jesus' full praxis. She is praying, fasting, and giving alms, combining private prayer and a good private life with a healthy concern for social justice. So what is missing in her life? Where is her spirituality inadequate?

She herself gives us the answer: "I had become like the older brother of the prodigal son." Fasting, as Jesus prescribes it, also includes fasting from bitterness of heart. Mellowness of heart is as nonnegotiable within the spiritual life as are an integral private life and a concern for justice. Why? Because otherwise, like the older brother of the prodigal son, we might succumb to the temptation that T. S. Eliot describes so well: "The last temptation that's the greatest treason is to do the right thing for the wrong reason."[6] In Jesus' view of things, we do not just need the right truth, we also need the right energy.

But even then, one might still be lacking an essential ingredient for full health. What else is demanded, beyond private prayer and private morality, social justice, and mellowness of heart? A final story . . .

d. Private Prayer and Private Morality, Social Justice, Mellowness of Heart—but Lack of Involvement Within a Concrete Community

I have a friend who, from every point of view, save one, is an exemplary Christian. She is a woman of faith, faithful in her marriage, a good mother, scrupulously honest; she reads spiritual books, prays daily on her own, and even leads retreats on spirituality and prayer for others. There are no major inconsistencies in her life regarding private prayer or personal integrity. As well, she has a deep concern for justice, is committed to various causes, and is involved with several groups who are trying to help the poor; in fact, some of her family and friends consider her a bit of a social justice radical. Moreover, she is a woman too of some warmth and graciousness. She enjoys celebrating life with others, has a good sense of humor, knows what to do with a bottle of wine, seemingly has little bitterness or anger about life, and does not put people on edge worrying that they might, through accident or ignorance, have a slip of the tongue, say something politically incorrect, and tragically alter the history of the planet. Her presence is a blessing rather than a judgment and, in it, you relax rather than grow anxious and pseudo-intense.

But she does not go to church. In her view of things, personal involvement within a concrete church community is not of high value. She is not particularly negative on church and even attends occasionally. Indifference is the bigger issue. For her, churchgoing is not considered important, but as a negotiable item, one of the accidentals, not essentials, within spirituality.

Thus, despite all her faith, concern for the poor, and her mellowness of spirit, she still lacks full balance. Why? What can be missing in a life so honest, prayerful, and gracious?

The grounding, earthiness, and necessary pain that only real involvement within a concrete, parish-type family can give you. In parishes, as we know, we do not get to pick who we will be standing beside as we worship and celebrate various things together. A parish-type family is a hand of cards that is randomly dealt to us, and precisely to the extent that it is truly inclusive, will include persons of every temperament, ideology, virtue, and fault. Also, church involvement, when understood properly, does not leave us the option to walk away whenever something happens that we do not like. It is a covenant commitment, like a marriage, and binds us for better and for worse.

Accordingly, if we commit ourselves to a church community and stay with that commitment, we will, at some point, have the experience that Jesus promised Peter would befall every disciple: Prior to this kind of commitment you can gird your belt and go wherever you want, but, after joining a concrete church community, others will put a belt around you and take you where you would rather not go.[7] And Jesus is right. What church community takes away from us is our false freedom to soar unencumbered, like the birds, believing that we are mature, loving, committed, and not blocking out things that we should be seeing. Real churchgoing soon enough shatters this illusion, and gives us no escape, as we find ourselves constantly humbled as our immaturities and lack of sensitivity to the pain of others are reflected off eyes that are honest and unblinking.

We can be very nice persons, pray regularly, be involved in social justice, and still not be fully responsible. It is still possible to live in a lot of fantasy and keep our lives safe for ourselves. This gets more difficult, however, if we start going to a church, most any church, especially one that is large enough to be inclusive. To be involved in a real way in a church community is to have most of our exemption cards taken away.

3. *Toward Fullness and Balance—Some Detail Regarding the Four Essential Pillars Within Christian Spirituality*

We get into trouble whenever we do not name things properly. The task for the rest of this chapter will be one of naming. It will not attempt to lay out a positive theology of prayer, social justice, health of soul, and ecclesiology. That comes later. Here we want only to name the four pillars that are so essential and non-negotiable and highlight some of the problems that result when we neglect that fact.

a. Private Prayer and Private Morality

Private prayer and personal moral integrity in things, even in the smallest private affairs, are things that Jesus makes nonnegotiable within the spiritual life. He asks us to "pray in secret,"[8] to have a private, personal relationship with him, and through him, with God. Moreover, in Jesus' mind, the test as to whether or not we are in fact doing this, having a personal relationship with God, is not a question of whether we feel we are having one or not, but of keeping the commandments: "If anyone loves me, he or she will keep my commandments."[9] In the Gospels, fidelity in keeping the commandments is the only real criterion to tell real prayer from illusion. One of the anchors of the spiritual life is private prayer and private morality.

In the past, this would not have had to be emphasized in a

book such as this one. When one looks at past Christian spiritual literature, this mandate was always the central focus and was sometimes seen as the only important component within spirituality. Many traditional Roman Catholics and most people within the evangelical Protestant churches still believe that this is so. For them, a personal relationship with Jesus Christ and the keeping of the ten commandments are still the centerpiece of spirituality.

For all kinds of reasons, many Christians in our culture, and liberal Christians in particular, do not share that view. Within liberal Christianity, and within the secular culture as a whole, there is a certain fear that having too-privatized a relationship with Jesus is dangerous, that this is something that takes us away from true religion. Thus, to speak of a personal relationship with Jesus today is to run the danger of being called a fundamentalist. Piety too is considered by many to be a conservative virtue.

While this critique of the private aspect of spirituality by liberal Christianity and secular culture is not without its merits (or historical reasons), it is itself spiritually dangerous. Irrespective of whatever else needs to be emphasized in religion, the question of private prayer and private morality may never be written off or trivialized in any way as unimportant. It is true, as one of the harsher criticisms of conservative Christianity states, that we can keep the commandments and not be loving; but it is also true, and Jesus teaches this very clearly, that we cannot pretend to be loving if we are not keeping the commandments.

There are real dangers in an overprivatization of spirituality. The spiritual life is not just about "Jesus and I." However, there are equal dangers in not having enough "Jesus and I" within our spiritual lives. The danger in not having the proper interiority (intimacy with God) and the personal moral fidelity to back up our faith preaching is that we end up turning Christianity into a philosophy, an ideology, and a moral code, but ultimately missing what Christianity is all about, a relationship with a real person. If we refuse to take seriously this first pillar of the spiritual life, we will continue to go through the motions, perhaps even with some passion, but we will be unable to inspire our own children or pass on our faith to them. Moreover, we will eventually find ourselves both empty and angry, feeling cheated, and struggling with the temptation of either becoming ever more bitter or of chucking it all.

St. Paul warns that we must always be solicitous, lest having preached to others, we ourselves might be lost. Private prayer and private morality may never be bracketed; otherwise, as Henri Nouwen so well puts it, I might find that "just when I was being praised for my spiritual insights, I felt devoid of faith. Just when people were thanking me for bringing them closer to God, I felt that God had abandoned me. It was as if the house I had finally found had no floors."[10]

In many of the spiritual classics of Christian literature, the writers, oftentimes saints themselves, suggest that we will make progress in the spiritual life only if we, daily, do an extended period of private prayer, and only if we practice a scrupulous vigilance in regards to all the moral areas within our private lives. In essence, that is the first nonnegotiable within the spiritual life.

b. Social Justice

More than a few Christians might be surprised to learn that the call to be involved in creating justice for the poor is just as essential and nonnegotiable within the spiritual life as is Jesus' commandment to pray and keep our private lives in order. Jesus' teaching on this is very strong, consistent throughout all the Gospels, and leaves no room for equivocation. In the Christian scriptures, one out of every ten lines deals directly with the physically poor and the call from God for us to respond to them. In the gospel of Luke, that becomes every sixth line, and in the epistle of James, that commission is there, in one form or another, every fifth line.

Moreover, the call to do justice as an integral part of relating to God is already strong within the Jewish scriptures. Beginning about 800 B.C., the Jewish prophets made one truth central to their teaching. They taught that the quality of faith in the people depends upon the character of justice in the land—and the character of justice in the land is to be judged by how we treat the most vulnerable groups in the society, namely, widows, orphans, and strangers. Thus, according to the Jewish prophets, where we stand with God depends not just upon prayer and sincerity of heart but also on where we stand with the poor.

Jesus never disputes that. He takes it further. He identifies his own presence with the poor and tells us that, ultimately, we will be judged on how we treat the poor. Bluntly put, we will go to heaven or hell on the basis of giving or not giving food, water, clothing, shelter, and justice to the poor.[11] How we treat the poor is how we treat God. For this reason, Jesus asks us to make a preferential option for the poor: "When you give a lunch or a dinner, do not invite your friends or your family or your relations or rich neighbors, in case they invite you back and repay you. No; when you have a party, invite the poor, the crippled, the lame, and the blind; then you will be blessed."[12] Reaching out, preferentially, to the poor is an essential component of the spiritual life.

This is not a new teaching, albeit our understanding of it is deepening. All Christian churches have always taught this, in one way or the other, and they have also always, in their best expressions, lived it out. Despite many embarrassing blemishes in the history of Christianity, it has too a proud history in terms of the poor. From the initial establishment of hospitals, orphanages, soup kitchens, and schools for the poor (long before secular society took any responsibility), to the role of the churches in overthrowing slavery, to the social gospel within many Protestant churches and liberation theology and the social encyclicals within Catholicism today, the Christian churches have always made the preferential option for the poor an integral part of the living out of one's faith.

The call to become involved in helping the poor to find justice is a nonnegotiable pillar within Christian spirituality. Much of our culture today, and conservative Christianity in particular, struggles with this, protesting that this is really a question of politics and not something that lies at the very heart of religion itself. But, as Jesus himself makes clear, there can be no real relationship with him when the poor are neglected and injustice abounds. When we make spirituality essentially a privatized thing, cut off from the poor and the demands for justice that are found there, it soon degenerates into mere private therapy, an art form, or worse still, an unhealthy clique.

God cannot be related to without continually digesting the uneasiness and pain that are experienced by looking, squarely and honestly, at how the weakest members in our society are faring and how our own lifestyle is contributing to that. This is not something that a few liberation theologians, feminists, and social justice advocates are trying to foist on us. This is not a liberal agenda item. It is something that lies at the very heart of the gospel and which Jesus himself makes the ultimate criterion for our final judgment.

c. Mellowness of Heart and Spirit

Sanctity has to do with gratitude. To be a saint is to be fueled by gratitude, nothing more and nothing less.

Søren Kierkegaard, as we saw, once defined a saint as a person who can will the one thing. What is missing in his definition, however, is the question of motivation, namely, the real energy behind the willing. We can will and do the right thing for the wrong reason. Thus, for example, I can do a selfless act for others, but be manipulative in that supposed generosity; I can die for a cause and simply be acting out of my own hurt or out of infantile grandiosity; and I can be a warrior for truth mainly because I energize through conflict. I can do all kinds of good things out of anger, guilt, grandiosity, or self-interest. Moreover, like the older brother of the prodigal son, I can be scrupulously faithful for years and years, but with a bitter heart.

Sanctity is as much about having a mellow heart as it is about believing and doing the right things, as much about proper energy as about truth. Gustavo Gutiérrez, the father of liberation theology, suggests that, to have a healthy spirituality, we must feed our souls in three ways: through prayer, both private and communal; through the practice of justice; and through having those things in our lives (good friendships, wine-drinking, creativity, and healthy leisure) that help keep the soul mellow and grateful.[13] For Gutiérrez, our task as Christians is to transform the world through love and justice, but he is clear that we will not succeed in this if our actions issue forth from anger or guilt. Only one kind of person transforms the world spiritually, someone with a grateful heart.[14]

Jesus too is clear on this: In the parable of the Prodigal Son, he teaches that we can be away from the father's house equally through infidelity and weakness ("the younger brother") or through bitterness and anger ("the older brother"), whereas what God is really asking of us is to have the compassion of the father (an empathy that can issue forth only from a very grateful heart).[15] In the Gospels, the call to have a mellow, grateful heart is just as nonnegotiable as are the demands to keep the commandments and practice social justice.

This challenge, to stay warm of heart, is an integral part of fasting. Asceticism is as much about disciplining the emotions as it is about disciplining the body. What good is a trim body, free of fat and toxins, but full of anger and unhappiness? What good is fidelity in terms of keeping the commandments and practicing justice if we end up as bitter as the older brother of the prodigal son?

Both as liberals and conservatives we too easily write off this third prong of the spiritual life, rationalizing that our causes are so urgent, we are so wounded, and our world is so bad, that, in our situation, anger and bitterness are justified. But we are wrong and, as the American poet William Stafford warns, "following the wrong God home we may miss our star."[16] The wrong God is the God of both the contemporary right and the contemporary left, that is, the God who is as wired, bitter, anxious, workaholic, neurotic, and unhappy as we are. But that is not the God who lies at the end of the spiritual quest, who, as Julian of Norwich assures us, sits in heaven, smiling, completely relaxed, looking like a marvelous sympathy[17] and who agrees with Albert Camus that the real revenge on our enemies, both to the right and to the left, and on the deepest demons that haunt us, is to be madly happy.[18]

d. COMMUNITY AS A CONSTITUTIVE ELEMENT OF TRUE WORSHIP

One of the great religious intellectuals of our century, Bernard Lonergan once tried to set out criteria to judge what constitutes a true religious conversion. He suggests that an authentic religious conversion has within it six dimensions: It is religious, theistic, Christological, ecclesial, moral, and intellectual.[19] Not all of these dimensions might be immediately evident and a person might sometimes be focused for a while on one to the neglect of another, but eventually, to meet God and uncover the face that we find there, we will have to deal with each of these dimensions, including the ecclesial, the element of concrete involvement within a historical worshiping community.

Jesus' way of stating this is less intellectual, though no less clear. He teaches us clearly that God calls us, not just as individuals, but as a community and that how we relate to each other is just as important religiously as how we relate to God. Or, more accurately, how we relate to each other is part of how we relate to God. For Jesus, the two great commandments, to love God and love one's neighbor, can never be separated.

Moreover, for Jesus, loving one's neighbor is not an abstract thing. Essentially it means that we must, in our worship of God in heaven, involve ourselves concretely with a worshiping community on earth. Hence, he tells us that anyone who claims to love God who is invisible but refuses to deal with a visible neighbor is a liar, for one can only really love a God who is love if one is concretely involved with a real community (ultimately an "ecclesial community") on earth.[20]

For a Christian, concrete involvement within a historical

community of faith (churchgoing) is a nonnegotiable within the spiritual life.

This is something that is difficult for our age to hear. As we saw in the previous chapter, our age tends to divorce spirituality from ecclesiology. We want God, but we don't want church. By doing this, however, we bracket one of the primary demands inherent right within the very quest for God.

Already a century ago, a prominent Protestant theologian, Frederick Schleiermacher, tried to point this out in a book with a curious, but revealing, title: *Speeches on Religion for Those Among the Cultured Who Despise It.* Schleiermacher pointed out that, separate from historical religion, namely, the churches with all their faults, the individual in quest of God, however sincere that search, lives the unconfronted life. Without church, we have more private fantasy than real faith. Like Lonergan, he submits that real conversion demands that eventually its recipient be involved in both the muck and the grace of actual church life.

Spirituality is ultimately communitarian, even within those faiths such as Buddhism, Hinduism, Islam, and Taoism that are not ecclesial within their essential makeup, as are Christianity and Judaism. Why? Because the search for God is not a private search for what is highest for oneself or even for what is ultimate for oneself. Spirituality is about a communal search for the face of God—and one searches communally only within a historical community.

To Walk on Earth Like Gods

Spirituality is partly a question of balance. Attention to the essential pillars can help provide us with that balance. However, balance is not the ultimate goal of spirituality. We want to walk the earth with balance . . . but we want too to walk it like gods and goddesses. We want, with our Creator, to continue to create; and with our Redeemer, to continue to redeem. We want to help

God bring this planet to completion, to a consummation of all that hope inspires in us. A key part of the spiritual life is to fulfill a vocation.

How do we, as Christians, walk this earth as gods? As co-creators? As persons, in God's image and likeness, who are trying to help God save the planet and everything on it? How do we fulfill our God-given vocations?

By being part of God's ongoing incarnation.

PART THREE

The Incarnation as the Basis for a Christian Spirituality

Sharon's Christmas Prayer

She was five,
sure of the facts,
and recited them
with slow solemnity
convinced every word
was revelation.
She said
they were so poor
they had only peanut butter and jelly sandwiches
to eat
and they went a long way from home
without getting lost. The lady rode
a donkey, the man walked, and the baby
was inside the lady.
They had to stay in a stable
with an ox and an ass (hee-hee)
but the Three Rich Men found them
because a star lited the roof
Shepherds came and you could
pet the sheep but not feed them.
Then the baby was borned.
And do you know who he was?

Her quarter eyes inflated
to silver dollars.
The baby was God.

And she jumped in the air
whirled round, dove into the sofa
and buried her head under the cushion
which is the only proper response
to the Good News of the Incarnation.
   —JOHN SHEA[1]

4

Christ as the Basis
for Christian Spirituality

Christ has no body now but yours,
no hands but yours,
no feet but yours.
Yours are the eyes through which
Christ's compassion must look out on the world.
Yours are the feet with which
He is to go about doing good.
Yours are the hands with which
He is to bless us now.[2]

The Centrality of Christ

We measure time in relation to the birth of Jesus. All dates end with a suffix, B.C. or A.D., indicating whether an event took place before Jesus' birth or after. The whole world does this. There are reasons beyond the purely religious why this is so. Nonetheless, the fact that the whole world records time in relation to the birth of Jesus does indicate something about his importance.

For those of us who are Christians, time obviously should be measured by when Jesus was born. For us, he is the center of everything: our meaning, our hope, our self-understanding, our church lives, our theologies, and our spiritualities. He is also the guide for our discipleship.

Spirituality, as we saw, is about creatively disciplining the fiery energies that flow through us. Hence a good spirituality requires a certain discipleship. A disciple is someone under a discipline. Jesus laid out a certain discipline to creatively channel our energies. But he did more than this and he was more than this.

Who is Jesus Christ? If Jesus himself did a survey today, asking each of us personally the question he once asked Peter, "Who do you say that I am?" he would, I am sure, get a wide variety of answers. Who is Jesus for us, really? A historical person, a God-man (whatever that means!), a great moral teacher, a philosophy, a church, a dogma, a figure for piety, a superstition, a mythical super-Santa, a household god? Who really is Jesus for us?

Most of us who are Christians have at least this in common about Jesus. We admire him. As Søren Kierkegaard once pointed out, however, this is not enough. What Jesus wants from us is not admiration, but imitation. It is far easier to admire figures of great morality and courage than to do what they do. Admiration alone is a weak thing. Imitation is more important, though we need to go even beyond that as regards Jesus. He is more than a model to be imitated. What Jesus wants is not admiration, nor simple imitation (no one does Jesus very well anyway!). What Jesus wants of us is that we undergo his presence so as to enter into a community of life and celebration with him. Jesus, as John Shea says, is not a law to be obeyed or a model to be imitated, but a presence to be seized and acted upon.[3] What exactly does that mean? The task of this chapter and the next will be to try to answer that question.

Undergoing Jesus must be the center of any Christian spirituality. Within Christian spirituality, long before we speak of anything else (church, dogmas, commandments, even admonitions to love and justice), we must speak about Jesus, the person and the energy that undergirds everything else; after all, everything else is merely a branch. Jesus is the vine, the blood, the pulse, and the heart.

But how to understand Jesus? There have been, easily, five

hundred serious theological books written about Jesus in the past thirty years. The intent here is not to try to summarize these, but to situate Jesus and the discipleship he asks of us within the context of the central mystery of Christianity, the incarnation, the mystery of the word made flesh.

Jesus, and the discipleship he asks of us, can best be understood within a single phrase: *The word was made flesh and it dwells among us.*[4]

The Concept of the Incarnation—"The Word Made Flesh."

The central mystery within all of Christianity, undergirding everything else, is the mystery of the incarnation. Unfortunately, it is also the mystery that is the most misunderstood or, more accurately, to coin a phrase, under-understood. It is not so much that we misunderstand what the incarnation means, it is more that we grasp only the smallest tip of a great iceberg. We miss its meaning by not seeing its immensity.

Generally, we think of the incarnation this way: In the beginning, God created the world and everything in it, concluding with the creation of humanity. But humanity soon sinned (original sin) and became helpless to save itself. God, in his goodness and mercy, however, decided to save humanity, despite its sin. So God prepared a people by calling the patriarchs and then the prophets. Through them, God slowly readied the people (the Jewish scriptures). Finally, when the time was right, God sent his own son, Jesus, who was born in Palestine nearly two thousand years ago. Jesus was God, but also fully a man. He had two natures: one human, the other divine. Jesus walked this earth for thirty-three years. He revealed God's nature, taught great truths, healed people, worked miracles, but eventually was falsely accused, arrested, crucified, and died. He rose three days later and, for the next forty days, made various appearances to his followers. At the end of this time, with his followers now more adjusted to the new reality of the resurrection, he took them to a hillside outside of Jerusalem, blessed them, and ascended, physically, to heaven.

In this concept, God walked this earth, physically, for thirty-three years, and then returned to heaven, leaving us the Holy Spirit, a real but less physical presence of God. The physical body of Jesus, the word made flesh, was with us for thirty-three years and is now in heaven.

What is wrong with this? It is right—in its own symbolic, beautiful language—about many things: our sin, God's mercy, God's coming physically to earth. Where it is wrong is that it gives the impression that the incarnation was a thirty-year experiment, a one-shot incursion by God into human history. In this version, God came to earth physically and then, after thirty-three years, went back home. It uses the past tense for the incarnation and that is a dangerous under-understanding. The incarnation is still going on and it is just as real and as radically physical as when Jesus of Nazareth, in the flesh, walked the dirt roads of Palestine. How can this be so?

The Hermeneutical Key—"Giving Skin to God."

The mystery of the incarnation, simply stated, is the mystery of God taking on human flesh and dealing with human beings in a visible, tangible way. The radical character of this, however, needs some explanation, especially as it pertains to three things: why God would act in this way; the shocking rawness of this kind of act; and its ongoing, rather than one-shot, character.

a. The Why of the Incarnation

Why would God want to take on human flesh? Why would an infinite power want to limit itself within the confines of history and a human body? Why incarnation?

There is a marvelous story told about a four-year-old child who awoke one night frightened, convinced that in the darkness around her there were all kinds of spooks and monsters. Alone, she ran to her parents' bedroom. Her mother calmed her down and, taking her by the hand, led her back to her own room, where she put on a light and reassured the child with these words: "You needn't be afraid, you are not alone here. God is in the room with you." The child replied: "I know that God is here, but I need someone in this room who has some skin!"

In essence, that story gives us the reason for the incarnation, as well as an excellent definition of it. God takes on flesh because, like this young girl, we all need someone with us who has some skin. A God who is everywhere is just as easily nowhere. We believe in what we can touch, see, hear, smell, and taste. We are not angels, without bodies, but sensual creatures in the true sense of the word sensuality. We have five senses and we are present in the world through those senses. We know through them, communicate through them, and are open to each other and the world only through them. And God, having created our nature, respects how it operates. Thus, God deals with us through our senses. The Jesus who walked the roads of Palestine could be seen, touched, and heard. In the incarnation, God became physical because we are creatures of the senses who, at one point, need a God with some skin.

Nikos Kazantzakis once explained this by way of a parable: "A man came up to Jesus and complained about the hiddenness of God. 'Rabbi,' he said, 'I am an old man. During my whole life, I have always kept the commandments. Every year of my adult life, I went to Jerusalem and offered the prescribed sacrifices. Every night of my life, I have not retired to my bed without first saying my prayers. But . . . I look at the stars and sometimes the mountains—and wait, wait for God to come so that I might see him. I have waited for years and years, but in vain. Why? Why? Mine is a great grievance, Rabbi! Why doesn't God show himself?' "

Jesus smiled and responded gently: "Once upon a time there was a marble throne at the eastern gate of a great city. On this throne sat three thousand kings. All of them called upon God to appear so that they might see him, but all went to their graves with their wishes unfulfilled.

"Then, when the kings had died, a pauper, barefooted and hungry, came and sat upon that throne. 'God,' he whispered, 'the eyes of a human being cannot look directly at the sun, for they would be blinded. How, then, Omnipotent, can they look directly at you? Have pity, Lord, temper your strength, turn down your splendor so that I, who am poor and afflicted, may see you!'

"Then—listen, old man—God became a piece of bread, a cup of cool water, a warm tunic, a hut, and in front of the hut, a woman nursing an infant.

" 'Thank you, Lord,' the pauper whispered. 'You humbled yourself for my sake. You became bread, water, a warm tunic and a wife and a child in order that I might see you. And I did see you. I bow down and worship your beloved many-faced face.' "5

God takes on flesh so that every home becomes a church, every child becomes the Christ-child, and all food and drink become a sacrament. God's many faces are now everywhere, in flesh, tempered and turned down, so that our human eyes can see him. God, in his many-faced face, has become as accessible, and visible, as the nearest water tap. That is the why of the incarnation.

b. The Shocking Raw, Physical Character of the Incarnation

The incarnation is shocking in the rawness of its physical character. The English word "incarnation" takes its root in the Latin word *carnus,* meaning flesh, physical flesh. But in Latin, as in English, this is a very unplatonic word. There is nothing spiritual about it. It emphasizes, as do its English derivatives *(carnality, carnal, carnivorous),* the body in its raw, brute, physical tangibility. Incarnation means *in—carnus;* literally in physical flesh.

We usually do not have much trouble conceiving of Jesus in this way, although, even there, we often hesitate to think of Jesus' body as mortal, sexual, and subject to illness, smell, and other humbling bodily processes. The problem rather, as we shall soon point out, is that we do not attribute the same physical reality to the whole Body of Christ, namely, to the Eucharist and the body of believers.[6]

c. Its Ongoing Character

Finally, and of critical importance, is the question of the ongoing nature of the incarnation. The incarnation is not a thirty-three-year experiment by God in history, a one-shot, physical incursion into our lives. The incarnation began with Jesus and it has never stopped. The ascension of Jesus did not end, nor fundamentally change, the incarnation. God's physical body is still among us. God is still present, as physical and as real today, as God was in the historical Jesus. God still has skin, human skin, and physically walks on this earth just as Jesus did. In a certain manner of speaking, it is true to say that, at the ascension, the physical body of Jesus left this earth, but the body of Christ did not. God's incarnational presence among us continues as before. What is being said here?

An initial distinction is key: "Christ," as you know, is not Jesus' surname. We do not say "Jesus Christ" in the same way as we say "Susan Parker" or "Jack Smith." Jesus did not have a surname in the way that we do. He may have been referred to as the son of Joseph (Jesus Gar Joseph), but we do not say that the word Christ is a title, connoting God's anointed, messianic presence on this earth. Scripture uses the expression the "Body of Christ" to mean three things: *Jesus,* the historical person who walked this earth for thirty-three years; the *Eucharist,* which is also the physical presence of God among us; and the *body of believers,* which is also the real presence. To say the word "Christ" is to refer, at one and the same time, to Jesus, the Eucharist, and the community of faith.

We are the Body of Christ. This is not an exaggeration, nor a metaphor.[7] To say that the body of believers *is* the Body of Christ is not to say something that scripture does not. Scripture, and Paul in particular, never tells us that the body of believers *replaces* Christ's body, nor that it *represents* Christ's body, nor even that it is Christ's *mystical* body. It says simply: "We *are* Christ's body."[8]

Scholars disagree among themselves as to precisely how literally Paul meant this.[9] When he says we are the Body of Christ, does he mean this in a corporate or a corporeal way? Are we Christ's body the way a group animated by a common spirit (say, for instance, the Jesuits) are a body? Or, are we a body like a physical organism is a body? With some qualifications (and, of course, some exceptions) scripture scholars agree that it is the latter. The body of believers, like the Eucharist, is the Body of Christ in an organic way. It is not a corporation, but a body; not just a mystical reality, but a physical one; and not something that represents Christ, but something that is him.[10]

This has immense implications. It means that the incarnation did not end after thirty-three years, when Jesus ascended. God is still here, in the flesh, just as real and just as physical, as God was in Jesus. The word did not just become flesh and dwell among us—it became flesh and *continues* to dwell among us. In the body of believers and in the Eucharist, God still has physical skin and can still be physically seen, touched, smelled, heard, and tasted.

But this is not simply a truth of theology, a dogma to be believed. It is the core of Christian spirituality. If it is true that we are the Body of Christ, and it is, then God's presence in the world today depends very much upon us. We have to keep God present in the world in the same way as Jesus did. We have to become, as Teresa of Avila so simply put it, God's physical hands, feet, mouthpiece, and heart in this world. Scripture scholar Jerome Murphy-O'Connor summarizes the importance of this less simply than Teresa, but very accurately: "The community mediates Christ to the world. The word that he spoke is not heard in our contemporary world unless it is proclaimed by the community. The power that flowed forth from him in order to enable response is no longer effective unless manifested by the community. As God once acted through Christ, so he now acts through those who are conformed to the image of his Son and whose behaviour-pattern is in imitation of his. What Christ did in and for the world of his day through his physical presence, the community does in and for its world. . . . In order to continue to exercise his salvific function the Risen Christ must be effectively represented within the context of real existence by an authenticity which is modelled on his."[11]

The Difference Between a Christian and a Theist

What difference does it make whether one believes in Christ or whether one simply believes in God? What does Christ add to God? What does being Christian add to theism?

The difference is huge, not just in theology, but especially in spirituality, in the way we are asked to live out our faith lives.

A theist believes in God. A Christian believes in God, but also in a God who is incarnate. What is the difference? To put the matter into street language, one might say: A theist believes in a God in heaven whereas a Christian believes in a God in heaven who is also physically present on this earth inside of human beings. The theistic God is transcendent and, if not wholly so, present in matter only as some vague ground of being. The Christian God is also transcendent, is also the ground of being, but has a physical body on earth. The Christian God can be seen, heard, felt, tasted, and smelled through the senses. The Christian God has some skin.

The Christian God is *in-carnus,* has concrete flesh on this earth. This may seem rather abstract to us, but its implications color every aspect of how we relate to God and to each other—how we pray, how we look for healing and reconciliation, how we seek guidance, and how we understand community, religious experience, and mission. This, however, needs explication. So let us turn to look at what it means concretely, in terms of spirituality, to believe in the incarnation.

5

Consequences of the Incarnation for Spirituality

For Understanding How We Should Pray

In Matthew's gospel, Jesus tells us that a prayer of petition, addressed to God, is infallible: "Ask, and you shall receive; search, and you shall find; knock, and the door will be opened to you. Everyone who asks receives; everyone who searches finds, and everyone who knocks will have the door opened."[1] Have you ever wondered why, in fact, that does not always work? Many times we ask and do not receive, seek and do not find, or knock and find the door firmly barred against us. Yet, Jesus seemingly promised the opposite. Why does God not always answer our prayers?

We have a whole stock of answers for that. Maybe we did not have sufficient faith. Maybe we asked for the wrong thing, for something that was not good for us. Maybe God gave us what we asked for in some other way. God is a loving parent who knows better than we do what is good for us—and what parent would give a child a knife to play with? Someday we will understand God's deeper wisdom in not answering that prayer.

C. S. Lewis once suggested that we will spend most of eternity thanking God for prayers that he did not answer!

He is right. There is wisdom and truth in all of those reasons, except that none of them are the real reason, in Matthew's gospel, why prayers of petition are often not answered. Matthew, among all the evangelists, is the one who most links prayer of petition to concrete action within the Christian community. He is a Christian theologian, not simply a theistic one. Thus, for him, prayers of petition have power to the extent that they are linked to concrete action within a community of faith and love—and vice versa. As Christians, we pray to God "through Christ," and in trying to answer that prayer, God respects the incarnation, namely, that God's power is now partially dependent upon human action.[2] What does this mean?

As Christians, we have a set formula for ending all of our prayers—"We ask this through Christ our Lord." This formula is more than a formality, a ritual signal to God that the prayer is over. When we pray "through Christ" we are praying through the Body of Christ, which then includes Jesus, the Eucharist, and the body of believers (ourselves) here on earth. We are praying *through* all of these. Thus, not only God in heaven is being petitioned and asked to act. We are also charging ourselves, as part of the Body of Christ, with some responsibility for answering the prayer. To pray as a Christian demands concrete involvement in trying to bring about what is pleaded for in the prayer. Consider, for example, the following case:[3]

An elderly nun came to see a spiritual director. She shared with him the story of a young nun who had just left their community. The elderly nun had very much liked this young nun and appreciated the spark and vigor she brought to the community. For a year, though, she'd noticed that the young nun was obviously in distress, agonizing as to whether or not she should leave the community and as to whether, indeed, the community even wanted her. So the elderly nun prayed for the young nun, prayed that she might stay, prayed that she might realize that she was wanted and valued, prayed that God might give her the strength to see beyond her doubts. But she never went, at any time, and talked to the young nun. She never told her how much the community appreciated the gift that she, the young nun, was. Now she was upset that the young nun had left.

The point is obvious. The elderly nun prayed as a theist and not as a Christian. She never put skin to her prayer. She never concretely involved herself in trying to bring about what she was asking God to do. She left things up to God. But how was God to let the young nun know that she was appreciated inside the community when the community itself would never tell her that? When we pray "through Christ" more is involved than merely asking God in heaven to make some kind of intervention. The community too, and we ourselves, must be involved not just in the petition but also in trying to bring about what the petition pleads for.

Hence . . . if my mother is sick and I pray that she gets better, but do not drive her to see the doctor, I have prayed as a theist, not as a Christian. I have not given any incarnational flesh, skin, to my prayer. It is more difficult for God to answer such a prayer. If I see a colleague or friend who looks depressed and pray for her, but do not speak to her, then I am praying like a theist, not as a Christian. How is God supposed to console her? Send her an e-mail from heaven? It is my voice and my compassion that is called for since I am part of the Body of Christ, am praying, precisely, through the Body of Christ, and am there, available to talk to her. If I pray for a close friend today but do not send him a postcard to tell him I am thinking about him, how is that prayer supposed to touch him? If I pray for world peace, but do not, inside of myself, forgive those who have hurt me, how can God bring about peace on this planet? Our prayer needs our flesh to back it up.

There is in Ingmar Bergman's movie *The Serpent's Egg* a scene that powerfully illustrates this. It runs along these lines: A priest has just finished presiding at the Eucharist and is in the sacristy taking off his vestments when a woman enters. Middle-aged, needy, lonely in her marriage, and suffering terribly from religious scruples, she begins to sob and protest that she is unlovable: "I'm so alone, Father, nobody loves me! God is so far away! I don't think he could love me anyway. Not the way I am! Everything is so dark for me!" At first, the priest is more irritated than compassionate, but at one point he says to the woman: "Kneel down and I will bless you. God seems far away. He cannot touch you right now, I know that, but I am going to put my hands on your head and touch you—to let you know that you are not alone, not unlovable, not in the darkness. God is here and God does love you. When I touch you, God will touch you."[4] This is someone who is praying as a Christian, someone who is giving incarnational flesh, skin, to his prayer.

For Understanding How We Should Seek Reconciliation and Healing

When Jesus walked this earth, people were healed and reconciled to God simply by touching him or by being touched by him. The motif of physical touch is everywhere present in Jesus' ministry. People are always trying to touch him and he often cures people by touching them.

One typical example suffices to illustrate this. In Mark's gospel we have the following story:[5] There was a woman who had been suffering from internal bleeding for twelve years. She had tried every kind of treatment and seen every kind of doctor, but to no avail. Finally, she said to herself: "If I but touch the hem of Jesus' garment, I shall be saved." And she did this. She came up behind him in a crowd and touched his cloak. Instantly the flow of blood stopped and she was healed. Jesus, however, sensing that power had gone out from him, turned and asked: "Who touched me?" His disciples answered: "You are being jostled in a crowd. Many people are touching you!" But Jesus continued to look around. Finally, the woman, frightened, realizing that she had been healed, came forward, and as scripture puts it, "told him the whole truth." Jesus then said to her: "Your faith has healed you—be at peace."

Notice in this story the woman is healed simply by touching Jesus, even before she actually speaks to him. As well there are two moments of healing: the initial, mute touch, and the explicit exchange between her and Jesus that later takes place. Why two different moments of healing? What does the explicit exchange add to the essential moment of touch? Risking an interpretation through other categories, one might say that when she touched the hem of Jesus' garment she was *essentially* healed and when she spoke with Jesus explicitly and told him the whole truth she was *fully* healed.

This text is a paradigmatic one. It lays out a pattern. In it we see, in terms of the incarnation, how healing and reconciliation work in our world. Simply put, what it tells us is that, just like this woman, we will find healing and wholeness by touching the Body of Christ and, as members of the Body of Christ, we are called upon to dispense God's healing and wholeness by touching others. Let me risk illustrating this through a series of examples:

1. Reconciliation and the Forgiveness of Sins . . .

What is the fundamental sacrament of reconciliation? How are our sins to be forgiven us?

Roman Catholics and Protestants have long argued over this, with Roman Catholics emphasizing the need to confess our sins, both in terms of genre and number, to a priest, and most Protestants suggesting that sincere contrition before God is sufficient. Who is right? That discussion is beyond the scope of this book, but suffice it here to say that both emphasize something very important, and both, at a more fundamental level, insist upon a more radical incarnational truth, namely, that the primary sacrament of forgiveness is touching the hem of Jesus' garment, the Body of Christ. We have our sins forgiven in the same way as the woman in Mark's gospel stopped her hemorrhaging, through contact with Christ's body, that is, the Eucharist and the community.

How can touching the community be healing? Imagine this scenario: You are sitting one night with your family. You feel irritated, overtired, and underappreciated. Something happens to push you beyond your patience and you suddenly lose your temper. You yell at everyone, tell them that they are selfish and stupid, throw your coffee cup across the room, and stamp out, violently slamming the door as a final statement. Then you sit in your room, alienated. Slowly sanity and contrition overcome self-pity, but wounded pride and the rawness of what has just happened prevent you from reentering the room and apologizing. Eventually, you fall asleep, leaving things in that unreconciled state. The next morning, now doubly contrite and somewhat sheepish, but still wounded in pride, you come to the table. Everyone is sitting there having breakfast. You pick up your coffee cup (which didn't break and which someone has washed and returned to its hook!), pour yourself some coffee, and without saying a word, sit down at the table—your contrition and your wounded pride showing in your every move. Your family is not stupid and neither are you. Everyone knows what this means. What is essential is being said, without words. You are touching the hem of the garment, you are making the basic move toward reconciliation, your body and your actions are saying something more important than any words: "I want to be part of you again." At that moment, the hemorrhaging stops (even if only for that moment). If you dropped dead on the spot, you would die reconciled to your family.

But this is more than an analogy of how reconciliation works within the incarnation. It is the reality. What has just been described is, in its rawest, most stripped-down form, the sacrament of reconciliation. We have our sins forgiven by being in community with each other, at table with each other. Bluntly put, we will never go to hell as long as we are touching the community—touching it with sincerity and a modicum of contrition. To state things rather crassly for the sake of clarity, if I commit a serious sin on Saturday night and, whatever my physical state on Sunday morning, enter a church with some sincerity and contrition in my heart, I am forgiven my sin. I am touching the hem of Christ's garment.

St. Augustine, whose depth in understanding the Body of Christ has few rivals, in some of the homilies that he would deliver on Easter Sunday to newly baptized adults, would tell Christians that when they stood around an altar, as a community, and prayed the Lord's Prayer, any sins they had ever committed would be forgiven.[6]

He is right. Such is the power of the incarnation. Such is the power, and the responsibility, that God has given us in Christ. We can forgive each other's sins; not we, but the power of Christ within us. As Jesus himself tells us: "In truth I tell you, whoever believes in me will perform the same works that I do myself, and will perform even greater works."[7]

2. Binding and Loosing . . .

What do we do when those whom we love no longer share our faith, our deep values, and our morals?

Suppose, to use a very common example, as a parent you have lost your own children in terms of practicing your faith. Your own children no longer go to church, no longer pray, no longer observe the church's rules (especially as these pertain to sex and marriage), and view your own faith practice as either a naivete or a hypocrisy. You have argued with them, fought with them, and tried in every way to convince them, but to no avail. Eventually you arrived at the unhappy truce you live today: you practice and they don't. One of the deepest bonds of all between you has been broken. Moreover, you worry about them, living, at least so it seems, godless lives. What can you do?

Obviously you can continue to pray and live out your own life according to your own convictions, hoping to challenge them with your life more than with your words. But you can do more.

You can continue to love and forgive them and, insofar as they receive that love and forgiveness from you, they are receiving love and forgiveness from God. You are part of the Body of Christ and they are touching you. Within the incredible mystery of the incarnation, you are doing what Jesus asks of us when he says: "Whatever you bind on earth shall be considered bound in heaven; whatever you loose on earth shall be considered loosed in heaven."[8] And "whose sins you forgive they are forgiven; whose sins you retain, they are retained."[9]

If you are a member of the Body of Christ, when you forgive someone, he or she is forgiven; if you hold someone in love, he or she is held to the Body of Christ. Hell is possible only when one has put oneself totally out of the range of love and forgiveness, human love and forgiveness, when one has rendered oneself incapable of being loved and forgiven in that he or she has actively rejected not so much explicit religious and moral teaching and practice as the love of sincere humanity. To make this more concrete:

If a child or a brother or a sister or a loved one of yours strays from the church in terms of faith practice and morality, as long as you continue to love that person, and hold him or her in union and forgiveness, he or she is touching the hem of the garment, is held to the Body of Christ, and is forgiven by God, irrespective of his or her official external relationship to the church and Christian morality.

Your touch is Christ's touch. When you love someone, unless that someone actively rejects your love and forgiveness, she or he is sustained in salvation. And this is true even beyond death. If someone close to you dies in a state which, externally at least, has her or him at odds ecclesially and morally with the visible church, your love and forgiveness will continue to bind that person to the Body of Christ and continue to forgive that individual, even after death.

One of the great Christian apologists of all time, G. K. Chesterton, once wrote a little parable on this: "A man who was entirely careless of spiritual affairs died and went to hell. And he was much missed on earth by his old friends. His business agent went down to the gates of hell to see if there was any chance of bringing him back. But though he pleaded for the gates to be opened, the iron bars never yielded. His priest also went and argued: 'He was not really a bad fellow, given time he would have matured. Let him out, please!' The gates remained stubbornly shut against all their voices. Finally, his mother came; she did not beg for his release. Quietly, and with a strange catch in her voice, she said to Satan: '*Let me in.*' Immediately the great doors swung open upon their hinges. For love goes down through the gates of hell and there redeems the dead."[10]

In the incarnation, God takes on human flesh in Jesus, in the Eucharist, and in all who are sincere in faith. The incredible graciousness, power, and mercy that came into our world in Jesus is still, at least potentially so, in our world in us, the Body of Christ. What Jesus did we too can do; in fact, that is precisely what we are asked to do.

3. Anointing Each Other for Death . . .

In the movie *Dead Man Walking,* there is a particularly poignant scene: Sister Helen Prejean, the Roman Catholic nun who is helping a prisoner on death row prepare to die, tells him that when he is strapped to the chair, injected with the lethal solutions, waiting to die, he should watch her face. "That way the last thing you will see before you die will be the face of someone who loves you." He does that and dies in love rather than in bitterness.

In the Gospel of John, Chapter 12, there is an incident in which a woman named Mary, in effect, does a similar thing for Jesus. At Bethany, in the days just prior to his death, she anoints his feet with a costly perfume and Jesus says: "She has just anointed me for my impending death."

There are various levels of meaning to that statement, but among other things, Jesus is saying: "Because of this it will be easier to not give in to bitterness, easier to die. Knowing that I am so loved it will be easier to leave this world without anger in my heart." This is what it means to be anointed.

In Roman Catholicism we have a ritual called the sacrament of the sick. It is an anointing with oil that is meant to fulfill what scripture calls for when it says: "If one of you is ill, he should send for the elders of the church, and they must anoint him with oil in the name of the Lord and pray over him. The prayer of faith will save a sick man and the Lord will raise him up again; and if he has committed any sins, he will be forgiven. So confess your sins to each other, and pray for one another, and this will cure you; the heartfelt prayer of a good person works very powerfully."[11]

An elder in the church is anyone sufficiently enough in grace and maturity to, like Sister Helen Prejean, say to another person: "In your bitterness and anger, in your sickness, watch my face and there you will see the face of someone who loves you. Hold my hand and resist bitterness. Forgive, let go, be at peace." Thus, any one of us who visits a sick or dying person, regardless of how inadequate and stuttering our actual words might be, anoints that person, just as a priest does in the sacrament of the sick. To touch a sick person's hand or to speak words of affection or consolation to a dying person, in its own way, does what the woman at Bethany did for Jesus and what Helen Prejean did for Patrick Sonnier. It anoints them for their impending death. The incarnation has given us incredible power.

4. A Few Concluding Notes in Response to Some Obvious Objections

a. If This Is True, It Is Too Good to Be True!

Some years ago, I wrote several short articles on the incarnation, suggesting essentially what has just been outlined here. There was a deluge of letters and complaints.

Many objected on this basis: "How can you say that we can forgive sins and do all these things when only Christ can do them?" That objection is very correct, except for the fact that the view of the incarnation being proposed here never says that we forgive sins, that we bind and loose, that we heal each other, or that we anoint each other. It is Christ, working through us, who does this. The power is still with God, not with us, but in the incarnation God has chosen, marvelously, to let his power flow through us, to let our flesh give reality to his power.

More curious, however, was the complaint of a very different nature. A good number of persons wrote to the various magazines that printed these articles with this objection: "This can't be true because, if it were, it would be too good to be true!" The response to that can only be: What a marvelous description of the incarnation. It is too good to be true. It is precisely because of this incredible, unimaginable, goodness that we sing so joyfully in the Christmas carol: "Joy to the world, the Lord has come!" In Jesus' birth, something fundamental has changed. God has given us the power, literally, to keep each other out of hell.

b. WHERE THEN DOES THIS LEAVE THE CATHOLIC SACRAMENT OF CONFESSION?

If we can be forgiven our sins simply by touching the community and by going to Eucharist, is there then any need or place for an explicit confession to a priest, as is done in Roman Catholicism? Granted, this is more of a concern for Roman Catholics than for other Christians, but it is an important question nonetheless. What is the place of explicit, person-to-person confessing of sins?

This question would need a much fuller discussion than can be given here. However, this, at least, should be said in this context. What has just been said about the forgiveness of sins through touching the Body of Christ does not in any way denigrate nor lessen the importance of explicit confession. Properly understood, it does the opposite. When one understands herself or himself as part of the Body of Christ and as touching the Body of Christ, the rationalizing individualism that precisely tempts us never to confess to another person, especially an official representative of the church, drops away and we, in fact, begin to sense a burning obligation (coming from far beyond any ecclesiastical law) to confess our sins. But what is at stake in explicit confession is not the radical question of whether God forgives our sins or does not forgive them.

We do not, at the most basic of all levels, need explicit confession to a priest to have our sins forgiven—that is an unequivocal truth taught in scripture, by the church fathers, in Christian theology of every kind, in dogmatic tradition (even in the Council of Trent and the theology and catechisms that ensued from it), in church tradition, and especially in the lived practice of the faith.[12] The essential sacrament of reconciliation has always been sincerity and contrition as one approaches Eucharist and touches the Christian community. But that does not say that confession is unnecessary and unimportant.

In the story of the woman touching the hem of Jesus' cloak, there are two moments of healing, the touch and the explicit confrontation. Confession to a priest and forgiveness through simply touching the community are related in the same way as that woman's explicit exchange with Jesus is to her touching the hem of his garment. The person-to-person exchange completes something very important and it is part of one organic movement toward full reconciliation, peace, and maturity. Explicit confession is to the sacrament of reconciliation what an explicit apology is to healing. Actions speak louder than words and essential reconciliation happens through an act. But words, at a certain point, become very important. Mature people apologize explicitly and we become mature by apologizing. Moreover, as anyone who has ever been abused will tell you, something is not complete until there has been an explicit confession, an acknowledgment of wrongdoing that is not rationalized. As well, anyone familiar with the healing of addictions, who understands how any twelve-step program works, will tell you that until one faces, with searing honesty, one's sins and tells them, face to face, to another human person, there will be no final healing and peace.

When one believes oneself to be essentially reconciled by touching the community of faith this does not lessen the need for private confession. It begins a process which, when it comes to maturity, will make one see, as did the woman who touched the hem of the garment, that now it is of critical importance that a deeply personal, and searing, face-to-face encounter take place.

For Understanding Guidance

What is the difference between how we seek guidance from God, depending upon whether or not we are a Christian?

The conversion of St. Paul to Christianity is most revealing in this regard, as indeed it is about the incarnation in general. In the Acts of the Apostles, his conversion is described this way.[13]

Paul (then called Saul) already is a sincere, pious believer, a theist. So fervent is he in the faith, in fact, that he is persecuting Christians, believing them to be straying from the true path of faith. One day, however, as he is walking to Damascus to arrest Christians he is felled by a light from heaven and he hears a voice saying: "Saul, Saul, why are you persecuting me?" Curious, Paul has never seen Jesus, yet he is being accused of persecuting Christ. Paul answers: "Who are you?" The answer comes: "I am Jesus, whom you are persecuting." Notice how the person of the historical Jesus and the body of believers are identified as a single identity.

And Paul is touched to the heart and there, on the spot, gives his life to Christ . . . but he immediately receives his first lesson as to the implications of that. Instead of a clear directive from heaven as to where to go and what to do, he is instructed to let himself be taken by the hand and be led into Damascus where the Christian community will tell him what to do. As a Christian, he is to receive guidance not only from God above but also from community below.

As Christians we seek guidance "through Christ." However, since Christ refers both to the historical Jesus, now exalted in heaven, and the concrete, historical body of believers here on earth, when we seek guidance in terms of discernment and decisions we need to look not just to God in heaven, but also to what is being pointed out to us by the Body of Christ on earth, namely, our families, our friends, our churches, and our communities.

To offer just one example: I spent some years as a spiritual director to seminarians. Very often a young man would come to me, struggling with his decision as to whether to accept ordination or to leave the seminary. Invariably, in trying to discern this, he would want to lean almost exclusively on a gut-feeling that would come to him on the basis of private prayer and private reflection. Rarely would he want to give equal weight to the assessment of the seminary community and the persons he had already, in various internship situations, ministered to. Bluntly put, he wanted to discern as a theist—"What does God in heaven want me to do?"—without doing what Paul was asked to do, let himself be taken by the hand by human beings and allow them some say in the matter.

John of the Cross once said that the language of God is the experience God writes into our lives.[14] That is a good incarnational comment. God does not speak to us through séances, and the most important things that God wants to say to us are not given in extraordinary mystical visions. The God of the incarnation has real flesh on earth and speaks to us in the bread and butter of our lives, through things that have skin—historical circumstance, our families, our neighbors, our churches, and that borderline-psychotic friend who painfully reminds us that we are not God. When we look for God's guidance these voices on earth must complement the voice from heaven.

For Understanding Community

The fact that God has human flesh has some rather hard consequences regarding spirituality and community. Spirituality, at least Christian spirituality, is never something you do alone. Community is a constitutive part of the very essence of Christianity and thus of spirituality. God calls us to walk in discipleship, not alone but in a group. Again, one scriptural text can suffice to teach this.

In each of the four gospels there is a certain pattern: Jesus' preaching initially fires a great popularity. People flock to listen to him, idolize him, and want to make him king. However, eventually something happens, a different understanding of his message seeps through, and his popularity degenerates and sours to the point where people want to, and do, kill him. John's gospel gives a very revealing reason for why, at a certain point, the crowds become disillusioned and angry with Jesus. What is that breaking point, as John describes it?[15]

In John's gospel, Jesus reaches the zenith of his popularity right after he has multiplied the loaves and fishes. At that point, he has to flee the crowds because they would like to make him king. However, right after this, he begins to explain more deeply what the bread of life means, and it is this that gets him into trouble. He tells the crowds: "In truth I tell you, if you do not eat the flesh of the son of man and drink his blood, you have no life within you."[16] And the reaction is astonishing. After that virtually everyone left him, saying: "This is intolerable language. How can anyone accept it?"[17]

What did Jesus say that was so strong and cutting that he went from someone whom they wanted to make king to someone whom they wanted to kill? How do you go from great popularity to a persona non grata on the basis of one homily?

By teaching as Jesus taught, namely, that "unless you eat my flesh and drink my blood, you will not have life in you." What does that mean?

Fierce debates have been waged about this line, with some commentators suggesting that what was so upsetting to Jesus' listeners is the implication of cannibalism. Anyone would be upset at the suggestion that he or she must literally eat human flesh.

Others have read Eucharist into this text and suggest that the people were upset because Jesus is implying that he is physically, flesh and blood, present in the Eucharist and to receive him there is to literally eat his flesh.

Both of these interpretations, ultimately, miss the point. They are correct only in that they sense that the question of Christ's physical body is somehow at issue here. However, neither cannibalism nor receiving a consecrated wafer at the Eucharist is what is being referred to. What divides wheat from chaff is not the capacity or incapacity to walk down a church aisle and receive holy communion. Jesus' challenge here is infinitely more demanding than that. What is it?

The key to understanding Jesus' demand here is the word that he chooses to use. He uses the word *sarx* to refer to his body. An astonishing choice of words. The New Testament, in its original Greek, uses two words for body, that is, for the whole human person—*sarx* and *soma*. Soma refers to the human person insofar as the person is good or neutral. Thus, for instance, if Robert Burns' famous line, "a body meet a body/Coming through the rye," had been sung by the Greek authors of the New Testament, they would have given it a voice in this way: "Gin a soma meet a soma/coming through the rye . . ." *Sarx*, on the other hand, always refers to the human person pejoratively, negatively. It refers to the human person insofar as there is something unfavorable about him or her. Thus, for example, I am a *sarx* insofar as I get sick, have bodily smells, sin, and die, but I am a *soma* insofar as I am healthy, attractive, do virtuous things, and rise from the dead.

Given this background—and the fact that the Body of Christ means not just the person of the historical Jesus and the real presence of God in the Eucharist, but also the concrete, historical body of believers on earth—we see more clearly some of what Jesus means here and why it is so strong and divisive. By using *sarx*, Jesus is referring to his body precisely insofar as it is not simply his sinless, glorified body in heaven, nor simply a sterilized, white communion wafer in a church. What we are being asked "to eat" is that other part of his body, the community, the flawed body of believers here on earth.

In essence, Jesus is saying: You cannot deal with a perfect, all-loving, all-forgiving, all-understanding God in heaven, if you cannot deal with a less-than-perfect, less-than-forgiving, and less-than-understanding community here on earth. You cannot pretend to be dealing with an invisible God if you refuse to deal with a visible family. Teaching this truth can ruin one's popularity in a hurry. People then found it to be "intolerable language" and it meets with the same resistance today.

To concretize this somewhat, let us imagine an example: You join a new parish community. Initially, meeting all these people for the first time, you find the community good and to your liking. You are so impressed in fact that you get involved both in the parish council and the choir. Eventually, however, as you get to know everyone more deeply, a certain disillusionment sets in. You learn that your pastor has some real faults, that your parish council can be petty and narrow, and the community itself can be quite self-absorbed and callous to the needs of those outside itself. It all comes to a head one evening at a board meeting when someone accuses you of being pushy and arrogant. The penny drops inside you, and as you walk out of that meeting, you say to yourself: "This is intolerable! I don't need to put up with this! I'm outta here!"

You have just walked away from the *sarx* . . . because that is what Christ's concrete body on earth will always look like. To say, "I don't have to deal with this!" goes against the teaching of Christ because this is precisely what he was referring to when he said: "Unless you eat my flesh you cannot have life within you." Jesus, at least in John's gospel, is clear. We cannot bypass a flawed family on earth to try to relate to an nonflawed God in heaven. Concrete community is a nonnegotiable element within the spiritual quest because, precisely, we are Christians not simply theists. God is not just in heaven, God is also on earth.

This has many far-reaching consequences. Among other

things, it exposes a major popular misconception (a viral heresy) that so negatively influences popular thought today.

This misunderstanding has different expressions but it can be summarized in a simple phrase: *"I am a good Christian, a sincere, God-serving person, but I don't need church—I can pray just as well at home."*

That can be true, if you are, precisely, a theist, but it can never be true for a Christian (or for anyone within Judaism as well). Part of the very essence of Christianity is to be together in a concrete community, with all the real human faults that are there and the tensions that this will bring us. Spirituality, for a Christian, can never be an individualistic quest, the pursuit of God outside of community, family, and church. The God of the incarnation tells us that anyone who says that he or she loves an invisible God in heaven and is unwilling to deal with a visible neighbor on earth is a liar since no one can love a God who cannot be seen if he or she cannot love a neighbor who can be seen.[18]

Hence a Christian spirituality is always as much about dealing with each other as it is about dealing with God.

For Understanding Religious Experience

There is also a fundamental difference between a theist and a Christian in how each actively seeks God and understands religious experience. Let me illustrate this with an example:

Some years ago, I was attending a seminar on prayer. The woman leading the seminar, an expert on Eastern methods of prayer, was explaining various methods of meditation and, at one point, shared with us her own prayer life. She described how she, using a particular method which involves sitting silently for two hours each day, would have some very moving experiences of God. During the question period, I asked her how those experiences of God that she had in prayer compared with the experiences she had in her ordinary everyday life, her day-to-day sharing of conversation, tasks, and meals with her family.

"No comparison," she replied. "Being with and eating with my family is a good human experience [mostly], but it is not religious. It's just human. In meditation I have true *religious* experience."

A Christian needs to be both pagan and incarnational enough to dispute her answer. While not disputing the importance of private prayer and meditation (which most of us should do more of), what must be challenged here, if one is a Christian, is the theistic rather than incarnational perspective. The God who has become incarnate in human flesh is found, first and foremost, not in meditation and monasteries, albeit God is found there, but in our homes. As Nikos Kazantzakis puts it: "Wherever you find husband and wife, that's where you find God; wherever children and petty cares and cooking and arguments and reconciliation are, that is where God is too."[19] The God of the incarnation is more domestic than monastic.

"God is love and whoever abides in love abides in God."[20] When scripture affirms this, the love of which it speaks is not so much romantic love as it is the flow of life within a family. God is not "falling in love," but family, shared existence. The God of the incarnation lives in a family, a trinity, a community of shared existence. Hence, to say that God is love is to say that God is community, family, shared existence, and whoever shares his or her existence inside of family and community experiences God and has the very life of God flow through her or him.

If this is true, and it is, then a lot changes in how we should seek to experience God. If God is incarnate in ordinary life then we should seek God, first of all, within ordinary life. Too often, even though we know this theoretically, practically we still look for God in the extraordinary.

To offer some examples: Why do we go on pilgrimages to holy places and not instead sit barefoot and feel the holiness of the soil of the earth? Why do we go to places like Lourdes and Fatima, to see where the Blessed Virgin might have cried, and not notice the tears in the eyes of the person sitting across the family table from ourselves? Why are we all enthralled by a person like

Padre Pio, who carried the wounds of Jesus in his hands and feet, and blind to the wounds of Christ in the face of the emotionally needy person we so much try to avoid? There is nothing wrong with pilgrimages, Marian shrines, and Padre Pio, but it is not through them that God says the most important things to us. A friend of mine shares how he used to golf regularly with a very sincere and enthusiastic, evangelical Christian who was always praying that God might give him a vision. One day my friend said to him: "Do you want to see a vision? Get up tomorrow and watch the sun rise. That's as good as God does!"

That is a Christian perspective on religious experience. The God who is love and family, who was born in a barn, is a God who is found, first of all, in our homes, in our families, at our tables, in sunrises, in our joys, and in our arguments. To be involved in the normal flow of life, giving and receiving, as flawed and painful as this might be at times within any relationship, is to have the life of God flow through us.

Christian spirituality is not as much about admiring God, or even trying to imitate God, as it is about undergoing God and participating, through taking part in the ordinary give and take of relationships, in the flow of God's life. The God who became flesh in order to be experienced by the ordinary senses, still has flesh and is primarily to be experienced through the ordinary senses.

For Understanding Mission

Some years ago a Christian journal carried the lament of a woman who, with some bitterness, explained why she did not believe in God. Never in her explanation did she mention dogma, morals, or church authority. For her, the credibility of God and of Christ depended more on something else, the faces of Christians. Her complaint went something like this:

> Don't come talk to me of God, come to my door with religious pamphlets, or ask me whether I'm saved. Hell holds no threat more

agonizing than the harsh reality of my own life. I swear to you that the fires of hell seem more inviting than the bone-deep cold of my own life. And don't talk to me of church. What does the church know of my despair—barricaded behind its stained-glass windows against the likes of me? I once sought repentance and community within your walls, but I saw your God reflected in your faces as you turned away from the likes of me. Forgiveness was never given me. The healing love that I sought was carefully hoarded, reserved for your own kind. So be gone from me and speak no more of God. I've seen your God made manifest in you and he is a God without compassion. So long as your God withholds the warmth of human touch from me, I shall remain an unbeliever.[21]

The last thing that Jesus asked of us before he ascended, was that we go to all peoples and nations and preach his presence.[22] However, that must be understood precisely in an incarnational, not theistic, way. The challenge is not, as the woman just quoted makes clear, to pass out religious tracts, establish religious television networks to make Jesus known, or even to try to baptize everyone into Christianity. The task is to radiate the compassion and love of God, as manifest in Jesus, in our faces and our actions.

When Israel's great prophets are called, God initiates them through an interesting ritual. They are asked to physically eat the scroll of the law, to eat their scriptures.[23] What a powerful symbolism! The idea is that they should digest the word and turn it into their own flesh so that people will be able to see the word of God in a living body rather than on a dead parchment. The task of taking God to others is not that of handing somebody a Bible or some religious literature, but of transubstantiating God, the way we do with the food we eat. We have to digest something and turn it, physically, into the flesh of our own bodies so it becomes part of what we look like. If we would do this with the word of God, others would not have to read the Bible to see what God is like, they would need only to look at our faces and our lives to see God.

Jean-Paul Sartre, even though he came at this from an atheistic perspective, adds a valuable insight here. He once suggested that human beings create their own faces. For Sartre, we are born without a face, at least without one that says very much. When a baby is born, three features characterize its face: First, its face exhibits very little in the way of individuality. Despite mothers' protests to the contrary, all babies look very much alike! Second, a baby's face tells little about the personality of that child. Looking at a baby's face gives you little indication as to what kind of character that person possesses and will develop. Finally, in a baby's face, beauty is almost totally genetic. A baby is good-looking or not depending almost entirely on its genetic endowment.

This holds true for a baby when it is first born, but, with each hour, day, and year of its life, this changes and, according to Sartre, culminates at age forty when, finally, a person has the essential lines of a face. At that age, we look different from anyone else in the world (even if we have an identical twin), our face speaks volumes about who we are, and our physical beauty has begun to blend with our general beauty so that we are now judged to be good-looking or not more on the basis of who we are than on the simple basis of physical endowment. From age forty onward, our faces manifest individuality, character, and a beauty-beyond-genes.

What is important about all of this is what, in the end, forms our faces. Up until age forty, genetic endowment is dominant and that is why, up until that age, we can be selfish and still look beautiful. From then onward, though, we look like what we believe in. If I am anxious, petty, selfish, bitter, narrow, and self-centered, my face will show it. Conversely, if I am warm, gracious, humble, and other-centered, my face will also show it. A scary thought; there can be no poker faces after forty.

Our mission as persons of faith is precisely to form our own faces in the correct way. The word has started to become flesh and it needs to continue to take flesh in that God must now be transubstantiated not only into the bread of the Eucharist but, even more important, into human faces.

Jesus taught us that the kingdom of God works like yeast. We are asked to let the things he taught transform us, from the inside, like yeast transforms dough and as summer transforms a tree. Our digestion of the word of God must make us look different physically. Thus, our first task in preaching is a silent one. We must transubstantiate God in order to give a human face to divine compassion and forgiveness. Only rarely need we preach using words.

For Understanding How We Remain in Contact with Our Loved Ones After Their Deaths

Finally, there is also a huge difference between how a theist and a Christian understand contact and intimacy with our loved ones after they have died.

Both, theists and Christians, believe in life after death and both too believe that there can be a rich contact between us on earth and our loved ones who have died. However, if one accepts the incarnation, there is a different spirituality as to how this contact takes place.

For a theist, in the best understanding of this, contact is understood to take place mystically, soul to soul, through a certain imaginative (though real) presence of the loved one inside of us. While the Christian does not dispute this, he or she goes further. How does a Christian remain in contact, love, communication, and in a real community of life with his or her loved ones after they have died? How do we find our loved ones after death separates them from us?

Through their word made flesh. By giving concrete expression in our lives to those virtues and qualities which they best incarnated. How does this work?

It was all explained to us at Jesus' resurrection. On Easter Sunday morning, Mary Magdala went to the tomb of Jesus, hoping to anoint his dead body with spices. She was confronted, however, with an empty tomb and an angel who said to her: *"Why do you seek the living among the dead?"*[24]

Curious words? Not really. In effect, the angel is telling her that cemeteries are not the real place where we find people who have passed from this world but are now alive in a new way. We do not find our deceased loved ones in their graves, good though it be to visit graves. Invisible angels sit there, at the graves of our loved ones, and send us back into life to seek for them at other places. Just as Mary Magdala did not find Jesus in his tomb, we too will not find our loved ones there. Where will we find them? We will meet the ones we can no longer touch when we put ourselves in situations where their souls once flourished. Our loved ones live where they have always lived and it is there that we will find them. What does that mean?

Simply put, we find our deceased loved ones by entering into life, in terms of love and faith, in the way that was most distinctive to them. We contact them and connect ourselves to them when, in our own lives, we shape the infinite richness of God's life and compassion in the way that they did, when we pour ourselves into life as they did.

Let me try to illustrate this with an example: My own parents died more than twenty years ago. Sometimes I visit their graves. That is a good experience. I feel some grounding in it, some deep rooting that helps center me. But this is not my real contact with them. No. I meet them among the living. I meet them when, in my own life, I live what was most distinctively them in terms of their love, faith, and virtue. Thus, for example, my mother was a very selfless woman, generous to a fault, always giving everything away. When I am generous and give of myself as she did, I meet my mother. She becomes very present, very alive. At those times, I do not experience her as dead at all. It is the same with my father. His great quality was his moral integrity, a unique stubbornness in faith, an uncompromising insistence that one should not give in to even the smallest moral compromise. At those times when I can be his son in these things, when I can, in fact, face down little and big temptations in my life, my father is present, alive, connected, in a vital community of life with me.

Less happily, but just as true, the reverse is also the case: At those times when I am selfish, when I cannot give myself over in sacrifice, my mother is more absent, more dead to me. The same with my father: When I compromise morally, be the issue ever so small, my father is not so alive to me. He recedes like the tide. It is not very helpful to visit their graves at those times for, in fact, in my actual life then, I am living among the dead. If I cry out to them in prayer at those times the only response I get is from the angel of the resurrection who tells me, gently, what was told Mary Magdala: Why do you seek the living among the dead?

Every good person shapes the infinite life and compassion of God in a unique way. When that person dies, we must seek him or her among the living. Thus, if we want a loved one's presence we must seek him or her out in what was most distinctively him or her, in terms of love, faith, and virtue. If your mother had a gift for hospitality, you will meet her when you are hospitable; if your friend had a passion for justice, you will meet him when you give yourself over to the quest for justice; if your aunt had a great zest for life, for meals with her family, and for laughter in the house, you will meet her when you have a zest for life, eat with your family, and have laughter in your house.

That is how a Christian searches for his or her loved ones after they have died. Theists visit graves (and Christians too visit graves because we are also theists) but, given the incarnation, given that we are all part of the word becoming flesh, as Christians, we search for our deceased loved ones outside of cemeteries, among the living—at our tables, in our places of work, and in the decisions, great and small, that we must daily make.

The Heart of Spirituality for a Christian

In the preface of his book on Jesus, John Shea makes this comment: "When the last syllable of the last word about Jesus the Christ has been spoken, a small, balding man who until now has been silent will say, 'Just a moment I . . .' After two thousand years people still journey to Jesus. They bring a vaunting ego and last year's scar, one unruly hope and several debilitating fears, and unwarranted joy and a hesitant heart—and ask Jesus what to make of it. We have only gradually become aware of the hook in Jesus' promise, 'I will be with you all days, even to the end of the world.' This not only means he will not go away but that we cannot get rid of him. He continues to roll back the stone from the caves we entomb him in."[25]

As we struggle to channel our eros, to find the spiritual disciplines that can bring us life, we need to bring our egos and our scars, our hopes and our fears, and our joys and our hesitancies to Jesus to see what he makes of them. But Christian spirituality is more even than that. The fire energy of God that so burns inside us will come to maturity, creativity, and calm when we shape our lives and our bodies in the way that Jesus shaped his, when we help him carry the incarnation forward. Spirituality, as we have already said, is not a law to be obeyed, but a presence to be seized, undergone, and given flesh to.

PART FOUR

Some Key Spiritualities Within a Spirituality

What we choose to fight is so tiny!
What fights with us is so great.
If only we would let ourselves be dominated
as things do by some immense storm,
we would become strong too, and not need names.

When we win it's with small things
and the triumph itself makes us small.
What is extraordinary and eternal
does not want to be bent by us. . . .

This is how one grows: by being defeated, decisively.
by constantly greater beings.
   —RAINER MARIA RILKE

The most intimate of all talk is talk about God.
   —ETTY HILLESUM

Christ is an extraordinary being with lips of thunder and acts of
lurid decision, flinging down tables, casting out devils, passing
with the wild secrecy of the wind from mountain isolation to a
sort of dreadful demagogy.
   —G. K. CHESTERTON

For happiness is not what makes us grateful. It is gratefulness that makes us happy.
    —David Steindl-Rast

God is self-evident, but what it is to be God is not self-evident to us.
    —Thomas Aquinas

Lost is a place, too.
    —Christina Crawford

A Spirituality of Ecclesiology

In the waters of baptism we are reminded that we are not born in a vacuum, nor do we journey entirely alone (although loneliness is often part of the burden). Being reborn, being made alive, involves being born into a community. So there are strings attached to this adventure. Far from being the spiritual journey of the solitary individual in search of God, it drags a people, a church, a nation, the human race, along with it.[1]

I Want the Kingdom but Not the Church

Already a century ago, a debate raged within Christian theology concerning the necessity or nonnecessity of the institutional church. A number of theologians were asking a tough question: "Jesus preached a kingdom—so why do we have the church?"

Whatever their fate in history, these theologians have a lot of sympathy today. Certainly in the Western world, an ever-growing number of people are questioning the validity of the church and are seeking to find God, moral guidance, and to express themselves religiously outside the walls of the Christian churches. Their critique of the church has both a theoretical and a practical side.

Theoretically, more and more people are simply divorcing their search for God from involvement within a church community. Not everyone does this for the same reason. For some, like

Sam Keen,[2] whose criticism we saw earlier, involvement in a church brings the spiritual quest to a premature end and thus negatively prejudices spirituality. His view is also that the churches demand an obedience that renders its members somewhat adolescent. Many agree with him. For others, their reluctance to darken the door of a church stems from the church's history. They see it as a compromised institution, one with too much blood on its hands, spiritual fat on its body, and too many skeletons in its closet. They no longer believe that it is an institution that meditates God's grace. Coupled with this criticism of the church's faults is the simple view that the Christian church has tried for two thousand years and not really changed anything, analogous to a two-thousand-year-old sports franchise that has never won a championship. It's time for a change!

Whether these criticisms are true and of substance or whether they are rationalizations and dangerous oversimplifications is not the point here. The point is their popularity, the fact that millions of people today are struggling theoretically with their churches and are antipathetic to the very idea of ecclesiology.

But more serious even than this theoretical criticism is the practical critique of ecclesiology today within Western culture. People are voting with their feet. They simply are going to church less and less. Church attendance and church involvement are falling off drastically. Statistics vary from country to country, but every country in the Western world is experiencing a major drop in church attendance.

Researchers studying this, however, note a couple of surprising things:[3] First, while church attendance is dropping alarmingly, the churches themselves have great staying power. Thus, while not wanting to attend regularly and be involved in their churches, people do continue to want to identify themselves religiously with a certain label ("I'm a Baptist, a Roman Catholic, an Anglican, a Presbyterian, a member of the United Church," and so on) and want, as well, to continue to receive rites of passage (baptism, marriage, and burial) within their churches.

Moreover, they want to see their churches continue, even though they are not attending them. They want the church to be there when they want it, even if they do not want it very often. As a Canadian sociologist of religion, Reginald Bibby, puts it: "People aren't leaving their churches, they just aren't going to them."[4]

As well, research on the question of declining church attendance shows that most people who do not practice regularly do not have the questions that the Sam Keens have nor the angers of the church's harshest critics. Anger and hard theoretical questions about the church are not the biggest problem; indifference and a culture of individualism are. Most people who are not at church on Sunday are not at home brooding about the church's faults or reading Sam Keen's book. They are sleeping, shopping, skiing, jogging in the park, watching baseball and football games, working on their lawns and gardens, and visiting with family and friends. They do not have huge ecclesiology questions. As regards church, they are on sabbatical. They want a kingdom, but not a church.

All of this points to many things: the church's faults, the church's dark history, a certain tiredness within Western Christianity, our culture's pathological individualism, the religious indifference of millions, and a perception problem as regards the Christian churches. Certainly it points to the need for a better understanding of the church. The churches may have the water of life, but less and less people want them anywhere near the fire. What's to be done about that?

Our theological libraries are full of excellent books on ecclesiology, but church attendance continues to plummet. Good theology is important, but something else too is needed, a better spirituality of ecclesiology, better practical, personal reasons why, to have a kingdom, we want and need a church.

So how might the church be understood?

Toward a Spirituality of Ecclesiology—Spiritual Images of the Church

1. The Church Is the People . . . Apostolic Community

Before all else, *the church is the people.* Long before there should be any mention of buildings, ministers, priests, bishops, popes, organizations, institutions, or moral codes, there should be mention of a community of hearts and souls, previously separated by many things, coming together. Jesus formed a community around himself, animated it, and then left it his word, his spirit, and the Eucharist. That community is the church and it is a particular kind of community, an apostolic one.

What is an apostolic community? What constitutes a church?

There are so many misunderstandings about this that, for purposes of clarity, it is best to approach it through the *via negativa,* namely, to begin by specifying what apostolic community is not. Church community, while it may contain some of these aspects, and these aspects may indeed even contribute something positive, is not, in essence, any of the following:

a. LIKE-MINDED INDIVIDUALS, GATHERING ON THE BASIS OF MUTUAL COMPATIBILITY

This is a very common misunderstanding, but gathering as church has little or nothing to do with liking each other or finding others with whom we are mutually compatible. The group of disciples that first gathered around Jesus were not individuals who were mutually compatible at all. They came from very different backgrounds and temperaments, had different visions of what Jesus was all about, were jealous of each other, and were, as scripture tells us, occasionally furious with each other. They *loved* each other, in the biblical meaning of that phrase, but they did not necessarily *like* each other—akin to a church member who says to a fellow member who is a constant source of irritation to her: "Janice, my love for you is entirely supernatural, of that I can assure you!"

That is what it means to be church. Too often we are disappointed in church because we find there such a diverse and motley collection of persons, some of whom do not like us and whom we would never pick to be our friends. We go to church looking for friendship or ideological soulmates and, often, do not find them. This does not necessarily mean that there is something wrong with the church, merely that we have false expectations. To be in apostolic community, church, is not necessarily to be with others with whom we are emotionally, ideologically, and otherwise compatible. Rather it is to stand, shoulder to shoulder and hand in hand, precisely with people who are very different from ourselves and, with them, hear a common word, say a common creed, share a common bread, and offer a mutual forgiveness so as, in that way, to bridge our differences and become a common heart. Church is not about a few like-minded persons getting together for mutual support; it is about millions and millions of different kinds of persons transcending their differences so as to become a community beyond temperament, race, ideology, gender, language, and background.

b. Huddling in Fear and Loneliness

Likewise, apostolic community is not a group of persons huddling in fear or loneliness—"you and me, against the world"—as is sometimes seen when two frightened persons marry each other or when small sectarian groups form because of a shared fear.

In both John's gospel and in the Acts of the Apostles, we see this kind of false community among the early disciples before they receive the Spirit.[5] They are described as "huddled in a room with the doors locked, out of fear." In that state, they are physically together, under one roof, in the same house, but not a real community. Ironically, after the Spirit descends upon them at Pentecost, they burst forth from that room, go to different parts of the world, and some never see each other again, but have genuine community.

Apostolic community is not had by joining others who share our fears and, with them, barricading ourselves against what threatens us. It is had when, on the basis of something more powerful than our fears, we emerge from our locked rooms and begin to take down walls. As Henri Nouwen so well describes it: "When the Spirit descended on the disciples huddling together in fear, they were free to move out of their closed room into the world. As long as they were assembled in fear they did not yet form community. But when they had received the Spirit, they became a body of people who could stay in communion with each other even when they were as far from each other as Rome is from Jerusalem. Thus, when it is the Spirit of God and not fear that unites us in community, no distance of time or place can separate us."[6]

Apostolic community never occurs when a few lonely or frightened people gang up against the world.

c. "Family" in the Psychological Sense

Some years ago, a young man joined the Oblates, the religious community of which I am a member. He was a very idealistic young person, but, emotionally, a very needy one. Time and time again, at our community meetings, he would complain about lack of community with this type of refrain: "I joined this order, looking for community, but everyone is always too busy to have time for me. We don't share deeply enough with each other. There is no real intimacy among us. We are too cold, too masculine. I'm forever lonely and nobody much cares!"

He was right about the community. No religious community is perfect and ours was far from it, but that was not really his main problem, false expectations were. Eventually he went for counseling. The counselor, a priest-psychologist who understood the dynamics of religious community, helped the young man clarify things and, at one point, told him: "What you are really looking for is not to be found in a religious order. You are looking for a lover, not a religious community."

We have often confused church community with family in

the psycho-sexual sense. This has brought us no end of disappointment. We speak of the church as a family, but it is not a family like a family created by a man and a woman and children is a family. A family in the normal, psycho-sexual, sense is made up of two persons coming together in love and sexual relation and eventually having children together. Within that framework, which includes the sexual, a whole range of intimate needs can be met that cannot be met in other kinds of families. Perhaps a few mystics, like Teresa of Avila, who would occasionally go into an emotional and bodily ecstasy after receiving holy communion, will find their need for emotional and sexual intimacy fulfilled within a church. They are the exceptions. The rest of us need to go to church looking for something else. Church community can never be a functional substitute for emotional and sexual intimacy. It is not intended to be. One shouldn't go to church looking for a lover.

We might well want to remember this at those times when we complain that our churches are too large, too impersonal, and we do not always find there the warmth and emotional support we legitimately desire and need. "How can I feel any warmth and intimacy," is the frequently asked question, "when I am worshiping in a huge church with six hundred other people?"

If our creeds are correct, and I believe that they are, we are destined to spend eternity with billions and billions of other people. Worshiping in large groups is a good way of getting some practice at this.

d. One Roof, One Ethnicity, One Denomination, One Rule Book, or One Book of Common Prayer

Apostolic community is also not a question of simply living together in one house, being united by common blood, being part of a single religious denomination, having a common rule book, or being bound by a common book of prayer.

I can live under the same roof with somebody, be his or her blood brother or sister, live a common rule with someone, and be part of the same religious denomination, and not really be in community with that person. The reverse is also true. I can be continents apart, of a different ethnicity, and of a different faith, and yet be in community with another person. A shared roof, a shared bed, a shared table, a shared blood, a shared family history, and a shared religious denomination does not, of itself, community make; just as physical distance, living alone, sleeping alone, a different color of skin, and a different faith do not necessarily separate us. Apostolic community, as we shall see, depends upon something else.

e. A Shared Task, a Common Mission

One of the things that apostolic community is often confused with, but is not, is the togetherness that is brought about by having a common mission. I remember, as an example, a pep talk I once heard a Catholic school principal give his staff on the opening day of the school year: "As a staff, we form a community together and we need that oneness to be effective. We don't have to like each other, we don't have to be emotional family for each other, and we don't have to pretend that there aren't huge differences and tensions among us. What is important is that we have a job to do together, a shared mission. Together we must give these kids the best education that's possible. To do this, we need to be a real team, not just a coalition of freelance individuals."

He was right about one thing, a common mission demands a team effort. But a common mission, precisely, creates a team—to win the Superbowl, to produce a product, to police the city, to run an organization, or even to catechize our children—but it does not, of itself, make for apostolic community. Church community must be founded on something else.

What? If church community is not to take its foundation in like-mindedness, a shared fear, the need for intimacy in our lives, a common roof, a common ethnicity, a common denomination, or a shared mission, on what basis does it found itself?

On gathering around the person of Christ and sharing his Spirit.

On the surface that might sound like a very pious and over-worked cliché; it is anything but that. It is the sole basis for real church community and it is a hard, not a pious, statement. What does it mean, to gather around the person of Christ and share in his Spirit?

An analogy can be helpful here: Imagine a woman, whom we shall call Betzy, who has a heart the size of the Grand Canyon. She is gracious, loving, devoid of prejudice, and with an understanding and empathy wide enough to encompass everything and everybody. Because she is so loving, she has a very wide variety of friends and one night she decides to have a party and invite them all. She rents a hall to hold everyone. And her guests begin to arrive. Men, women, and children show up, of every description, ideology, background, temperament, taste, social standing, and religion. A curious mixture of persons fills the hall. Liberals and conservatives, fundamentalists and feminists, Promise Keepers and New Agers, priests and anticlerics, union presidents and bankers, animal rights activists and persons involved in the seal hunt, meat-eaters and militant vegetarians mingle with each other. Present is the president of the local pro-life association, but the president of pro-choice is also there. Ian Paisley is there, as is the leader of the Irish Republican Army.

Given the mix, there is a fair amount of tension, but because Betzy is there, because she is in the center of the room, and because they respect who she is and what she stands for, everyone, for that night at least, is polite to one another and is enough engulfed in a certain spirit of tolerance, respect, decency, and charity to stretch them beyond how they would normally feel, think, and act.

As you can imagine, such a gathering would work only while Betzy was actually present. Should she have to excuse herself and leave, or should persons get preoccupied in ways that would make them forget the real reason why they are there, you would soon enough get a combination of fireworks and dissipation that would empty the room. This particular mix of persons can be brought together and kept together only around one person, Betzy. Everything depends upon her presence and upon those present having her wide empathy while they are in that presence, that is, upon being in her spirit.

That is an image of the Christian church around Jesus Christ. Outside of a focus on his person and what we are drawn to spontaneously live when we sense his presence, we have angry fireworks and constant dissipation, as the state of our families, communities, nations, and world gives ample testimony to. Nothing else, ultimately, holds us together.

Hence the basis for Christian ecclesial community, church, is a gathering around the person of Jesus Christ and a living in his Spirit. And that Spirit too is not some vague bird or abstract tonality. The spirit of Jesus, the Holy Spirit, is defined in scripture as charity, joy, peace, patience, goodness, long-suffering, fidelity, mildness, and chastity.[7] Living in these virtues is what binds us into community in such a way that we are immune from separation by distance, temperament, race, color, gender, ideology, social status, history, creed, or even death. All who live in these virtues are one body with each other and constitute the church.

Given this criterion for apostolic community, we see that the church is both something abstract and partly outside of history and yet, at the same time, something very concrete and historical.[8] At one level, it includes all persons, regardless of where they stand in their explicit understanding of religion, who are living in charity, joy, peace, patience, goodness, long-suffering, mildness, and chastity. At another level, it comprises the historical Christian churches, those that are visibly called into community by the word of Christ and the Eucharist that he left us.

To be church is, therefore, to celebrate the word of Christ and the Eucharist.[9] But, properly understood, that implies more than simply going to church on Sunday. The Christian scriptures speak of church community as somehow meaning a common life, of "having everything in common."[10]

What is meant by that? What are the constitutive parts of concrete, ecclesial community? Beyond the level of soul, where we can be a single heart by living the same fruits of the Spirit, what concretely, other than simply attending church, is asked of us in order to have a common life?

Some Christian groups have interpreted this more literally and teach that a common life implies precisely somehow physically living together and sharing money and property in common. Thus, there have always been religious communities, both clerical and lay, within Christianity who have tried to live this out through religious vows and promises that physically create a common house, common food, and a common purse. This has, however, always been seen as a special calling for some and has never been proposed as ideal for everyone.

Instead the churches, in their best ecclesiologies, have defined common life ("fellowship," some call it) as something which is real but which does not demand, literally, one roof and one purse. What does it demand?

It demands that there be some real sharing of life together, namely, that we pray together; that we celebrate our rites of passage together; that we celebrate some of our everyday joys, fears, and feasts together; that we are responsible to each other and open to each other as regards mutual correction and challenge; that we are responsible together for the ministry of the church; and that we have some common sharing of finances (even if this means only that we contribute financially to the support of our local church and its projects).

All these things together, in essence, mean that, in some form or other, we are mutually accountable to each other for our lives. We may still live in our private houses and have our private bank accounts, but, once we belong to a church, we no longer fully own our lives. We now have to answer to each other and may no longer claim our own lives as an exclusive piece of private property. As a woman in a prayer group once put it: "I knew we had the reality of church when, after some years of praying together, we gave each other permission to mess with each others' lives. I mean, if anyone began to do things that went against what our prayer and what our lives were all about, the group would go to him or her and challenge that person to straighten himself out . . . and he or she couldn't protest and say: 'This is my life, butt out, that's none of your business!' "

That, in essence, is church community. The church is the people.

2. The Church Is the Rope—Baptism and Conscription

The church is the people, but it is also the rope that consecrates us and takes us where we would rather not go. To be baptized into a Christian church is to be a consecrated, displaced person. What is implied in that?

In the epilogue of John's gospel, there is recorded a very revealing exchange between Jesus and Peter. Three times Jesus asks Peter: "Do you love me?" Three times, Peter replies that he does. On the basis of that confession of love, Jesus tells him: "In truth I tell you, when you were young you gird your own belt and you walked where you liked; but when you grow old you will stretch out your hands, and someone else will put a rope around you and take you where you would rather not go."[11]

What has just been described is, in essence, Peter's baptism—and the dynamics of any real baptism into the church. Baptism consecrates us and consecration is a conscriptive rope that takes us to where we would rather not go, namely, into that suffering that produces maturity. This, however, needs considerable explanation.

The word consecration is, for most of us, a sacristy word. When we think of something as being consecrated we think of a church building, an altar, a sacred chalice, or a blessed Bible. When we think of a person as being consecrated we think of someone who has made special religious vows and wears a special habit, like monks, nuns, and Mother Teresa. Of itself, that conception is not wrong. To consecrate something means to displace it from normal usage: as an ordinary cup is set aside to be a chalice, an ordinary table is set aside to be an altar, an ordinary building is set aside to be a church, and an ordinary person is set aside to be a monk.

However, to think of consecration in this sense, while not wrong, gives the word a connotation of piety and of extraordinary religious separateness that deflates it of most of its punch. What does it mean to consecrate something or somebody?

To consecrate means to set aside, to displace from ordinary usage, to derail from normalcy. Long before this had to do with sacred buildings, altars, chalices, and vowed religious, it was descriptive of something within ordinary life. Consider the following examples:

In the early 1960s in New York City, there was an infamous murder. A woman was stabbed and murdered in the street while more than thirty people watched from their apartment windows. None of the onlookers called the police. They did not want to get involved. Later, when this came to light, there was a heated debate as to how guilty these innocent onlookers really were. Were they not somehow guilty because they saw the murder and did nothing about it?

For a Christian the answer is clear. Seeing that woman being stabbed consecrated them, set them aside, displaced them, and derailed them from normalcy. At that moment, they lost their freedom and were conscripted to act. If you look out of your window and see a person being stabbed in a park you are, in that instant, baptized and consecrated in the true meaning of those words. Up until that time, you could gird your belt and go where you liked, but now, seeing this, someone has put a rope around you and is taking you to where you would rather not go. Tragically, that night, in New York, more than thirty people resisted their baptism. A woman died as a result.

To offer a less dramatic, though no less clear, example: Imagine you are setting out one night to visit some friends and enjoy a barbecue on a warm summer's night. That is a perfectly legitimate agenda and God, no doubt, is hoping you will enjoy yourself. However, just as you turn out of your driveway onto the main street, you are the first person to witness a major traffic accident. Some people are seriously hurt, perhaps dying. At that moment, you lose your freedom. You are baptized, consecrated, set aside, derailed, and your perfectly legitimate agenda has to be suspended, not because it is wrong, but because something higher has literally usurped your freedom. Until you came upon that accident, like the preconfessional Peter, you could gird your belt and walk wherever you wished; now this accident is putting a belt around you and taking you where you would rather not go. The accident has made you a consecrated person—and baptized you into the church.

What is implied in that is partly captured right within the very word church. We use the term ecclesiology to refer to the theology of the church. The etymology of this word is most revealing. Ecclesiology comes from the Greek word for church, *ekklesia,* which itself comes from two Greek words, *ek kaleo (ek*—meaning *out of*—and *kaleo,* being the verb *"to call"*). Thus, *ekklesia,* church, literally means to *"be called out of."* But what are we called out of?

We are called out of what our normal agenda would be if we had not come upon the traffic accident, seen the woman being stabbed outside our window, or, in our case, met the person and the gospel of Christ and the community of faith on earth. Church puts a rope around us, takes away our freedom, and takes us where we would rather not, but should, go.

Thus, the best example of what church, baptism, and consecration really mean is the example of having and raising children. A home is a church and, in a manner of speaking, it is true to say that most parents are baptized by their own children—and raised by them!

Imagine a typical scenario. A young woman and a young man meet, fall in love, and get married. At this stage of their lives they are fairly immature. Their agenda is their own happiness and, notwithstanding that they are good-hearted and sincere, they are both still selfish with the natural self-centeredness of youth. Then, without really realizing all the implications of this for their lives, they begin to have children. From the moment their first child is born, unless they are very calloused human beings, they will, without necessarily wanting to, start to mature. What happens is that for the next twenty-five to fifty years, every time they turn around, a number of tiny and not so-tiny hands will be stretched out, demanding something of them—their time, their energy, their money, their car keys, their telephone, their sympathy, their understanding, their hearts. Whether they want to or not, they will mature. For twenty-five years to fifty years they will be forced, by a clear conscription, to think of others beyond themselves. All those years of practice will eventually pay dividends. By the time their children are grown, they will be mature.

And, during all these years of having and raising children, they are, in the deep meaning of those terms, consecrated, displaced, and baptized. They are at the scene of an accident that has usurped their freedom and made them put their normal, perfectly legitimate, agenda on hold. Instead of their normal agenda, they are conscriptively asked to make a lot of sacrifices in terms of lifestyle, career, hobbies, meals out, vacations, travel, and so on. Their children stand before them daily, like Jesus before Peter, asking: "Do you love me?" If the parents say "yes," then, biblically speaking, the children reply: "Up until now, you have gird your belts and walked wherever you wanted to, but now we are putting a rope around you and taking you where you would rather not go, namely, out of your natural selfishness and into self-sacrificing maturity."

Such is baptism. Such is the church. When St. Paul converts to Christianity, he is immediately given a lesson in fundamental ecclesiology, one not very different from the one that Jesus gave Peter. Paul is told how much he will have "to suffer for the name," for the commitment he has just made.[12] Scripture then points out that he got up off the ground and walked into his ecclesial future "with his eyes wide open, seeing nothing"[13]— which is a marvelous description of basically all of us on the day when we made our commitments in marriage, parenthood, priesthood, religious life, or any other deep vocation; we stared ahead into the future with our eyes wide open, seeing nothing, and walked, probably with some enthusiasm, into that future. How blind we were—and yet, usually, how lucky we were too. The conscriptive demands of that baptism is, to the extent that we have any, what has given us maturity and grace.

I have a friend, a layman, who works full-time in church ministry. His work is very demanding and, because that is often the only time when people in parishes can meet, he has to work most evenings. Sometimes, he tells me, on a given evening when he is driving to the church for yet another meeting, his car, almost all on its own, tries to turn into a movie theater or a sports stadium and he, behind the wheel, envying the people who are going to these events or who are sitting watching Seinfeld on television, tells God: "If there is reincarnation and I get another life, the next time, I want nothing to do with family, church, neighbor, and community. I want to come back to earth as a Yuppie and have season's tickets to everything . . . and I am not going to work a single evening in my whole life!" That is a healthy thought; he is feeling what it means to be church, to have the conscriptive rope of ecclesiology around his waist.

One last thing about the conscriptive rope: It is not one which we may let go of after we have accepted it. Ecclesial commitment does not work that way. One does not keep an exit visa in his or her back pocket and, consciously or unconsciously, emotionally blackmail the family he or she belongs to with the attitude: "I will stay with you as long as I deem you worth it or until you radically disappoint me!" The church has always taught, and rightly so, that baptism is irrevocable, that it leaves an indelible mark on the soul. Anyone who has ever had a child knows exactly what that means; when you hold your own child for the first time it scars your soul indelibly.

That is also true for being a child in the church. In scripture, we are told that, after Noah finally gets all the animals and his family into the ark (the symbol of the church), God *"locks them in."*[14] Any covenant commitment, if authentic, does precisely that; it locks us in. Like a mother who has given birth to a child or a couple who have promised lifelong fidelity to each other, we cannot opt in and out of the church as fits our moods and phases of growth. As long as we do not understand this, we are still, in terms of ecclesiology, a child or an adolescent who needs to be carried, as opposed to an adult who is helping to take responsibility for carrying the family.

3. The Church Is the Sarx—the Exzemed Body of Christ

"Unless you eat my flesh, you cannot have life within you." When Jesus says this, as we have already seen, he is referring to his *sarx,* his flawed, exzemed body, as it is met in the community of believers and he is mandating that we must also deal with this if we wish to deal with God.

In essence, this means two things: First, that community is a constitutive element within the Christian quest. My task is not to walk to God as an individual but to be within a community that is worshiping God. Second, what is taught here is that, in this life, whenever I meet the presence of God within community I will not meet it in its pure form. All communities of faith mediate the grace of God in a very mixed way. Sin, pettiness, and betrayal are always found alongside grace, sanctity, and fidelity.

The crucifixion scene is a good image of church. Jesus dies between two criminals. Anyone at the time, looking at that scene, would not have made a distinction between who was guilty and who was innocent. There was just one landscape— God on a cross between two thieves. That is the perennial ecclesial image. Grace and sin, sanctity and pettiness, and fidelity and betrayal, all part of a single horizon.

And there are no communities or families, ecclesial or other, where this is not the case. Today we have a rich literature which analyzes dysfunctional families and often names the church the prime analogate of such a family. This analysis is, for the most part, quite accurate. Its fault is not in what it says, but in what it subtly intimates, namely, that there are somewhere families and organizations that are functional, that deliver grace without sin. No such families exist. All human families and organizations are dysfunctional, it is merely a question of degree. An old Protestant axiom has it: "It is not a question of whether you are a sinner or not, but only a question of what is your sin?" The same holds true for families, organizations, and churches—all of them. It is never a question of whether your family is dysfunctional, it is only one of—what is its particular canker and how bad is it?

This is an important horizon against which to understand the negative aspects of the church. Today, many people cannot understand how, given certain aspects of the church's history and some of its present infidelities, it can be seen as a privileged instrument of grace.

Is God really to be found in an organization that slaughtered so many innocent people in the Crusades, that used the Inquisition as a divine tool, that sanctioned racism and sexism for centuries, and that has in its history so much in the way of religious wars, sinful silences, and blind imperialism? Is God really to be found in an organization that has some pedophiles among its ministers? How many millions of people have been hurt by the church? How can the church be forgiven for some of its history and parts of its present practice?

These are not irreverent questions, though, ultimately, not iconoclastic ones either. The church is always God hung between two thieves. Thus, no one should be surprised or shocked at how badly the church has betrayed the gospel and how much it continues to do so today. It has never done very well. Conversely, however, nobody should deny the good the church has done either. It has carried grace, produced saints, morally challenged the planet, and made, however imperfectly, a house for God to dwell in on this earth.

To be connected with the church is to be associated with scoundrels, warmongers, fakes, child-molesters, murderers, adulterers, and hypocrites of every description. It also, at the same time, identifies you with saints and the finest persons of heroic soul within every time, country, race, and gender. To be a member of the church is to carry the mantle of both the worst sin and the finest heroism of soul . . . because the church always looks exactly as it looked at the original crucifixion, God hung among thieves.

Carlo Carretto, the great Italian spiritual writer, once wrote a little tribute to the church which captures well both its scandal and its grace. In the closing section of perhaps his most mature book, *I Sought and I Found,* Carretto addresses the church in these words:

How much I must criticize you, my church and yet how much I love you!

You have made me suffer more than anyone and yet I owe more to you than to anyone.

I should like to see you destroyed and yet I need your presence.

You have given me much scandal and yet you alone have made me understand holiness.

Never in this world have I seen anything more compromised, more false, yet never have I touched anything more pure, more generous or more beautiful.

Countless times I have felt like slamming the door of my soul in your face—and yet, every night, I have prayed that I might die in your sure arms!

No, I cannot be free of you, for I am one with you, even if not completely you.

Then too—where would I go?

To build another church?

But I could not build one without the same defects, for they are my defects. And again, if I were to build another church, it would be my church, not Christ's church.

No. I am old enough. I know better![15]

Anyone who searches for God and perseveres in that quest will, at some point, look at the role that human community plays in that quest and resonate with what Carretto has written.

4. The Church Is the House of Many Rooms—Catholicity

One of the marks of being a church is catholicity. All Christians, not just Roman Catholics, teach that. What is meant by that?

To be catholic is not the opposite of being protestant. Protestants too claim the name catholic and the "protest" of the original Protestant reformers was not, in essence, so much a protest against the pope and Roman Catholicism as it was a protest, a witness, for God, for God's holiness, and against anything that would limit the catholicity of God's heart.

What does it mean to be catholic? Jesus gave the best definition of the term when he said: "In my Father's house there are many rooms."[16] This is not a description of a certain geography in heaven but a revelation of the breadth of God's heart. The bosom of God is not a ghetto. God has a catholic heart—in that catholic means universal, wide, all-encompassing. The opposite of a catholic is a fundamentalist, a person who has a heart with one room.

Thus, any spirituality of the church needs to emphasize wide loyalties and inclusivity.

To belong to a church is to be loyal to many things, not just to one thing. A healthy member of a church community does not pick, in an either/or fashion, between having boundaries or emphasizing freedom, between believing in defined doctrines or emphasizing individual conscience, between the gift of legitimate institutionalized authority or the importance of individual charisma, between the role of ordained ministers and the priesthood of all people, between the needs of the local community and the needs of the larger universal church, between what the gifted artist brings to the community and what the poorest of the poor brings, between liberal and conservative, between old and new, or even between what is being said by those church members who are still alive and those others who have died but with whom we are still in vital communion. To be a member of a church is not to choose among these. It is to choose them all.

Like our God in heaven, we too need a heart with many rooms. The true mark of church is wide loyalties.

The same holds true regarding inclusivity. When scripture tells us that, in Christ, there should be no male or female, no slave or free person, and no Jew or Gentile, it is telling us that there should also be no liberal or conservative, white or colored, new or traditional, feminist or antifeminist, pro-life or pro-choice, Democrat or Republican, Tory or Labor, or any other such ethnic or ideological pocket that matters in terms of church. John Shea once suggested that the heavenly banquet table is open to everyone who is ready to sit down with everyone.[17] That names the inclusivity required of any true church member. The task of church is to stand toe to toe, shoulder to shoulder, and heart to heart with people absolutely different from ourselves— but who, with us, share one faith, one Lord, one baptism, and one God who is Father and Mother of all. To live and worship beyond differences is what it means to have a bosom that is not a ghetto.

5. The Church Is the Banquet Table—the Ointment

The church is also the place we go to help anoint each other for our impending deaths. What is meant by that?

The essence of what church is can be understood by highlighting an incident that occurred in Jesus' life in the weeks just before his death. Although all four gospels report this event, a sure sign that it is important, we rarely reflect or homilize about it or are too timid in accepting the raw truth of its revelation. The incident being referred to is the anointing of Jesus' feet in Bethany by a woman named Mary.[18]

To understand what is revealed in this incident it is helpful to highlight the lavishness of the images used to describe it. Thus, if one were to take all four gospels' accounts of it and run them through a blender what emerges is this:

One evening Jesus was at dinner. This dinner, it seems, was a rather lavish one. At one point, a woman with a bad reputation

in the town enters carrying an alabaster jar of spikenard ointment. Both the jar and the ointment are very expensive. Alabaster was the Waterford crystal of the time and spikenard was a
very expensive perfume. She breaks the jar—a wasteful act, but
one signifying how deeply she loves Jesus and how much she
wants this giving to be a singular thing. Then she pours the
perfume on him and its aroma permeates the room. Finally, she
cries and her tears wash Jesus' feet and she dries his feet with her
hair.

It is hard to paint a scene that is as crass in its depiction of
raw affection. That rawness was not lost on the original audience. The evangelists say that people in the room began to grow
uncomfortable, as well they might—and as we would in a similar
situation. Some began to voice objections to what was happening. A few objected to the fact that Jesus, who was supposed to
be a holy man, was letting a woman with a bad reputation touch
him. That, however, was not the main objection, nor was it discomfort. What was making those present uncomfortable was
something that also makes us uneasy—raw gift; lavish, gratu-
itous affection. Those present voiced their discomfort by pointing to waste and excess: "What wastefulness! That jar and
ointment could have been sold and the money could have been
given to the poor."

Jesus, however, answered the objection by completely affirming what the woman had done and telling his uneasy, ob-
jecting hosts: "Leave her alone! She has done a good thing. The
poor you will always have with you, but you won't always have
me. She has just anointed me for my impending death." That is
the key line. Jesus told his hosts that this woman had just helped
ready him for death. What did he mean by that?

There are levels of meaning here. One of those, however, is
brilliantly captured by John Powell in a short book he wrote
some years ago. Entitled *Unconditional Love*,[19] it contains
within it the story of a young man, Tommy, one of Powell's
students, who is twenty-four years of age and dying of cancer. At
one stage, before his death, Tommy comes to Powell and shares

with him that he feels there are worse tragedies in life than dying young. I quote part of their conversation:

> "What's it like to be only twenty-four and dying?"
> "Well, it could be worse."
> "Like what?"
> "Well, like being fifty and having no values or ideals, like being fifty and thinking that booze, seducing women, and making money are the real 'biggies' in life. . . .
> "The essential sadness is to go through life without loving. But it would be almost equally sad to go through life and leave this world without ever telling those you loved that you had loved them."[20]

From the mouth of a dying young man we hear a great truth: There are only two potential tragedies in life and dying young is not one of them. What is tragic is to go through life without loving and without expressing love and affection toward those whom we do love. With that truth in hand, let us return to Jesus' comment that someone had just anointed him for his impending death:

What Jesus is saying, in effect, might be paraphrased this way: "When I come to die, I will be more ready for death because tonight, of all nights in my life, I'm experiencing the reason this universe was made, the giving and receiving of love and affection, pure gift. This is a moment to die for!"

There is a great irony here. If this woman had gone to Jesus' grave with this outpouring of affection and perfume, it would have been accepted, even admired. You were allowed to anoint a dead body, but it was not acceptable to express similar love and affection to a live one. Nothing has changed in two thousand years. We still save our best compliments and flowers for the funeral. Jesus' challenge here is for us to anoint each other while we are still alive: Shower those you love with affection and flowers while they are alive, not at their funerals.

There are many lessons in this but, at one level, it is also a lesson about church. What is church? Church, ultimately, whether we do it in a church building or around our kitchen tables, is about people getting together for no reason other than to take the ointment, that is, to offer each other love and affection, to bask in the perfume and the hair. That reason alone is enough to justify ecclesiology.

We go to church so as not to be alone—alone in our joys, alone in our sufferings, alone in the everydayness of our lives, alone in the important passages of our lives, alone on our birthdays, alone on a Sunday morning, and alone on Christmas, Easter, New Year's and Mother's Day. We go to church for the ointment. That is not an abstract concept. I know some people who like to go to church for reasons that, on the surface, appear immature and unspiritual. They like to go to church simply to socialize, to see people, to chat with people, and to enjoy the coffee, juice, and doughnuts after the service. Not bad. Together with worshiping God, this is one of the more salient reasons for being there. We go to church to tell people we love them and, hopefully, to hear them tell us the same thing. In the end, we go to church to help ready each other for death.

So Why Go to Church?

No spirituality of the church today is complete without a section that tries to answer, within the present antiecclesial climate, the question: "Why go to church?"

Indeed, why go? What is your *apologia pro vita sua* for going? What do you tell your friends or perhaps even your own children who no longer go but wonder why you do? Why might you consider going if you are not going?

The reasons given here are confessional and personal as well as theological and objective. Moreover, they are rational rather than emotional, hoping for intellectual respect more than for emotional sympathy. What is being proposed is not a series of reasons why you *might want to go* to church but why you *should go* to church; but that is not necessarily a bad thing. An old philosophical dictum suggests that love follows knowledge, that the heart needs a vision, that we can think ourselves into a new way of feeling. Scripture affirms the same thing when it says that without vision the people perish.

So what can be a vision, a reason for going to church and committing ourselves in an irrevocable covenant to a group of very flawed men and women and agreeing to journey with them for the rest of our lives? What are the reasons that one should go to church?

Most of these have already been seen, in one guise or other, in the preceding pages. Thus, here, the effort will be more to name than to explain. Hence, the present antiecclesial (and antishould) climate notwithstanding, I should go to church for these reasons:

1. Because It Is Not Good to Be Alone

We are essentially social by nature. To be a human being is to be with others. We wake up to consciousness not as an isolated ego, but as one among many. When scripture says, "it is not good to be alone," it means that for every man, woman, and child forever. Hell is not the other person, as Sartre once suggested, but the reverse. Our quest for God must be consistent with our nature. Hence, it must have, as a nonnegotiable part, a communitarian dimension. Ecclesiology, church, by definition, is precisely that, walking to God within a community. To attempt to make spirituality a private affair is to reject part of our very nature and walk inside of a loneliness that God himself has damned.

2. To Take My Rightful Place Humbly Within the Family of Humanity

There are three major stages to life. Different ages have had different ways of teaching this. Contemporary psychology speaks of the process of individuation and what lies before and beyond that. The ancient biblical sage Job spoke of two kinds of nakedness ("Naked I came from my mother's womb, and naked shall I return again."[21]) and what lies between them. Essentially what both, new and old, teach is the following:

The first stage of life is birth. We emerge from our mothers, from nature, naked and helpless, more of an acorn than a tree, not very actuated in terms of self and not very differentiated in terms of others. At this stage, smelling of the earth and of the womb, we are still primordially linked to the family of humanity. We are humble.

But, almost immediately, we begin the second stage—washing the smell of the earth off ourselves, clothing, accumulation, distinction, separation, and actualization. We spend our early years—and, if we never really grow up, the rest of our lives—trying to distinguish ourselves, to set ourselves apart from others, to accumulate things, to have successes, to create some privacy for ourselves. This stage is characterized by the urge to separate and clothe ourselves (in Job's terms). For the first part of our lives this is a healthy thing.

But at the point when adulthood is reached, something else is asked of us, not just by God but also by nature. Our task now is no longer to try to emerge, but to merge—to go back into community, to lose our separateness, to not stand out, to become naked again. This is the real meaning of humility and it describes perfectly what is contained in the great imperative that asks us to take our place within the family of humanity. To be human is, ultimately, to be part of the group, naked and unmarked.

But how to achieve this? What concrete community can offer us that place to merge? Our blood families can help, but they are too narrow and exclusive to fully identify us with all of humanity. Humanity as a family is inclusive enough, but is too abstract. The church—infinitely more inclusive than blood family and infinitely less abstract than humanity—offers us that place. The church gives us the place to die to elitism.

To join a church is to give up elitism. That is both perhaps the greatest obstacle to church participation and the greatest benefit of it.

3. Because God Calls Me There

The Holy Spirit is not a piece of private property, neither is God's call. The Judeo-Christian God is clear. Spirituality is not a private search for what is highest in oneself but a communal search for the face of God. The call of God is double: Worship divinity and link yourself to humanity. There are two great, equal commandments: Love God and love your neighbor. There can be no real Christian spirituality divorced from ecclesiology. To deal with Christ is to deal with church.

4. To Dispel My Fantasies About Myself

Away from actual, historical church community, whatever its faults, we have an open field to live the unconfronted life, to make religion a private fantasy that we can selectively share with a few like-minded individuals who will never confront us where we most need challenge. The churches are compromised, dirty, and sinful, but, just like our blood families, they are also real. In the presence of people who share life with us regularly, we cannot lie, especially to ourselves, and delude ourselves into thinking we are generous and noble. In community the truth emerges and fantasies are dispelled. Not being involved with church because of the church's faults is often a great rationalization. What is too painful to deal with is not the church's imperfection but my own fantasies about my own goodness, which, in the grind of real community, will become painfully obvious. Nobody deflates us more than does our own family. The same is true of the church. Not all of this is bad.

5. Because Ten Thousand Saints Have Told Me So

I go to church because by far the majority of good and faith-filled persons that I know go there. Moreover, not only do they go to church but they tell me that whatever goodness and faith they carry is, in an essential way, fostered there. The saints of old and the saints of the present day are fairly unanimous regarding the importance of church. It is hard to imagine Mother Teresa or Francis Assisi apart from their connection to ecclesiology.

Of course, I know too some good and faith-filled individuals who do not go to church. However, even there, I see in their lives, in their commitment to their families and communities, the functional dynamics of church. In every case, they are in real commitments that give them community, keep them humble, dispel their fantasies, and let them know, in whatever shape this takes in their minds, that God wants them to walk the spiritual road not alone but with others.

6. To Help Others Carry Their Pathologies and to Have Them Help Me Carry Mine

Anthropologists tell us that one of the primary functions of any family is to carry the pathologies of its members. In past times, when families were stronger, there was a lot less need for private therapy. The therapy of a public life helped provide what today individuals must seek elsewhere. To go to church is to seek the therapy of a public life and to be part of that therapy for others. Simply put, I go to church so that other people might help me carry what is unhealthy inside of me and so that I might help them carry what is unhealthy inside of them.

If this is true, and it is, then we should also not be surprised that we find every kind of sickness within our churches. But the presence of those pathologies should then not deflect us from going to church but, instead, positively beckon us there.

7. To Dream with Others

Edward Schillebeeckx once said: What we dream alone remains a dream, but what we dream with others can become a reality.

I go to church because I realize the impotence of my individuality, the limits of my private self. Alone, standing apart from community, I am no more powerful than my own personality and charisma, which, in a world of six billion people, will not make much of a difference.

When I watch the news at night and see all that is still needed in our world, I go to bed somewhat depressed, painfully aware of my own powerlessness to change anything. That depression is well founded. Alone, I am pretty powerless, able to make a splash, but not a difference. A very large group of people watching the news together could change the world. The church is that group of persons. As a world organization—with a heart for justice, peace, and the poor—it is far from perfect, but it is the best of a bad lot and it offers positive hope. The first thing I should do, if I hope to help bring about some justice and peace on this planet, is to begin to dream with others within a world-wide body of persons committed to the same dream. If I hope to do that I should go to church.

8. To Practice for Heaven

Heaven, the scriptures assure us, will be enjoyed within the communal embrace of billions of persons of every temperament, race, background, and ideology imaginable. A universal heart will be required to live there. Thus, in this life, it is good to get some practice at this, good to be constantly in situations that painfully stretch the heart. Few things—and we certainly all admit this—stretch the heart as painfully as does church community. Conversely, when we avoid the pain and mess of ecclesial encounter to walk a less painful private road or to gather with only persons of our own kind, the heart need not and generally does not stretch. Going to church is one of the better cardiovascular spiritual exercises available.

9. For the Pure Joy of It . . . Because It Is Heaven!

Carol Shields ends her recent novel, *Larry's Party*, with a scene depicting a dinner party. Larry, the bungling hero of her story, has invited a motley group of persons to join him for a Saturday night dinner. The guests include his two ex-wives, his present girlfriend, and an array of disparate individuals, each of whom is well equipped to illustrate all the virtues and sins in the world. The party goes as go all dinner parties. There is banter, jealousy, and argument about politics, religion, and life.

Old wounds raise their ugly heads and new wounds are created as the evening progresses. People are reminded in subtle ways of their past stupidities and infidelities, even as these are being washed clean by the celebration taking place. Food and wine get passed around and, underneath it all, despite everything that has been wrong and still is wrong, there is a deep joy present. A wee messianic banquet is taking place. Redemption is happening.

Most of our family or church gatherings pretty much mimic this scene. The family is home for Christmas, but your spouse is in a sulk, you are fighting tiredness and anger, your seventeen-year-old is pathologically restless and doesn't want to be there, your aging mother isn't well and you are anxious about her, your uncle Charlie is as batty as an owl (and you are worried that he's a pervert), your thirty-year-old unemployed son sits in the bathroom most of the day, and everyone is too lazy or selfish to help you prepare the dinner. You are readying to celebrate but things are far from idyllic. Your family is not the holy family, nor a Hallmark card for that matter. Its hurts, pathologies, and Achilles' heels lie open not very far below the surface . . . but you are celebrating Christmas and, underneath it all, there is joy present. A human version of the messianic banquet is taking place and a human family is meeting around Jesus' birth.

That is what church, in this world, perennially looks like. Most of the time, it is so frustrating that we do not see the joy that is, in fact, underneath. In the end, we go to church for the same reason that we continue to have Christmas dinner together as a family—for the pure joy of it.

7

A Spirituality of the Paschal Mystery

Unless a grain of wheat falls into the ground and dies, it remains but a single grain; but if it dies it yields a rich harvest.[1]

The Timeless Issues of Suffering, Death, and Transformation

Some of Christianity's harshest critics have suggested that what is wrong with it is that it sets itself the absurd task of teaching happy people to be unhappy so that it can minister to their unhappiness.[2] Christianity, they say, focuses too much on suffering, death, and the next life, effectively destroying our capacity to enjoy this one. Freud, it seems, was of this mind. He blamed Christianity for a certain neurotic anxiety within the Western soul that, among other things, prevents us from being properly responsive to where the soul's real happiness lies.[3]

Not all of this is wrong, a lot of anxiety has been taught in the name of Christian spirituality, but the critics of Christianity are naive if they suppose that humans are naturally content and that the issues of suffering, death, and the next life do not, without undue attention from Christianity, make us pathologically anxious. No philosophy of life, no anthropology, no psychology, and, *a fortiori,* no spirituality can pretend to be mature without grappling with the timeless, haunting questions of suffering and death. These are realities that gnaw at the heart. No amount of denial, disciplined focus on the present moment, or effort to ex-orcise what some perceive as the neurotic ghosts of Christianity immunizes us against the realities of suffering and death and the need for transformation to which these call us.

Hence, Christian spirituality does not apologize for the fact that, within it, the most central of all mysteries is the paschal one, the mystery of suffering, death, and transformation. In Christian spirituality, Christ is central and, central to Christ, is his death and rising to new life so as to send us a new Spirit.

This is the central mystery within Christianity. Unfortu-nately, it is also one of the great misunderstood and ignored mysteries within Christian theology and spirituality. We pay lip-service to the fact that the key thing that Jesus did for us was to suffer and die, but we seldom really try to understand what that means and how we might appropriate it within our own lives.

What is the paschal mystery of Christ? How do we enter that mystery and live it?

The Pattern of the Paschal Mystery

1. *An Umbrella Under Which to Understand:*
Some Paschal Stories

Before looking explicitly at the theology that underlies the pas-chal mystery, it can be helpful to get a certain feel for it by examining a few stories within which we see it incarnate. Hence, simply for some flavor, let us look at three stories, coming from very different places, each of which tells us something key about paschal transformation.

The first story comes from the novelist Brian Moore. One of his early books, *The Lonely Passion of Judith Hearne,*[4] is truly a paschal story. Roughly, it might be summarized as follows:

Once upon a time, in Dublin, there lived a woman named Judith Hearne. In many ways, Judith is a very gifted woman. Healthy, bright, attractive, a respected teacher, comfortable financially, and solidly connected to family and a number of trusted friends, she is loved and respected. There is one problem, however. She is approaching menopause, is unmarried and without children, and both her biology and psyche are consciously and unconsciously reminding her of that fundamental anthropological axiom, "It is not good be alone"—especially when your biological clock is running down!

Hence, without really realizing it, Judith becomes desperate. Everything in her life—her health, her job, her family, and her friends—begins to count for nothing in face of the fact that what she really wants, a husband and children, is denied her. A great restlessness besets her, and in that unconsciously desperate state, she meets a man, an American, with whom she falls in love. The man, however, is not interested in her romantically and is pursuing the relationship only because he thinks she has money and that they might open up a restaurant together.

One night, after a date, Judith takes the initiative. She proposes marriage to the American. But he rejects her offer, telling her the truth of his intention. That rejection is the final straw. Judith snaps. She goes on an alcoholic binge, has a nervous breakdown, and ends up in a church, cursing at God and trying to tug the Blessed Sacrament out of the tabernacle. She is taken away to a hospital where she receives good care and eventually recovers.

The story has a redemptive ending. Shortly before she is to be released from the hospital, she receives a visit from her American friend, the man who had previously rejected her. He arrives in her room contrite, carrying a dozen roses, telling her he has been wrong, and proposing marriage. Her response to him, far better than most theology books, lays out the dynamics of Pentecost. She hands the roses back to her friend with these words:

"Thank you, but no thank you. I am not interested in marrying you and, to tell you why, I need to tell you a story. When you are a little girl you dream a dream of the perfect life you will have. You will grow up to have a beautiful body, meet the perfect man, marry him, have wonderful children, live in a wonderful home in a wonderful neighborhood, and have wonderful friends. But . . . as you get older and that dream doesn't happen, you begin to revise it, downward. You scale down your expectations and begin to look for someone to marry who doesn't have to be so perfect . . . until you get to be like I was, where unconsciously you get so desperate that you would marry anyone, even if he's common as dirt! Well, I learned something by losing myself and then refinding myself; I learned that if receive the spirit for who I am, it doesn't matter whether I am married or unmarried, I can be happy either way. My happiness doesn't depend upon somebody outside of me, but upon being at peace with what's inside of me."[5]

The story ends with her leaving the hospital, strong and happy again, making a paper airplane out of the man's business card and floating it out of the cab window.

Pentecost has just taken place because, as scripture tells us, the Holy Spirit is not a generic spirit, but a spirit that is given to each of us in a most particular way for the particular circumstances that each of us finds himself or herself in.[6] Pentecost is not just social, it is also personal and, for Judith Hearne, this meant receiving the spirit for somebody who was approaching menopause without a husband and children.

The second story is one shared by John Shea at the beginning of his book *Stories of Faith*.[7]

Shea tells the story of young man who is tending to his dying father. The father, still quite young himself, is dying of cancer and is dying hard. The disease is terminal, has literally wasted his body, and now, long after he should already be dead, he lies in a hospital still clinging to life. His body is full of tubes and, despite the best efforts of morphine, he is in constant pain.

Each night, after work, his son comes, sits by the bed, holds his father's hand, and watches helplessly while he suffers. This goes on for a number of days. Finally, one night, sitting like this, the son says to the father: "Dad, let go! Trust God, die; anything is better than this." Within a short time, the father grows peaceful and dies and the son realizes that he had just given voice to a very important truth—a truth about letting go and trusting God.

For this man, coached into death by a loving son, Good Friday has just taken place. Like Jesus, he was finally able to give his spirit over to his Father.

The last story is from the Jewish scriptures and recounts the story of the death of King David's illegitimate son.[8]

One day David's son became seriously ill and David, for his part, did what was expected then of a father. He donned sackcloth, sat in ashes, and prayed and fasted, pleading with God to spare his son. However, the son died. Immediately upon hearing this, David got up off the ground, took off his sackcloth, bathed off the ashes, went to the temple, prayed, returned to his house, ate a good meal, and went and slept with his wife, who then conceived Solomon.

This behavior struck some of his friends as rather odd. They ask David whether perhaps he has not got things somewhat backward: "While your son was alive you fasted and prayed; and now that he is dead you eat and drink?" But David, in words to this effect, explains some of the paschal mystery to them: "While the child was still alive, I fasted and prayed, hoping God might spare him. Now that he is dead there is nothing I can do to bring him back—but I'm still alive and I must go on living in the face of this and must continue to create new life."

For King David, a certain resurrection has just occurred. His son is dead, but he is still alive, not in the same way as he was alive before his son died, but with a new life which he, in faith, begins to move into with some strength.

The paschal mystery is the mystery of how we, after undergoing some kind of death, receive new life and new spirit. Jesus, in both his teaching and in his life, showed us a clear paradigm for how this should happen.

We turn now to examine that paradigm.

2. The Paschal Mystery—a Cycle for Rebirth

"Unless a grain of wheat falls into the ground and dies, it remains only a single grain; but if it dies it yields a rich harvest."[9]

These words of Jesus define the paschal mystery; namely, in order to come to fuller life and spirit we must constantly be letting go of present life and spirit. However, to understand that and to see how Jesus both taught it and illustrated it in his own life, a few preliminary distinctions are necessary. We must distinguish between *two kinds of death, two kinds of life,* and *between life and spirit.*

First, regarding two kinds of death: There is *terminal* death and there is *paschal* death. Terminal death is a death that ends life and ends possibilities. Paschal death, like terminal death, is real. However, paschal death is a death that, while ending one kind of life, opens the person undergoing it to receive a deeper and richer form of life. The image of the grain of wheat falling into the ground and dying so as to produce new life is an image of paschal death.

There are also two kinds of life: There is *resuscitated* life and there is *resurrected* life. Resuscitated life is when one is restored to one's former life and health, as is the case with someone who has been clinically dead and is brought back to life. Resurrected life is not this. It is not a restoration of one's old life but the reception of a radically new life. We see this difference in scripture by comparing the resurrection of Jesus and the so-called resurrection (which is really a resuscitation) of Lazarus. Lazarus got his old life back, a life from which he had to die again. Jesus did not get his old life back. He received a new life—a richer life and one within which he would not have to die again.

The paschal mystery is about paschal death and resurrected life.

Finally, we must also distinguish between *life* and *spirit.* They are not the same thing and are often given to us at a different time. For example, after the resurrection of Jesus, the disciples are given the new life of Christ, but only some time after, at Pentecost, are they given the spirit for the new life that they are already living. As we will see in the examples given later in this chapter, that is also the case for us in our own lives. We live by both life and spirit and our peace of soul depends upon having a happy synthesis between the two.

The paschal mystery, as we shall see shortly, is a process of transformation within which we are given both new life and new spirit. It begins with suffering and death, moves on to the reception of new life, spends some time grieving the old and adjusting to the new, and finally, only after the old life has been truly let go of, is new spirit given for the life we are already living.

We see all of this, first, in the great mystery of Jesus' own passover from death to life.

Theologically, looking at Jesus' teachings and especially at his death and resurrection and what follows from them, we can see that there are five clear, distinct moments within the paschal cycle: *Good Friday, Easter Sunday,* the *forty days leading up to the Ascension,* the *Ascension,* and *Pentecost.* Each of these is part of a single process, an organic one, and each needs to be understood in relation to the others to make sense of the paschal mystery. Each is part of one process of transformation, of dying and letting go so as to receive new life and new spirit.

In caption, the paschal cycle might be diagrammed as follows:

1. Good Friday . . . "the loss of life—real death"
2. Easter Sunday . . . "the reception of new life"
3. The Forty Days . . . "a time for readjustment to the new and for grieving the old"
4. Ascension . . . "letting go of the old and letting it bless you, the refusal to cling"
5. Pentecost . . . "the reception of new spirit for the new life that one is already living"

Put into a more colloquial language and stated as a personal, paschal challenge for each of us, one might recast the diagram this way:

1. "Name your deaths"
2. "Claim your births"
3. "Grieve what you have lost and adjust to the new reality"
4. "Do not cling to the old, let it ascend and give you its blessing"
5. "Accept the spirit of the life that you are in fact living"

This cycle is not something that we must undergo just once, at the moment of our deaths, when we lose our earthly lives as we know them. It is rather something we must undergo daily, in every aspect of our lives. Christ spoke of many deaths, of daily deaths, and of many rising and various pentecosts. The paschal mystery is the secret to life. Ultimately our happiness depends upon properly undergoing it.

All of this is perhaps, at this stage, a bit abstract. Concretely, what does this all mean? How, in our daily lives, should we be living out the paschal mystery?

What follows are a number of examples, taken from the bread and butter of our everyday lives, that try to illustrate how our happiness, peace, and maturity depend upon appropriating properly this mystery in our lives. Unless we die in infancy, we will have many deaths in our lives and within each of these we must receive new life and new spirit. Daily we must undergo the paschal mystery. Let us examine some of these deaths.

Undergoing the Various Deaths Within Our Lives

1. The Death of Our Youth . . .

Imagine this scenario: You wake up one morning, look at your calendar, and come to the unwelcome realization that it is your seventieth birthday. You are seventy years old! At seventy, in terms of this life, you are no longer a young person—and all the cosmetics, exercise, plastic surgery, tummy tucks, and positive attitude in the world cannot change that. Your youth is dead.

But you are not dead! You look at yourself in the mirror and see there a very vibrant person, despite the physical limitations of age. In fact, you are richer now, full of a deeper life, than when you were twenty or forty or sixty. But you are alive as a seventy-year-old, not as a twenty-year-old.

Paschally, in terms of your youth, this is your status: Good Friday has already happened, your youth has died. Resurrection too has happened; you have already received the life of a seventy-year-old, a new life, different from and richer than the life of a twenty-year-old. And now you have a choice: You can refuse to grieve and let go of your lost youth and, like Mary Magdala on Easter morning trying to cling to a Jesus she once knew, try to hold on to your youth. If you do that you will be blocking ascension and you will be an unhappy, fearful, and frustrated seventy-year-old because, like Judith Hearne before her breakdown, you will be trying to live your life with someone else's spirit. A schizophrenic endeavor at best. Pentecost cannot happen for you and you will daily grow more fearful and unhappy about aging.

However, should you let your youth ascend, should you be able to say: "It was good to be twenty, good to be thirty, good to be forty, and fifty, and sixty; but it's even better to be seventy!"—then pentecost will happen. You will receive the spirit for the life that you are already in fact living, the life of a seventy-year-old, which is a different spirit than for somebody who is twenty.

Some of the happiest people in the whole world are seventy years old and some of the unhappiest people in the world are that age. The difference is not in who has kept himself or herself the slimmest and most youthful-looking, but in pentecost. The happy seventy-year-old is a woman or a man who has received the spirit for someone that age—that spirit which scripture says is given to each of us in a most particular way for each particular circumstance in life.

It is interesting in this context to note that the ancient Egyptians used to mummify their dead, soaking dead bodies in form-aldehyde so as somehow to keep them intact forever. As an image, this is the antithesis of the paschal mystery. The Christian idea is to let go, to let nature take its course, to trust that the God who once gave life will now give it in an even deeper way. If I am seventy, but trying, through every technique and cosmetic known, to preserve my youth, I am in my own way attempting to mummify my body.

The paschal mystery should set us free from that kind of unhappiness.

2. The Death of Our Wholeness . . .

Another death each of us in his or her own way must undergo is the death of our wholeness, the death that results when part of us is fractured and dies. Here too we need paschal transformation so as to receive the spirit for one who is no longer whole. Allow me to share a story that illustrates this.

Some years ago, in one of my theology classes, there was a woman who, for many reasons, was not a very happy person. From outside appearances, however, she had enough reasons to be happy. She was forty-nine years old, healthy, attractive, very bright, a published artist with a career, financially secure, married, and the mother of two healthy young adolescents. But she was far from happy. Inside of her was a cancerous anger that was consuming her and threatening to choke off every potential area of happiness. Her presence in class was a continual disruption for the rest of us and everyone had to tiptoe around her sensitivities for fear of triggering her anger. At this stage of her life, she had constellated many of her angers around a feminist agenda.

At one stage, some time after that particular class ended, she shared her story with me. It was indeed a tragic one. Her father had been an alcoholic, and one night when she was nine years old, he had raped her. This was now forty years later but here is how she describes what happened to her then and how she now feels:

"Something inside of me died then. It's forty years later and, really, I'm still in shock. My whole life really ended then. I remember once reading a book by Joyce Carol Oates where she says: 'and the spirit went out of the man.' That's what happened to me. The spirit left me at age nine. I've had no enthusiasm, really, for life ever since.

"I went through some times when I was able to bury it, to leave it behind, to pretend, to go on with life, to act normal, like everyone else. Yeah, I went through the motions—I fell in love [kind of], got married, had two kids—and for a while I even thought it was behind me. I was even able to forgive my dad [kind of]. I remember coming home for his funeral and seeing him there in the coffin. His face looked peaceful, more peaceful than I'd ever remembered him in life. The tension and the anger that were always there seemed to have drained away with his life. He looked peaceful. I kissed him—I forced myself to, I made my peace. He was dead and I wanted to let him and *it* go! But it didn't die, it didn't go away. The older I got the worse it got. I ended up getting angrier and angrier.

"It started with my reading feminist books, but I know that feminism wasn't the reason. It would have come out anyway, in a different way. I read feminist books and it helped put me in touch with my wound. I understood a lot. And I got angrier: If only! If only! . . . If only my dad hadn't been so sick, if only society were fairer, if only women had equality, if only men weren't so macho and thick-headed! If only! Well, I got angrier and angrier. I froze up inside like an iceberg. I was hardest on my family—my husband and kids, and then on those around me—the parish, my friends, everyone.

"I began to fight everyone . . . and I was right too! It is unfair. It's a shame that lives, especially women's lives, can be forever ruined so easily. It is unfair to have to live in a world that is so unfair. I would like for those in power, those men, from the pope down, to have to taste the death I've tasted. They tell me I'm an angry feminist. Yeah, I'm angry. Anger is threatening to ruin my marriage, to ruin my relationship to a church I once loved, to ruin my happiness . . . but something ruined me long before that. I wish somebody understood that.

"I'm right, but I'm so full of cancer inside. I'd like to scream, just shout to the world how unfair it all is, but I know that nobody would hear—or care! I want my life back! I wasn't born this angry. I don't want to die this angry. I don't want this god-awful death that wasn't my fault!"

Let us look at that story in terms of the paschal mystery. This woman is right. At that moment of abuse, something inside of her, her wholeness as a person, died—and died irrevocably. No therapy, positive attitude, or sheer willpower can ever undo that any more than they can undo the original Good Friday. Like Jesus, she has been crucified.

But she isn't dead. She is a woman full of life, exceptional in fact. She has so many things going for her—physical health, artistic talent, intellectual brightness, attractiveness, a loving and respectful husband, children, and, underneath her anger, a very honest and gracious spirit. But she is alive with the life of someone who has been violently abused, not with the life of someone who has not been.

Her task is to manage an ascension. She must grieve what has died and then, when the time is right, let it go, let it ascend, so that she can receive the spirit for someone who has been abused, which is a different spirit than for someone who has not been so violated. Some of the happiest people in the world have been abused and some of the most unhappy ones have been. The difference lies not so much in extent of the trauma of the original abuse or the quality of the subsequent therapy but in the ascension and pentecost.

That, in fact, is what happened to the woman whose story we just heard. Ascension and pentecost did take place. Largely through the encouragement of another woman who had herself been sexually abused, this woman eventually gave herself over to a therapy that led to pentecost. Grief therapy helped lessen the shock to her psyche, physical massage helped lessen the shock to her body, and good paschal direction helped lessen the shock to her soul. At one stage of the therapy—a session that included persons from various healing professions: a doctor, a psychiatrist, a nurse, and a priest—someone told her: "Jesus gave the disciples forty days to grieve and adjust. He has given you forty years! It is time to let go."

Like the man dying of cancer who was coached into death by his son—with the words: "Let go! Trust God, die"—she too was eventually able to let go. Today she is a happy woman, pursuing a career in art, content within her family, and using all her free time to work with others who have been sexually abused. She walks the earth happily, but with the spirit of someone who was once violated. She has been able to bring together life and spirit.

Some years ago, in spiritual direction, a woman shared with me: "My husband and I never understood fully what ascension and pentecost meant until I had to have a double mastectomy. There was, at first, a lot of anger, a lot of grieving, over what we'd lost. Eventually though we had to let go of a wholeness we once had. Now our relationship is great again . . . in every aspect . . . but my husband had to learn to see me differently and I had to learn to see me differently too! We know now what it means to have to let a body float up to heaven so as to receive a new spirit."

3. The Death of Our Dreams . . .

One of the deaths that Jesus talked about is the death of our dreams, not the dreams we dream at night, but the dreams of specialness and consummation we nurse in our hearts. Again, let me share one person's story to illustrate this.

Some years ago on a retreat I was directing a man who

shared his story with me. He was forty-seven years old, about forty-five pounds overweight (mostly around his waistline), and he came from a small town in northern Canada where he worked in a Safeway store. In essence, this is what he shared:

"Father, I came on this retreat because I need something new in my life. I am sick of myself, that's what it comes down to! I'm forty-seven years old and it's time I got into my own skin and stopped living a damned daydream.

"My daydream started when I was a little kid, growing up on a farm in northern Alberta. I remembering listening to hockey broadcasts on our radio and hearing the announcer shout: 'He shoots, he scores!' And that was me. In my daydream I was going to be a famous hockey star. And it almost happened. I was a very good player and for three years I played tier-one, junior hockey. That's the best hockey outside of the National Hockey League. And I was a star too, good enough to have some professional teams interested in me. So at age nineteen, I tried to play pro hockey. Sad part is, I wasn't quite big enough, nor good enough. By age twenty-two the dream was over. I was told I would never really make it. But I was young then and had been a big star in my little town. So I went home and began, for lack of another job, to work at the local Safeway store.

"Well it's twenty-five years later now and I'm still working at that same store. Along the line I got married [basically a good marriage] and we have four kids—all healthy and pretty decent. But this is the sad part. I should be happy. I've a good wife, a good marriage, good kids, our house is paid for, my job is boring but secure, I'm healthy—and probably a lot of people in the world would trade lives with me—but, best as I can describe it, for these last twenty-five years I've not been inside my own skin. I've been too restless, still living that damn daydream, always thinking to myself—'What if? What if I would have made the National Hockey League? What if I hadn't quit school so young? What if I hadn't married so young? What if I wasn't stuck in this godforsaken little town in the middle of nowhere?' You know, all my life I've nursed a daydream that I would be big time . . .

big star, big city, big salary, my name in lights. Well, look at me, I'm small time . . . small salary, small town, small everything, except the size of my waist!

"What's wrong with me can all be seen in one thing. I've been an autograph collector. Look at these, autographs of famous athletes and country and western singers! It's pathetic when you stop to think about it. Me, forty-seven years old and the highlight of my year is to show the guys at work an autograph I've picked up at a hockey game!

"I had a realization in church last year. I don't know what Sunday it was, but I was listening to the readings a little more closely because my daughter was the reader. Well, just after my daughter finished, the priest started reading how Jesus' body went up into heaven. A thought struck me then: That's what has to happen to my daydream—I have to let it go up to heaven, like Jesus' old body. It was a good dream, but it's over! I have to stop living that dream so that I am not so damn restless and can get inside my own skin. I have every reason to be happy, but I'm not. There must be people like me, forty-seven years old and forty-five pounds overweight, living in small towns and working in Safeway stores, who are happy—and I want to be one of them! It's a shame for my wife and kids—who are really good and in the end the only thing that's important—that I haven't been there for them like I should have been. I got to be who I am and get inside of my own life instead of trying to live somebody else's life or trying to live a dream that was over a long time ago."

This man is ready for the ascension. He has had his "forty days," twenty-five years of grieving and adjustment. Now he is ready to let the old ascend so that he can receive the spirit for someone who is forty-seven years old, overweight, and living and working in a small town in northern Canada. Some of the happiest people in the world fit that description, as do too some of the most restless people in the world. Happiness and restlessness are not determined by who makes it big time and who ends up in the small towns. They depend upon the ascension and pentecost and whether these have happened or not.

This man's story, in one form or other, is lived out by all of us. Like Judith Hearne, we all nurse the dream of a perfect life that will bring us perfect consummation. Eventually all of us will need to grieve that dream so as to receive the spirit of somebody who lives alone and unconsummated. The Bible offers a powerful, archetypal story that tries to teach us this. It is a story that both shocks and fascinates by its sheer earthiness.[10]

A certain king, Jephthah, is at war and things are going badly for himself and his army. In desperation he prays to God, promising that if he is granted victory he will, upon returning home, offer in sacrifice the first person he meets. His prayer is heard and he is given victory. When he returns home he is horrified because the first person he meets, whom he must now kill in sacrifice, is his only daughter, in the full bloom of her youth, whom he loves most dearly. He tells his daughter of his promise and offers to break it rather than sacrifice her. She, however, insists that he go through with his promise, but there is one condition: She needs, before she dies, time in the desert to bewail the fact that she is to die a virgin, incomplete, unconsummated. She asks her father for two months during which she goes into the desert with her maiden companions and mourns her unfulfilled life. Afterward she returns and offers herself in sacrifice.

Despite the unfortunate patriarchal character of this story, it is a parable that in its own earthy way teaches something profound about the paschal mystery, namely, that we must spend our forty days mourning what is incomplete and unconsummated within our lives. As Karl Rahner once put it, in the torment of the insufficiency of everything attainable we begin to realize that here, in this life, all symphonies remain unfinished. He is correct. In the end, we all die, as did Jephthah's daughter, virgins, our lives incomplete, our deepest dreams largely frustrated, still looking for intimacy, never having had, in terms of consummation, the finished symphony—and unconsciously bewailing our virginity. This is true of married people as much as of celibates. Ultimately, we all sleep alone.

And this must be mourned. Whatever form this might take,

each of us must, at some point, go into the desert and bewail her or his virginity. It is when we fail to do this, and because we fail to do it, that we go often through life demanding, angry, bitter, disappointed, and too prone to blame others and life itself for our frustrations. When we fail to mourn properly our incomplete lives then this incompleteness becomes a gnawing restlessness, a bitter center, that robs our lives of all delight. Because we do not mourn our virginity we demand that someone or something—a marriage partner, a sexual partner, an ideal family, having children, an achievement, a vocational goal, or a job—take all of our loneliness away. That, of course, is an unreal expectation, which invariably leads to bitterness and disappointment. In this life, there is no finished symphony. We are built for the infinite, Grand Canyons without a bottom. Because of that we will, this side of eternity, always be lonely, restless, incomplete, still a virgin—living in the torment of the insufficiency of everything attainable.

The dream for perfect consummation, like the dream to become a superstar, must, at some point, be mourned and left to ascend. Otherwise, as was the case for the man whose story we just heard, our daydreams will perennially rob us of the simple happiness of life.

4. The Death of Our Honeymoons . . .

Imagine this typical occurrence: A man and a woman meet and fall in love. They marry and the honeymoon period of their relationship is the stuff of Romeo and Juliet. They feel themselves as a one-in-a-million couple and the passion they feel for each other is so overpowering as to relativize anything either has felt ever before.

Now, fifteen years after that honeymoon, with each of them fifteen years older and fifteen pounds heavier, and with fifteen years of shared life between them, they are looking at each other across the breakfast table. Both know, and have sensed for a while, that the honeymoon is over. Those overpowering feelings of passion that they once had for each other are dead. A certain relational domesticity has set in. Where are they in their relationship in terms of the paschal cycle?

The honeymoon period of their relationship is dead, but their relationship, their marriage, is far from dead; in fact they are bonded more strongly and more deeply now than they were during their honeymoon. But they are living the life of a couple who have been married for fifteen years, not fifteen days or fifteen minutes. Thus the choice that now sits before them, however unconscious it may be:

They can cling to what they once had, that special passion, and crucify what they have at present by that romantic ideal. Each can accuse the other of being to blame for the loss of the passion ("You don't send me flowers anymore!") and each may be tempted to search for romantic passion in another relationship. Or, they can grieve their honeymoon and receive the spirit for a couple who have been married for fifteen years—which is a different spirit than for one who have been married for fifteen minutes. If they do this, then their marriage will be infinitely deeper than it was way back then, during the passion of the honeymoon. A couple who have shared life for fifteen years should (barring some major pathology, dysfunction, or infidelity in the relationship) have a far deeper and more life-giving bond than a couple who are on their honeymoon.

Some of the happiest couples in the world have been married for fifteen years and some of the unhappiest ones also fit that description. However, and this is the point, happiness and unhappiness within an ongoing relationship are not contingent upon the length of time we interrelate, but upon undergoing the paschal mystery, that is, upon constantly naming the relational deaths we are undergoing, claiming the new relationship that has been given us, grieving what has died, letting it go, and then receiving the spirit for the relationship we are, in fact, living. The couple who have been married for fifteen years must receive the spirit for those who have been married for fifteen years—and not try to live with the spirit of those who have been married for fifteen minutes.

This is not just true for the honeymoons we enjoy in our romantic relationships, but is also true and important for understanding our relationship to our friends, neighbors, vocations, and even to our jobs. All honeymoons die. To sustain anything in this life we must continually recognize that that first fervor, that special electricity that we would die for, never lasts and that we must be open to receive a new spirit within the relationship. The downside of this is that all honeymoons die, but the upside is that God is always giving us something richer, deeper life and fuller spirit.

5. The Death of a Certain Idea of God and Church . . .

All of this is also true for how we conceive of God and church. Here too we constantly need to be letting go of what we once had to receive what God is giving to us now. To take an instance from my own life:

As a young boy, I grew up in the Roman Catholic Church as it existed prior to the changes ushered in by the Second Vatican Council in the 1960s. Thus, I spent my childhood in an immigrant community within which the church was the center of life. Everyone went to church and the church's rhythms pretty much dictated things. The Eucharist (we called it "the mass" then) was celebrated in Latin and virtually all Roman Catholics identified strongly with a number of common devotional and ascetical practices—ranging from not eating meat on Fridays, to not dancing during Lent, to praying the rosary. At school we were, along with all other Roman Catholic children in North America, made to memorize a common catechism and, from shore to shore, we would regale and amuse each other by our virtuosity in reciting these questions and answers, so familiar to everyone. Rectories, convents, and seminaries teemed with life and, by and large, the church enjoyed considerable respect within the larger culture.

For Roman Catholics, in the Western world, this was a certain golden time. There was a universal ethos within the body of Roman Catholicism that we may perhaps never again approximate and there was a confidence within Roman Catholicism that bordered on intolerance. Whatever its dysfunctions, and there were some of those too, the Roman Catholic Church of my youth was a powerful incarnational expression of the Body of Christ. And, for me, it was the vehicle through which I received the Christian faith.

But now, forty years later, the God and the church of my youth have, like the original body of Jesus, been crucified—by time, circumstance, culture, and countless other forces. The church in which I grew up, that very particular expression of ecclesiology, is dead—as is everything else from the fifties, sixties, seventies, and eighties. But the church is not dead. It is very much alive, bursting with life in many ways. However, it is alive with the life of today, the life that we are actually living at the turn of the millennium, and not with the life of the 1950s. Thus, along with the other Roman Catholics of my generation, I have a choice:

I can try to cling to the church of my youth. This clinging can take different forms. If I am of a conservative bent and lament the passing of the church of my youth, I can try to restore that church—"Give me that old-time religion!"—by challenging the changes that Vatican II has asked for, by denying the changes that have in fact already taken place, and by living in an unhealthy nostalgia, yearning always for the good old days. If I am liberal by temperament and am happy that the old ecclesiology has died, I can still cling to that church, and not receive the spirit of the present one, through my hatred of my past, through continually lamenting how bad things were, how much change was and is needed, and how my conservative brothers and sisters are narrow and backward. In both cases, I am still Mary Magdala trying to cling to an old body even as she is looking at a new reality. It is no accident that, in Roman Catholicism, among those over forty years of age, conservatives and liberals are equally obsessed with the pre-Vatican II church for there has been an equal failure on both sides to grieve that church and to let it go.

On the other hand, I can accept the paschal mystery as it applies to the God and church of my youth. I can look at the church that gave me the faith, recognize that it (like my own youth) has died, grieve its passing, let it bless me, let it go, and then receive the spirit for the church within which I am actually living. In biblical terms, what all Roman Catholics of my generation, liberal and conservative alike, would need to do is to go out to the Mountain of the Ascension and let the church of our youth bless us and then let it reverently ascend so that we can all receive the new spirit for the ecclesial life we are in fact already living. Unfortunately, too often, Roman Catholics of my generation are blocking the ascension and, in that way, are also blocking pentecost. Small wonder we struggle to pass our faith on to our children. We have been given new life but we have not yet received the spirit for that new life.

The example given here is from Roman Catholicism, but the dynamics of what was described are universal. All of us must continually let go of the God of our youth in order to recognize the God who actually walks beside us today.

We see a poignant example of this in Luke's gospel in the famous incident where Jesus walks with the disciples on the road to Emmaus.[11] What is curious in this incident is that the disciples, the friends of Jesus, do not recognize him, even though he has been dead and absent for only a day and a half. Why can they not recognize him? Because they are too focused on his former reality. They are so focused on their former image of him, their former understanding of him, and the way he was formerly present to them that now they are not open to seeing him as he walks among them.

Sadly, that is often true for us, both in terms of our understanding of God and of the church. By clinging to what once was we cannot recognize God's presence within a new reality. Rabbi Abraham Heschel, the great Jewish spiritual writer, shared a story that illustrates this. A young student came to him one day, complaining of religious confusion and doubts about God's existence. The young man had grown up in a family that was full of faith; he had attended the synagogue regularly, read the scriptures daily, and had been quite pious. Now, as a university student, his religious life had dissipated considerably and he was beset with every kind of doubt. He shared with Rabbi Heschel his pain about these doubts and how he could no longer find the God of his youth in his present situation. Rabbi Heschel asked him: "And what makes you think that God wanted your former peace but does not want your present pain?"[12] A wise, paschal, counsel.

Like all things temporal, our understanding of God and the church too must constantly die and be raised to new life. Our intentions may be sincere and noble, but so too were Mary Magdala's on Easter morning when she tried to ignore the new reality of Jesus so as to cling to what had previously been.

A Note on Grieving and on Letting Ourselves Be Blessed by the Past

Imitating the voice of the Jewish prophets, Henri Nouwen once began one of his articles with these words:

> "Mourn, my people, mourn. Let your pain rise up in your heart and burst forth in you with sobs and cries. Mourn for the silence that exists between you and your spouse. Mourn the way you were robbed of your innocence. Mourn for the absence of soft embrace, an intimate friendship, a life-giving sexuality. Mourn for the abuse of your body, your mind, your heart. Mourn for the bitterness of your children, the indifference of your friends, and your colleagues' hardness of heart. . . . Cry for freedom, for salvation, for redemption. Cry loudly and deeply, and trust that your tears will make your eyes see that the Kingdom is close at hand, yes, at your fingertips!"[13]

These words are indeed prophetic because perhaps the greatest spiritual and psychological challenge for us once we reach mid-life is to mourn our deaths and losses. Unless we mourn properly our hurts, our losses, life's unfairness, our shattered dreams, our radical inconsummation, and all the life that we once had but that has now passed us by, we will live either in an unhealthy fantasy or an ever-intensifying bitterness.

Spiritually we see an illustration of this in the story of the older brother of the prodigal son.[14] His bitterness and unwillingness to take part in the celebration of his brother's return points to what he is still clinging to—life's unfairness, his own hurt, and his own unfulfilled fantasies. He is living in his father's house but he is no longer receiving the spirit of that house. Consequently, he is bitter, feels cheated, and lives joylessly.

Swiss psychologist Alice Miller, in her famous essay "The Drama of the Gifted Child,"[15] has analyzed this brilliantly from a psychological point of view. Her thesis, as it pertains to our point, runs like this:

Most of us are "gifted children." For Alice Miller this does not mean that we necessarily have extraordinary intelligence or are specially gifted in terms of talent, but that we are extraordinarily sensitive and are specially equipped to pick up the expectations of life and of those around us. Soon enough we realize that our lives are not fair, that we are not loved and valued as we deserve, and that our dreams can never really be fulfilled. When we are young our sheer energy and the seemingly limitless future that still lies before us compensates for this and we can generally keep the demons of anger and bitterness at bay. This, however, changes with mid-life. At that point in our lives, our own sensitivity and giftedness makes us aware, too aware, that life has cheated us, that things are unfair, that we have been abused in many ways, and that we are so rich and that all of this richness has really no place to go.

At this point, according to Alice Miller, the task of our lives is to mourn. We must, as she says, cry so as to shake the very foundations of our lives (and of our bitterness). We have no other options because life, in fact, for all of us, is unfair. We have been cheated, dropped too often, and never valued or loved properly. What we have dreamed for our lives can never be. Thus we have a choice: We can spend the rest of our lives angry, trying to protect ourselves against something that has already happened to us, death and unfairness, or we can grieve our losses, abuses, and deaths and, through that, eventually attain the joy and delights that are in fact possible for us.

Alice Miller states this all in psychological language, but the choice is really a paschal one. We face many deaths within our lives and the choice is ours as to whether those deaths will be terminal (snuffing out life and spirit) or whether they will be paschal (opening us to new life and new spirit). Grieving is the key to the latter.

Good grieving, however, consists not just in letting the old go but also in letting it bless us. What is meant by that? How do we let the old give us its blessing, particularly if it was a painful or abusive experience?

Again, a personal example: My origins are rather humble. As a young boy, I grew up on a farm outside an obscure little hamlet on the vast Canadian prairies. My family was poor, as were all the families around us, and all of us, my family like all the other families in the area, had to struggle to learn to speak English and most of us spoke it with a foreign accent. We lived in houses without indoor plumbing and, in some cases, without even electricity. But almost all of those people—Eastern European folk mostly, displaced by war—were highly industrious persons, enduring a temporary economic setback as they resettled. Within a single generation, their farms were prosperous, their children were educated, and the foreign accents had all but vanished. Most of my classmates and boyhood friends have done very well for themselves and now live in big cities and are economically and otherwise quite prosperous. They are, however, very divided in how they treat their origins.

Half of my peers, with a good distance between themselves and their humble origins, do not let themselves be blessed by their past. They have changed their names (so that Muckenheimmer became Muse and Jabonokoski became Jones) and speak of where and how they grew up only with disdain—"I was raised in that godforsaken rathole!" They never bring their children back to the old houses and farms where they grew up and their early years are a part of their lives that they are ashamed of and are trying to leave behind.

The other half of my boyhood peers—with the same geographical, economic, and social distance between them and their origins—are completely the opposite. They are proud of their humble origins, proud of their long, difficult-to-spell, European names, and proud of the fact that they once lived in houses without indoor plumbing. They visit the district frequently, proudly bring their children to see where they grew up, and recognize what these kinds of roots have given them. In doing that, they are letting themselves be blessed by their roots and they are continuing to drink from a very rich stream. Ironically too they are more free of their roots than those who are living in a certain shame because of them.

It is necessary to let our roots bless us. This is true not only if those roots were healthy but even if they were negative or positively abusive. One of the great anthropological imperatives, innate in human nature, is that we eventually must make peace with the family. No matter how bad your father and mother may have been, some day you have to stand by their graveside and recognize what they gave you, forgive what they did to you, and receive the spirit that is in your life because of them. Making peace with the family depends upon proper mourning and letting the ascension and pentecost happen.

Refusing to Cling . . .

There are two images of the ascension within scripture. In the gospels of Matthew, Mark, and Luke, the ascension is depicted pictorially. Jesus blesses the disciples and then floats bodily upward into the heavens. Thus, his earthly body is understood to be taken off the earth. In John's gospel, the same theology is given but through a different image. On Easter Sunday morning,

Mary Magdala meets the resurrected Jesus.[16] Initially she does not know who he is and she supposes him to be the gardener, but immediately upon recognizing him, she tries to throw her arms around him. Jesus, for his part, tells her: "Mary, do not cling to me!"

What lies behind Jesus' reluctance to let Mary touch him?

Mary Magdala herself, had we ever found her gospel, would, I suspect, explain it this way:

I never suspected
  Resurrection
    and to be so painful
to leave me weeping
With joy
    to have met you, alive and smiling, outside an empty
  tomb
With regret
not because I've lost you
but because I've lost you in how I had you—
    in understandable, touchable, kissable, clingable
    flesh
    not as fully Lord, but as graspably human.

I want to cling, despite your protest
  cling to your body
cling to your, and my, clingable humanity
cling to what we had, our past.

But I know that . . . if I cling
you cannot ascend and
I will be left clinging to your former self
. . . unable to receive your present spirit.[17]

8

A Spirituality
of Justice and Peacemaking

Strength without compassion is violence
Compassion without justice is mere sentiment
Justice without love is Marxism
And . . . love without justice is baloney!
—CARDINAL SIN

Act Justly—the Great Imperative

God asks only one thing of us, that we "act justly, love tenderly, and walk humbly with our God."[1] We have already seen how the first of these prescriptions, the invitation to work for social justice, is one of the essential, nonnegotiable pillars within Christian spirituality. However, some rather important questions still remain concerning precisely what social justice is, what energies should motivate it, and how it needs to be practiced so that it is itself nonviolent.

What does it mean to act justly? How is justice different from private charity? Moreover, what should be the energy behind our actions for justice so that our actions do not mimic the violence and injustice they are trying to change? How do we help victims without creating further victims ourselves?

To act justly requires some clarity about what social justice is and how it should be practiced within a Christian context.

What Is Christian Social Justice?

1. *Justice Is Beyond Private Charity—a Parable*

There is a story told, now quite famous within social justice circles:

Once upon a time there was a town that was built just beyond the bend of large river. One day some of the children from the town were playing beside the river when they noticed three bodies floating in the water. They ran for help and the townsfolk quickly pulled the bodies out of the river.

One body was dead so they buried it. One was alive, but quite ill, so they put that person into the hospital. The third turned out to be a healthy child, who they then placed with a family who cared for it and who took it to school.

From that day on, every day a number of bodies came floating down the river and, every day, the good people of the town would pull them out and tend to them—taking the sick to hospitals, placing the children with families, and burying those who were dead.

This went on for years; each day brought its quota of bodies, and the townsfolk not only came to expect a number of bodies each day but also worked at developing more elaborate systems for picking them out of the river and tending to them. Some of the townsfolk became quite generous in tending to these bodies and a few extraordinary ones even gave up their jobs so that they could tend to this concern full-time. And the town itself felt a certain healthy pride in its generosity.

However, during all these years and despite all that generosity and effort, nobody thought to go up the river, beyond the bend that hid from their sight what was above them, and find out why, daily, those bodies came floating down the river.

2. *Justice as demanding the Transformation of Systems*

What this parable highlights in a rather simple way is the difference between private charity and social justice. Private charity responds to the homeless, wounded, and dead bodies, but it does not of itself try to get at the reasons why they are there. Social justice tries to go up the river and change the reasons that create homeless, wounded, and dead bodies.[2]

Social justice, therefore, tries to look at the system (political, economic, social, cultural, religious, and mythical) within which we live so as to name and change those structural things that account for the fact that some of us are unduly penalized even as others of us are unduly privileged. Thus, social justice has to do with issues such as poverty, inequality, war, racism, sexism, abortion, and lack of concern for ecology because what lies at the root of each of these is not so much someone's private sin or some individual's private inadequacy but rather a huge, blind system that is inherently unfair.

Hence justice differs from private charity: Charity is about giving a hungry person some bread, while justice is about trying to change the system so that nobody has excess bread while some have none; charity is about treating your neighbors with respect, while justice is about trying to get at the deeper roots of racism; and charity is about helping specific victims of war, while justice is about trying to change the things in the world that ultimately lead to war. Charity is appeased when some rich person gives money to the poor while justice asks why one person can be that rich when so many are poor.

Thus, for example, a recent commentary in *Sojourners* magazine was less than fully impressed by the fact that multibillionaire American Ted Turner recently gave one billion dollars to the United Nations, stating, "I'm putting the rich on notice. They are going to be hearing from me about giving money away." Instead of celebrating Turner's huge gift, *Sojourners* commented that "God put the rich on notice a long time before Ted Turner did" and the more important question is "why one man can have so much to spare (and get praised for it!) in a country where poverty (especially among children!) is on the rise."[3] That kind of comment helps clarify what social justice is.

Social justice has to do with changing the way the world is organized so as to make a level playing field for everyone. In simple terms this means that social justice is about trying to organize the economic, political, and social structure of the world in such a way so that it values equally each individual and more properly values the environment. Accomplishing this will take more than private charity. Present injustices exist not so much because simple individuals are acting in bad faith or lacking in charity but because huge, impersonal systems (that seem beyond the control of the individuals acting within them) disprivilege some even as they unduly privilege others. This is what social justice language terms systemic injustice and systemic violence.

To offer just one example of this, we might look at the issue of abortion. Despite the bitter rhetoric that often exists between those who favor legalized abortion and those who oppose it, nobody, ultimately, wants abortion and everyone on both sides recognizes that whenever an abortion happens something is far from ideal. Too often, though, neither side acknowledges the deeper, systemic issues that underlie the problem. Ultimately abortion takes place because there is something wrong within the culture, within the system, and not simply because this or that particular woman is seeking to end an unwanted pregnancy. When a particular woman enters a hospital or a clinic seeking an abortion she is more than a simple individual making a private decision. She is the tip of a cultural pinecone. Behind her, helping push her into that clinic and that decision, stands an entire system (economic, political, cultural, mythical, and sexual). Her problem is as much political as it is personal. How so?

First, there is our political structure, democracy itself, at least in how it is presently understood and lived out. We know of course no better way to organize ourselves politically than through the democratic process, but democracy is far from perfect. At one level, it works by the free bartering of rights and skills. Capital, labor, management, workers, business corporations, elected governments, entrepreneurs, and the down-and-out all bargain and jostle with each other for resources, privileges, and power. In the ideal it is a fair system, but in practice it is not. Those who enter the arena with historical privileges, with stronger voices, and with more valued skills reap more benefits than the others. Conversely, those who have not been historically privileged, who have weaker voices, or possess less valued skills end up being disprivileged and find themselves at the bottom of the chain. It is no accident that laissez-faire democracy has rarely been kind to the poor.

In such a system, to be entirely voiceless, as are the unborn, is to be exceedingly vulnerable and in the ever-present danger of being decertified right out of existence. That is one of the systemic issues underlying abortion. There is another, more important, one.

We live in a system, a cultural one, within which it is acceptable for men and women to have sex with each other even though they are in no way committed to each other and do not wish to have children with each other. In such a system, abortion is inevitable and no laws and no law enforcement can stop it because the system will continually keep producing someone (who could be anyone) who finds herself pregnant and isolated in a way that would make the birth of this child from this man at this time an existential impossibility for her. In such a climate you will always have abortion and the particular woman who is seeking the abortion is dealing as much with a political issue as she is with a personal one. She is the tip of a pinecone behind which stands a whole culture that has chosen to dissociate sex from marriage and procreation. In such a system, wherein sex is an extension of dating, abortion will always happen. Abortion can stop only if the system changes. This does not excuse abortion, but it does explain it.

It is the same for every other social justice issue: war, poverty, racism, sexism, the ecology. There can be no peace, universal prosperity, equality, harmony between the sexes, and proper respect for the environment until there is universal justice, that is, until the systems we live within are made to be fair to and respectful of everyone and everything.

Former Jesuit Superior General Pedro Arrupe was once asked why there is such an emphasis today on social justice when, in the past, many saintly persons and good spiritual writings appeared to almost entirely neglect this, at least in terms of an explicit development. He answered rather simply: "Today we know more!"

He is right. Today we know more, not just because modern communications daily show us the victims of injustice on our television screens and in our newspapers, but also, and especially, because we are less sociologically naive. Put positively, this lack of naivete means that we understand better how social systems affect us, both for good and for bad. Social justice is about how systems affect us, especially adversely.

It is very important that this be understood. It is not enough simply to be a good person within our own private lives. We can be morally impeccable within our private lives (churchgoing, prayerful, kind, honest, gentle, and generous in our dealings with others) and still, at the same time, unknowingly, participate in and help sustain (through our work, our political affiliations, our economic ideology, our investments, and simply by our consumeristic lifestyle) systems which are far from charitable, gentle, prayerful, and moral. While the system gives us a good life, it is far less benign to others. In such a situation, our moral status is analogous to that of the spouse of an abusive parent who does nothing to stop the abuse—we ourselves may be kind and nonabusive, but we are helping prop up and legitimize a situation within which someone is being abused.

When Pedro Arrupe said: "Today we know more!" he was referring precisely to the fact that current sociological and economic analysis has shown us, with a clarity that defuses all further rationalization, how our political, economic, social, and ecclesial systems, irrespective of how individually sincere we might be in our support of them, are unfair and wounding to many others. Given this insight, daily, our ignorance becomes less inculpable.

Hence one might define the practice of social justice as follows: To practice social justice is to examine, challenge, refuse as far as possible to participate in, and try to change those systems (economic, social, political, cultural, mythic, and religious) that unjustly penalize some even as they unjustly reward others.

However, that is a generic definition, not yet fully adequate for a Christian. For a Christian, the practice of social justice demands what has just been defined, but it demands some other things as well.

For a Christian, the question of social justice has not only to do with truth, but also with energy, with motivation for the quest. Not just any motivation for justice is adequate since justice is not first of all a question of politics and economics, but a question of helping God build a kingdom of peace and joy for all. Thus, for a Christian, the ultimate motivation in working for justice may never be simple ideology, irrespective of how noble that particular ideology may appear. Rather both the truth that inspires the quest for justice and the energy that fuels it must ground themselves in something beyond any ideology.

Ultimately, both justice and our motivation for seeking it must be grounded in the equality of all human persons before God and in our respect for nature as also being God's child. This has important ramifications, namely, any motivation for justice that grounds itself simply in liberal ideology or in indignation and anger at inequality will ultimately not change the world's heart, even when it manages to change some of its structures. The frustration of Marxism and of most other political and social movements for justice (which have attempted to ground themselves on a purely secular basis) provide ample proof of this.

To have a just world we need a new world order. Such an order, however, can never be imposed by force of any kind, but must win the world's heart by its own intrinsic moral merit.

Simply put, to change the world in such a way that people want justice and are *willingly willing* to live in a way that makes justice possible requires an appeal to the heart that is so deep, so universal, and so moral that no person of good conscience can walk away from it. No human ideology, no private crusade, and no cause that takes its origins in guilt or anger can ever provide that. One can walk away from liberal ideology—as it is expressed in Marxism, Green Peace, feminism, or any number of other major forces for justice on this planet—with a sincere conscience. The vast majority of persons, in fact, in good conscience, do walk away from these. Why? Because despite their obvious merit in terms of the truth of the justice they promote, too often the energy driving their quest is not as morally compelling. In simple terms, the truth is right, but the energy often is not. Sadly, the same thing can also be said many times of the Christian churches and our own social justice groups as we try to challenge the world to be more just.

The same, however, cannot be said of Jesus, of his person and of the gospel he left us. One does not walk away from the Sermon on the Mount or the challenge Jesus gave to feed the hungry, clothe the naked, and give of our lives and resources to those less fortunate than ourselves with a clear conscience. Thus, the fuel that fires our quest for justice must be drawn from the same source as the truth of justice itself, namely, from the person and teaching of Jesus. Only by rooting ourselves there, or in similar principles that somehow take their root in God, will we find both the right vision and the right energy to offer a new order, a just one, to the world.

If this is true, and it is, then it is important that we turn to scripture to see what it says about social justice.

A Biblical Foundation for Social Justice

The foundations for social justice are laid within the story of creation itself. The Book of Genesis makes four major, interpenetrating affirmations that provide the ultimate basis for social justice: It affirms that God made all people equal in dignity and rights; that the earth and everything in it belongs equally to everyone; that all human beings, equally, are co-responsible with God in helping to protect the dignity of everybody and everything; and that the physical earth itself has rights and needs to be respected in and of itself, and not just as a stage for human activity. These affirmations are the basis for all subsequent moral teaching regarding the social order.

Israel's prophets affirm and deepen these principles. Already some eight hundred years before Christ, virtually all the Jewish prophets begin to affirm, over and over again, one singular truth which, ultimately, encapsulates and focuses in practical life the principles laid down at the dawn of creation: The quality of our faith depends upon the character of justice in the land and the character of justice is to be measured by how we treat three groups—widows, orphans, and foreigners (those with the least status in society). Thus, for the Jewish prophets, our standing with God depends upon where we stand with the poor and no private faith and piety, be they ever so pure and sincere, can soften that edict.

Jesus unequivocally affirms this. Like the Jewish prophets, he too affirms that our standing with God depends upon how we stand in relationship to the weakest members within society. Indeed, Jesus takes this further. He teaches that, in the end, when we stand before God in judgment, we will indeed be judged on the basis of how we treated the poor in this life. He makes the practice of justice the very criterion for salvation.[4] Moreover, he identifies God's presence with that of the poor. In Jesus' view, if you wish to find God, go look among the poor.[5] Conversely, he tells us that there are immense spiritual and psychological dangers in being rich and privileged.[6]

Social Justice and the Churches

Throughout the centuries, the Christian churches have developed these social principles as an integral part of Christian spirituality.

Obviously, as in most everything else, there are some major differences among the various denominations as to how these teachings of Jesus are understood and applied. However, despite these differences, there is essential consensus on the major points. With few exceptions, all Christian denominations hold and teach the following principles:

1. All people in this world have equal dignity and should enjoy equal rights in terms of respect, access to resources, and access to opportunity.

2. God intended the earth for all persons equally. Thus the riches of this world should flow equally and fairly to all people. All other rights, including the right to private property and the accumulation of riches that are fairly earned, must be subordinated to this more primary principle.

3. The right to private property and the accumulation of wealth is not an absolute one—but must be subordinated to the common good, namely, to the fact that the goods of the earth are intended equally for everyone.

4. No person, group of persons, or nation may have a surplus of goods if others lack the basic necessities. That is the present situation within our world, where some individuals and nations have excess while others lack the basic necessities. This is immoral, goes directly against the teachings of Christ, and must be redressed.

5. We are obliged, morally, to come to the aid of those in need. In giving such aid, we are not doing charity, but serving justice. Helping the poor is not an issue of personal virtue and generosity, but something that is demanded of us by the very order of things.[7]

6. The laws of supply and demand, free enterprise, unbridled competition, the profit motive, and private ownership of the means of production may not be seen as morally inviolate and must, when the common good, justice, demands it, be balanced by other principles. No one has the moral right to earn as much

as he or she can without concern for the common good (even if he or she is a celebrity).

7. Physical nature too has inherent rights, namely, rights that are intrinsic to itself and not simply given to it because of its relationship to humanity. The earth is not just a stage for human beings to play on. It too is a creature of God with its own rights, which humans may not violate.

8. The condemnation of injustice is part of the church's essential ministry of preaching and is an essential aspect of the church's prophetic role.

9. Movement toward the poor is a privileged route toward God and toward spiritual health. There can be no spiritual health, individually or communally, when there is no real involvement with the struggles of the poor. Conversely, riches, of any kind, are spiritually dangerous.

It is interesting to note how these teachings on justice—these moral principles that emphasize social rather than private morality—constellated within the teachings of the various churches. When someone asked Pedro Arrupe why the churches today are more concerned about social justice (when previously they emphasized more private morality) he might also have answered in this way.

The world has changed in a way that has necessitated a growing emphasis on social justice: Until the industrial revolution, the moral focus of the churches was on the family. It was a well-merited focus. The family was the unit upon which the very existence of the culture depended. Hence it drew most of the moral ink. Thus, until the industrial revolution radically changed things, Christian moral theology was focused quite strongly on the moral contours of the family—monogamy, sex as linked to marriage and procreation, mutual respect within marriage, the duties of parents and children toward each other, and the like.

Then, as the industrial revolution brought forth a whole wave of new issues (exploitation of workers, urban poverty, slums, anonymous urban living, isolation from family structures) the Christian moral agenda also widened. Churches began to teach about the necessity of just wages, moral checks to unbridled capitalism, the rights of unions to exist, private and government responsibilities to the poor, and most of the other social justice principles just cited. As the world's moral problems widened, so too did the church's spirituality.

Finally, just within the past generation or two, there has been another major development. As the questions of world community, gender, race, overpopulation, ecology, and abortion begin constellating in a new way, the churches' moral agenda as regards social justice is also widening and refining in a way so as to reflect this development. Hence, today the Christian churches are very much focused on the moral issues surrounding gender, race, class, and historical privilege.

This most recent development within Christian spirituality is well summarized by Elizabeth Johnson. In her view, Christian spirituality today "seeks wisdom, not in the clear and distinct ideas of what is claimed to be universal reason but what is in fact the thought of privileged men; rather, it honors the plurality and ambiguity of human consciousness, sensitive to the difference that difference makes according to one's social location in gender, race, class, and culture. The compass of postmodern spirituality points not to rampant individualism and its violent outcroppings but to the importance of community and tradition, prizing human solidarity and peace. It prizes not human supremacy over the earth but affective kinship with the whole community of the cosmos. In a word, postmodern spiritual experience prizes not isolation but essential connectedness; not body-mind dualism but the holistic, embodied person; not patriarchy but inclusive feminism; not militarism but expenditure for the enhancement of life; not tribal nationalism but global justice."[8]

But how is this global justice to be achieved?

Nonviolent Peacemaking

1. *Our Naivete*

Lack of success in achieving a more just world order has not always been because of lack of effort. Many justice and peace groups, including many Christian ones, have for a long time been trying to prophetically challenge the world toward greater justice. Too often though they have not been very effective. Why? A too simple answer is that justice makes little headway because the world's hardness of heart is not easily dissolved and the entrenched powers of privilege are not easily moved. While that is true, there is also another reason why justice and peace groups have not been more effective. Simply put, we are often somewhat naive about what is really asked of us if we are to challenge the world toward more peace and justice.

What is this naivete? It can be summarized in six fallacies that too frequently permeate justice and peace groups. These fallacies, as expressed in their prime analogates, sound like this:

a. "The urgency of my cause is so great that it is okay in this instance for me to bracket the normal laws that govern public discourse. Hence I can be disrespectful, arrogant, and ugly toward those who oppose me."

b. "Only the truth of the cause is important here, not my own private life. My own private life, whether it pertains to anger, sex, or envy, is of no relevance to the cause of justice for which I'm fighting; in fact, all focus on private morality is a hindrance to working for justice."

c. "Proper ideology alone can ground this quest—I don't need talk of God and Jesus. I don't need to pray for peace, I only need to work for it."

d. "I judge success and failure on the basis of measurable political achievement. I am less interested in a long-range kingdom of God than in real short-term political and social gain."

e. "I may exaggerate and distort the facts a bit to make the case for justice clearer, but the situation is so horrendous that I need not be very scrupulous about exact truth."

    f. "I am a victim and thus outside the rules!"

2. The Painful Truth

What we are coming more and more to realize, however, is that one of the reasons why the world is not responding more to our challenge to justice is that our actions for justice themselves often mimic the very violence, injustice, hardness, and egoism they are trying to challenge.

Our moral indignation very often leads to the replication of the behavior that aroused the indignation. As Gil Bailie puts it in his masterpiece on nonviolence: "Moral outrage is morally ambiguous. The more outraged it is, the less likely it is to contribute to real moral improvement. Righteous indignation is often the first symptom of the metastasis of the cancer of violence. It tends to provide the indignant ones with a license to commit or condone acts structurally indistinguishable from those that aroused the indignation."[9]

Sadly, more often than not, this is the case in our struggle for justice, even when we do so under a Christian banner. The anger, crass egoism, bitterness, hardness, and aggression of so many peace groups and movements for justice can never serve as the basis for a new world order. It will convert few hearts, even when it is politically effective. In the end, it is, as Bailie puts it, essentially indistinguishable from the egoism, aggression, and injustice that it is trying to change.

3. A Prescription for Nonviolence

A prophet, Daniel Berrigan submits, must make a vow of love not of alienation. The great modern-day prophets of social justice (persons such as Gandhi, Dorothy Day, Thomas Merton, Gustavo Gutiérrez, William Stringfellow, Oscar Romero, Jim Wallis, and Richard Rohr) would all agree with that. Love, not anger, is the basis for nonviolence and nonviolence is the only possible basis for a new world order of justice and peace.

Thus, for example, Jim Wallis would propose the following prescription for any nonviolent effort at creating justice and peace:[10]

> All of our actions for peace must be rooted in the power of love and the power of truth and must be done for the purpose of making that power known and not for making ourselves known. Our motivation must always be to open people to the truth and not to show ourselves as right and them as wrong. Our best actions are those which admit our complicity and are marked by a spirit of genuine repentance and humility. Our worst actions are those that seek to demonstrate our own righteousness, our purity, and our moral distance from the violence we are protesting.
>
> Whenever pride overtakes our protest we are simply repeating in a political form the self-righteousness judgement of the fundamentalist: "I'm saved and you're not." Action done in public always carries with it the great danger of presumption. Hence it should always be done in the spirit of humility and invitation.
>
> Judgement, arrogance, and exclusiveness, which so often mark our protest, are signs of spiritual immaturity and protest characterized by such things will have the effect of hardening people in their present opinions. Protest just as easily perpetuates as dispels public blindness.
>
> Moreover, never has the need for genuine non-violence been greater than now. However, its chief weapon is the application of spiritual force and not the use of coercion. A very serious problem in the peace movement is sometimes the hidden aggression, the manipulation, the assertive ego, the desire for provocation that can work beneath the surface of moral platitudes about the commitment to non-violence. The rhetorical cloak of non-violence can be used to hide the will to power which is the very foundation of violence. The desire to win over others, to defeat one's enemies, to humiliate the opposition, are all characteristics of violence and are still too painfully evident in almost all of our peace efforts.
>
> Our anger, our infighting, and our lack of respect for others, is hardly evidence that the will to power has been overcome. We should know by now that violence is all one piece. If that is true, then the

violence of dissent is directly linked to the violence of the established order. In fact, it is a mere reflection of it.[11] Nor may we justify excesses in the peace movement and in ourselves by appealing to a greater violence in the system. The urgency of the present situation calls for more, not less, care in the actions we undertake. At its heart, non-violence does not try to overcome the adversary by defeating him, but by convincing him. It tries to turn an adversary into a friend, not by winning over her, but by winning her over.

As well, patience is central to non-violence. Non-violence is based upon the patience which the Bible speaks of as "enduring all things." Thomas Merton taught that the root of war is fear. If that is true, then we must become more understanding of the fears that people have. The most effective peacemakers are those who can understand the fears of others.

Finally, non-violent peacemaking must spring from genuine hope in the power of God to change things. William Stringfellow once scolded a peace group in words to this effect: "I notice in your conversations one major omission, mention of the resurrection of Jesus. The victory of God over the forces of death is already assured and our modest task in peacemaking is simply to live in a way that reveals that fact. We do not have to triumph over the forces of death by our own inspiration, efforts, and strategy. We do not have to defeat death all over again. Psalm 58 tells us: 'Surely there is a God who rules the earth.' We must never forget that. Hope, and not anger, must direct our protest. Moreover that hope, belief in the power of the resurrection, is not a feeling or a mood, it is a necessary choice for survival."

Jesus, of course, is the ultimate example of the nonviolent peacemaker. He never mimics the violence and injustice that he is trying to change. Thus, for example, in an incident which illustrates the anatomy of both violence and nonviolence with exceptional clarity, we see him defuse and convert a crowd that is bent on violence.

The incident takes place when an angry crowd brings Jesus a woman who has been caught in adultery.[12] To understand fully the nonviolence of Jesus' action here, it is helpful to contrast this story to a similar incident (with a different ending) in the Book of Daniel.[13] There is a striking parallel between these two stories. In each, an innocent woman, threatened by a crowd, is saved because one person intervenes and alters things. The stories, however, end very differently, one in peace and the other in violence.

The Book of Daniel contains a story of Daniel saving a beautiful, innocent woman named Susanna. It goes this way: One day, two elderly men see Susanna taking a bath and lust after her. They approach her with their evil intent, but she rejects them, holding firm to virtue. Bitter and jealous of her power, they falsely accuse her of committing adultery, turning both the crowd and the ancient law against her. She is condemned to die and is being led to her death when Daniel, sensing lies and injustice, confronts the crowd. He accuses the two men of lying and to prove his point has them separated and questioned separately. Of course, they contradict each other, proving Susanna's innocence. Daniel, though, is not finished. He turns the crowd against the accusers, demanding their deaths, and the crowd, in a frenzy of emotion, obliges. The two men are stoned to death, the very death they had decreed for Susanna.

How parallel, yet how different, is the story of Jesus, calmly backing down the accusers of the woman caught in adultery. A woman is condemned to die, accused of adultery. Unlike Susanna, this woman is guilty, but that is incidental to what is happening. Clearly, like Susanna, she is there because of jealousy and mob frenzy and is, therefore, structurally innocent, despite her guilt. And Jesus, like Daniel, confronts the crowd. His protest to the crowd is more penetrating in conscience than is Daniel's—*"Let the one who is without sin cast the first stone!"*—and it also has a very different effect.

Like Susanna, the woman is saved, but no mob scene follows. What ensues is the exact opposite of lynch-mob hysteria: "They all went away one by one, beginning with the eldest." Jesus' words not only save a woman but, defuse a potential explosion. Nobody dies that day. Instead, everyone goes home considerably more attuned to humility and truth.

Nonviolent efforts for justice and peace work that way. Like Jesus, they do not turn the crowd against anyone, innocent or guilty. Rather they gently touch that part of the conscience that is still soft and inviolate, where truth still rings true and where peace is still a tender longing.

4. A Nonviolent God Who Underwrites Justice and Peace

G. K. Chesterton, commenting upon church doctrine, once said: "The church announces terrible ideas and devouring doctrines, each one of them strong enough to turn into a false religion and lay waste the world. . . . Thus, if some small mistake is made in doctrine, huge blunders might be made in human happiness."[14]

This is particularly true as it pertains to our concept and theology of God. Ultimately, how we conceive of God will color how we conceive of everything else, especially justice and peace and the road that leads to them. If we conceive of God as somehow violent, however redemptive we imagine this violence to be, we will then conceive of the road to peace as also lying in violence.

Sadly that is often the case, within Christian and secular circles alike. We too often think of God as someone who will use violence to overthrow evil and bring about justice and peace. We conceive of God as a force for redemptive violence.

What is redemptive violence? It is what happens at the end of a movie, storybook, or song, when the hero finally beats up the bully who has been terrorizing everyone. Basically, as we see it expressed in countless films, books, and songs, redemptive violence works this way:

Some good people find themselves being terrorized by a bully. Among the good people, there is one good man (it is always a man because straight muscle-power will ultimately be the redeeming force!) who is actually stronger than the bully. He will eventually be the hero and save the situation. We sense it already since we know that, in the end, he is stronger than the bully. But, for now, the bully continues his evil ways, intensifying his cru-sade against the good. Also, the bully senses the presence of the good man and he begins particularly to humiliate him. The good man, however, does not fight back, much to our mounting cha-grin and impatience. He accepts the bullying, quietly, for his time has not yet come.

Finally, the story reaches its climax. The bully corners the hero, who now has no choice—either fight or die. Then redemp-tion takes place. The hero, pushed beyond the limit, takes off his jacket, calmly rolls up his sleeves, and beats the bully to death . . . and tears come to our eyes because now, finally, justice has been done. Evil has been crushed and goodness has been vindi-cated.

We hardly stop to think that what has really happened is that goodness has now been more violent even than evil. We fail to notice that our good hero began as Mother Teresa but ended as Rambo and Batman. We certainly fail to see that the ending of this redemptive story is radically opposite to the story of Jesus. When he, Jesus, was finally cornered and the choice was to fight or die ("If you are the son of God, come off that cross!") he, unlike our mythical heroes, chose the latter.

We must be careful, particularly in trying to create justice and peace, not to confuse the Christian story of redemption with the myth of redemptive violence. We must try to bring about justice and peace as Jesus did, recognizing that the God whom Jesus called "Father" beats up no one. He does not vanquish the bad and vindicate the good through superior muscle-power, speed, or sharpshooting with a gun. In the Gospels, Jesus is de-scribed as powerful, more powerful in fact than anyone the crowds had yet encountered. However, the word that is used to describe Jesus' power, *exousia* (in Greek), does not refer to the power of muscle, speed, or even extraordinary grace or bril-liance. It refers to something for which, in the English language, we have no easy translation. What is *exousia?* What constitutes Jesus' real power? What ultimately brings about justice and peace?

Daniel Berrigan provides a good answer to this question. He was once asked to give a talk at a university gathering. The topic was something to the effect of "God's Presence in Today's World." His talk, I suspect, surprised a number of people in his audience, both in brevity and content.[15]

He simply told the audience how he, working in a hospice for the terminally ill, goes each week to spend some time sitting by the bed of a young boy who is totally incapacitated, physically and mentally. The young boy can only lie there. He cannot speak or communicate with his body nor in any other way express himself to those who come into his room. He lies mute, helpless, by all outward appearance cut off from any possible communication. Berrigan then described how he goes regularly to sit by this young boy's bed to try to hear what he is saying in his silence and helplessness.

After sharing this, Berrigan added a further point: The way this young man lies in our world, silent and helpless, is the way God lies in our world. To hear what God is saying we must learn to hear what this young boy is saying.

This is an extremely useful image in helping us understand God's power and it manifests itself in our world. God's power is in the world like that young boy. It does not overpower anyone or anything. It lies muted, at the deep moral and spiritual base of things. It does not overpower with muscle, or attractiveness, or brilliance, or grace, as does the speed and muscle of an Olympic athlete, the physical beauty of a young film star, or the gifted speech or rhetoric of the brilliant orator or author. These latter things—muscle, swiftness, beauty, brilliance, grace—reflect God's glory, but they are not the primary way God shows power in this world. God's power in the world has a very different look and a very different feel to it.

What does God's power look like? How does it feel to feel as God in this world?

If you have ever been overpowered physically and been help-less in that, if you have ever been hit or slapped by someone and been powerless to defend yourself or fight back, then you have felt how God feels in this world.

If you have ever dreamed a dream and found that every effort you made was hopeless and that your dream could never be realized, if you have cried tears and felt shame at your own inadequacy, then you have felt how God feels in this world.

If you have ever been shamed in your enthusiasm and not given a chance to explain yourself, if you have ever been cursed for your goodness by people who misunderstood you and were powerless to make them see things in your way, then you have felt how God feels in this world.

If you have ever tried to make yourself attractive to someone and were incapable of it, if you have ever loved someone and wanted desperately to somehow make him or her notice you and found yourself hopelessly unable to do so, then you have felt how God feels in this world.

If you have ever felt yourself aging and losing both the health and tautness of a young body and the opportunities that come with that and been powerless to turn back the clock, if you have ever felt the world slipping away from you as you grow older and ever more marginalized, then you have felt how God feels in this world.

And if you have ever felt like a minority of one before the group hysteria of a crowd gone mad, if you have ever felt, firsthand, the sick evil of a gang rape, then you have felt how God feels in this world . . . and how Jesus felt on Good Friday.

God never overpowers. God's power in this world is never the power of a muscle, a speed, a physical attractiveness, a brilliance, or a grace which (as the contemporary expression has it) blows you away and makes you shout: "Yes! Yes! There is a God!" The world's power tries to work that way. God's power though is more muted, more helpless, more shamed, and more marginalized. But it lies at a deeper level, at the ultimate base of things, and will, in the end, gently have the final say.

To work for justice and peace in this world is not to move

from being Mother Teresa to being Rambo or Batman. The God who undergirds justice and peace beats up no one and His or Her cause is not furthered when we do.

Sustaining Ourselves for the Long Haul

After the Gulf War of 1991, Jim Wallis, the founder of *Sojourners,* was being interviewed on national radio in the United States. Wallis had expressed considerable reservations about that war and especially about the victory celebrations that followed it. At one point, the man interviewing him said to him: "This time the protesters of war have to admit that they were wrong. The American people supported the war, not the protests." Wallis answered simply: "We weren't wrong—we just lost! There is a difference."

To sustain ourselves, as Christians, in the struggle for justice and peace, it can be helpful to remember Wallis' words. The struggle for justice and peace is not ultimately about winning or losing but about fidelity.

The gospel of Jesus makes the nonnegotiable demand that we work for justice and peace in the world, but does not demand that we win. Short-term political effectiveness is not as important as long-term fidelity to personal conscience, personal faith, and personal charity. We do not know how things will turn out in the end, but we do know what the gospel tells us, namely, that we ourselves must be loving, charitable, understanding, compassionate, forgiving, and morally integral within our own private lives. We will not always know what political strategy is best, but do know that God cares about all victims, that Jesus stands in the midst of brokenness, and that we are being faithful to the gospel when we stand there too.

There is a story told of a Norwegian pastor, a Lutheran, who, during the Second World War was arrested and interrogated by the Gestapo. As the Gestapo officer entered the room he placed his revolver on the table between them, commenting: "Father, this is just to let you know that we are serious!" The Lutheran pastor, instinctually, pulled out his Bible and laid it beside the revolver. The officer asked: "Why did you do that?" The pastor replied: "You laid out your weapon, and so did I!"[16]

In South Africa, prior to the abolition of apartheid, people used to light a candle and place it in their windows as a sign of hope, a sign that one day this evil would be overcome. At one point, this was declared illegal, just as illegal as carrying a gun. The children used to joke about this, saying: "Our government is scared of lit candles!" Eventually, as we know, apartheid was overcome. Reflecting upon what ultimately brought its demise, it is fair to suggest that "lit candles" (which the government so wisely feared) were considerably more powerful than were guns.

In the struggle for justice and peace our true weapons, as Christians, are not ideology and guns, but lit candles, hope, personal integrity, charity, and prayer.

A Lord's Prayer for Justice

In the world's schema of things, survival of the fittest is the rule. In God's schema, survival of the weakest is the rule. God always stands on the side of the weak and it is there, among the weak, that we find God.

Given the truth of that, we might occasionally pray the Lord's Prayer in this way:

Our Father . . . who always stands with the weak, the powerless, the poor, the abandoned, the sick, the aged, the very young, the unborn, and those who, by victim of circumstance, bear the heat of the day.

Who art in heaven . . . where everything will be reversed, where the first will be last and the last will be first, but where all will be well and every manner of being will be well.

Hallowed be thy name . . . may we always acknowledge your holiness, respecting that your ways are not our ways, your standards are not our standards. May the reverence we give your name pull us out of the selfishness that prevents us from seeing the pain of our neighbor.

Your kingdom come . . . help us to create a world where, beyond our own needs and hurts, we will do justice, love tenderly, and walk humbly with you and each other.

Your will be done . . . open our freedom to let you in so that the complete mutuality that characterizes your life might flow through our veins and thus the life that we help generate may radiate your equal love for all and your special love for the poor.

On earth as in heaven . . . may the work of our hands, the temples and structures we build in this world, reflect the temple and the structure of your glory so that the joy, graciousness, tenderness, and justice of heaven will show forth within all of our structures on earth.

Give . . . life and love to us and help us to see always everything as gift. Help us to know that nothing comes to us by right and that we must give because we have been given to. Help us realize that we must give to the poor, not because they need it, but because our own health depends upon our giving to them.

Us . . . the truly plural us. Give not just to our own but to everyone, including those who are very different than the narrow us. Give your gifts to all of us equally.

This day . . . not tomorrow. Do not let us push things off into some indefinite future so that we can continue to live justified lives in the face of injustice because we can make good excuses for our inactivity.

Our daily bread . . . so that each person in the world may have enough food, enough clean water, enough clean air, adequate health care, and sufficient access to education so as to have the sustenance for a healthy life. Teach us to give from our sustenance and not just from our surplus.

And forgive us our trespasses . . . forgive us our blindness toward our neighbor, our self-preoccupation, our racism, our sexism, and our incurable propensity to worry only about ourselves and our own. Forgive us our capacity to watch the evening news and do nothing about it.

As we forgive those who trespass against us . . . help us to forgive those who victimize us. Help us to mellow out in spirit, to not grow bitter with age, to forgive the imperfect parents and systems that wounded, cursed, and ignored us.

And do not put us to the test . . . do not judge us only by whether we have fed the hungry, given clothing to the naked, visited the sick, or tried to mend the systems that victimized the poor. Spare us this test for none of us can stand before your gospel scrutiny. Give us, instead, more days to mend our ways, our selfishness, and our systems.

But deliver us from evil . . . that is, from the blindness that lets us continue to participate in anonymous systems within which we need not see who gets less as we get more.

Amen.

9

A Spirituality of Sexuality

Perhaps there is nothing in this world as powerful to break self-ishness as is the simple act of looking at our own children. In our love for them we are given a privileged avenue to feel as God feels—to burst in unselfishness, in joy, in delight, and in the desire to let another's life be more real and important than our own.[1]

Sexuality as Divine Fire

The Greek philosophers used to say that we are fired into life with a madness that comes from the gods and that this energy is the root of all love, hate, creativity, joy, and sadness. A Christian should agree with that, then add that God put that great power, sexuality, within us so that, ultimately, we might also create life and, like God, look upon what we have helped create, overflow with a joy that breaks the very casings of our selfishness, and say: "It is good; indeed, it is very good!" A mature sexuality is when a person looks at what he or she has helped create, swells in a delight that breaks the prison of his or her selfishness, and feels as God feels when God looks at creation.

For this reason sexuality lies at the center of the spiritual life. A healthy sexuality is the single most powerful vehicle there is to lead us to selflessness and joy, just as unhealthy sexuality helps constellate selfishness and unhappiness as does nothing else. We will be happy in this life, depending upon whether or not we have a healthy sexuality.

One of the fundamental tasks of spirituality, therefore, is to help us to understand and channel our sexuality correctly. This, however, is no easy task. Sexuality is such a powerful fire that it is not always easy to channel it in life-giving ways. Its very power, and it is the most powerful force on the planet, makes it a force not just for formidable love, life, and blessing but also for the worst hate, death, and destruction imaginable. Sex is responsible for most of the ecstasies that occur on the planet, but it is also responsible for lots of murders and suicides. It is the most powerful of all fires, the best of all fires, the most dangerous of all fires, and the fire which, ultimately, lies at the base of everything, including the spiritual life.

But how should sexuality be understood? What are the central prongs within a Christian spirituality of sexuality?

Toward a Christian Understanding of Sexuality

1. Sexuality as an Awareness of Having Been Cut Off

To understand the meaning of sexuality, one must begin with its definition. The roots of a word are not always helpful in clarifying its meaning, but they are in the case of the words *sex* and *sexuality*. The word *sex* has a Latin root, the verb *secare*. In Latin, *secare* means (literally) "to cut off," "to sever," "to amputate," "to disconnect from the whole." To be "sexed," therefore, literally means to be cut off, to be severed from, to be amputated from the whole. Thus, to use a simple example, were you to take a chain saw and go to a tree and cut off one of its branches, you would have "sexed" that branch. This branch, could it feel and think, would wake up on the ground, severed, cut off, disconnected, a lonely little piece of wood which was once part of a great organism. It would know in its every cell that if it wants to continue living and especially if it wants to produce flowers and bear fruit, it must somehow reconnect itself to the tree.

That is precisely how we wake up in the world. We wake up in our cribs, not serene, but crying—lonely, cut off, severed from the great whole. Long before we even come to self-consciousness and long before we reach puberty when our sexuality constellates so strongly around the desire for sex, we feel ourselves painfully sexed in every cell of our body, psyche, and soul. Sex is a dimension of our very awareness. We wake up in the world and in every cell of our being we ache, consciously and unconsciously, sensing that we are incomplete, unwhole, lonely, cut off, a little piece of something that was once part of a whole. Karl Jung once compared the incompleteness we feel in sexuality to the separated white and yolk of an egg. Together they make a one, a whole. Apart they are incomplete. The sexes are like that. Alone we are essentially incomplete and aching at every level for a wholeness that, at some dark level, we know we have been separated from. We experience ourselves as white or yolk, separated from our other half.

And this is experienced as exceedingly painful—an aching loneliness, an irrational longing, a madness from the gods (as the Greeks put it). But this madness is also a great energy; in fact, it is the greatest energy of all inside us. It is the engine that drives everything else, body and spirit. If this is true, and it is, then we see that sexuality is more than simply a question of having sex and it becomes very important that we make a critical distinction between *sexuality* and *genitality*. Sex and having sex are not simply identifiable.

2. Sexuality Versus Genitality

Sexuality is an all-encompassing energy inside of us. In one sense, it is identifiable with the principle of life itself. It is the drive for love, communion, community, friendship, family, affection, wholeness, consummation, creativity, self-perpetuation, immorality, joy, delight, humor, and self-transcendence. It is not good to be alone.[2] When God said this about Adam at the dawn of creation, God meant it about every man, woman, child, animal, insect, plant, atom, and molecule in the universe. Sex is the energy inside of us that works incessantly against our being alone.

Genitality, having sex, is only one aspect of that larger reality of sexuality, albeit a very important one. Genitality is particularized, physical consummation, a certain privileged constellation of many of the energies that are contained within our wider erotic energies in one bodily encounter with another person which we commonly term making love.

Upon making this critical distinction, a couple of cautions must immediately go out. On the one hand, genitality (having sex) may never be trivialized or denigrated and seen as something that is too earthy and carnal to be spiritual, as countless Manicheans, Gnostics, and other spiritualists have believed and taught through the centuries. Christianity has for the most part been so influenced by negative and unchristian views on sex that it has never really developed a life-giving spirituality of genitality. For this reason, among others, celibacy has been made too much of a spiritual ideal. This is wrong. Having sex is admittedly not the whole reality of sex, but it is perhaps God's greatest gift to the planet and it offers humans the opportunity for genuine intimacy available this side of eternity. Indeed, some theologians see in sexual encounter a foretaste of the eternal life of heaven and many of the classical mystics use the image of sexual encounter to describe our ultimate union with God and creation.

On the other hand, Christians must also avoid the popular contemporary view that genitality somehow can carry all the things that sexuality is supposed to carry. Popular culture today teaches that one cannot be whole without being healthily sexual. That is correct. However, for the most part, it thinks of sex only as having sex. That is a tragic reduction. Sex is a wide energy and we are healthily sexual when we have love, community, communion, family, friendship, affection, creativity, joy, delight, humor, and self-transcendence in our lives. Having these, as we know, depends on many things and not just on whether or not we sleep alone. One can have a lot of sex and still lack real love, community, family, friendship, and creativity, just as one may be celibate and have these in abundance. We all know the popular dictum (and how true it is) that it is often easier to find a lover than a friend. Sexuality is as much about having friends as it is about having lovers. It is painful to sleep alone but it is perhaps even more painful to sleep alone when you are not sleeping alone. Thus, while genitality should never be denigrated and seen as something that is not spiritual or important, it should not be asked, all by itself, to be responsible for community, friendship, family, and delight within our lives.

The ancient Greek philosophers gave us the word *eros*. For them, however, it meant much more than it does for us today. Generally today we understand it to mean mainly sexual attraction. For the ancient Greeks, eros was a reality with six interpenetrating dimensions: It referred, at one and the same time, to *ludens* (love's playfulness, teasing, and humor); *erotic attraction* (sexual attractiveness and the desire to have sex); *mania* (obsessiveness, falling in love, romance); *pragma* (sensible arrangement in view of family life, home, and community); *philia* (friendship); and *agape* (altruism, selflessness, sacrifice). Unlike us, the ancient Greeks did not ask one aspect of love to carry all the others.

3. A Christian Definition of Sexuality

How then might a Christian define sexuality? Sexuality is a beautiful, good, extremely powerful, sacred energy, given us by God and experienced in every cell of our being as an irrepressible urge to overcome our incompleteness, to move toward unity and consummation with that which is beyond us. It is also the pulse to celebrate, to give and to receive delight, to find our way back to the Garden of Eden where we can be naked, shameless, and without worry and work as we make love in the moonlight.

Ultimately, though, all these hungers, in their full maturity, culminate in one thing: They want to make us co-creators with God . . . mothers and fathers, artisans and creators, big brothers and big sisters, nurses and healers, teachers and consolers, farmers and producers, administrators and community builders . . . co-responsible with God for the planet, standing with God and smiling at and blessing the world.

Given that definition, we see that sexuality in its mature bloom does not necessarily look like the love scenes (perfect bodies, perfect emotion, perfect light) in a Hollywood movie. What does sexuality in its full bloom look like?

• When you see a young mother, so beaming with delight at her own child that, for that moment, all selfishness within her has given way to the sheer joy of seeing her child happy, you are seeing sexuality in its mature bloom.

• When you see a grandfather so proud of his grandson, who has just received his diploma, that, for that moment, his spirit is only compassion, altruism, and joy, you are seeing sexuality in its mature bloom.

• When you see an artist, after long frustration, look with such satisfaction on a work she has just completed that everything else for the moment is blotted out, you are seeing sexuality in its mature bloom.

• When you see a young man, cold and wet, but happy to have been of service, standing on a dock where he has carried the unconscious body of a child he has just saved from drowning, you are seeing sexuality in its mature bloom.

• When you see someone throw back his or her head in genuine laughter, caught off guard by the surprise of joy itself, you are seeing sexuality in its mature bloom.

• When you see an elderly nun who, never having slept with a man, been married, or given birth to a child, has through years of selfless service become a person whose very compassion gives her a mischievous smile, you are seeing sexuality in its mature bloom.

• When you see a community gathered round a grave, making peace with tragedy and consoling each other so that life can go on, you are seeing sexuality in its mature bloom.

• When you see an elderly husband and wife who after

nearly half a century of marriage have made such peace with each other's humanity that now they can quietly share a bowl of soup, content just to know that the other is there, you are seeing sexuality in its mature bloom.

• When you see a table, surrounded by a family, laughing, arguing, and sharing life with each other, you are seeing sexuality in its mature bloom.

• When you see a Mother Teresa dress the wounds of a street-person in Calcutta or an Oscar Romero give his life in defense of the poor, you are seeing sexuality in its mature bloom.

• When you see any person—man, woman, or child—who in a moment of service, affection, love, friendship, creativity, joy, or compassion is, for that moment, so caught up in what is beyond him or her that for that instant his or her separateness from others is overcome, you are seeing sexuality in its mature bloom.

• When you see God, having just created the earth or just seen Jesus baptized in the Jordan river, look down on what has just happened and say, "It is good. In this I take delight!" you are seeing sexuality in its mature bloom.

Sexuality is not simply about finding a lover or even finding a friend. It is about overcoming separateness by giving life and blessing it. Thus, in its maturity, sexuality is about giving oneself over to community, friendship, family, service, creativity, humor, delight, and martyrdom so that, with God, we can help bring life into the world.

4. A Few Nonnegotiable Christian Principles

Beyond the wide definition just given, what other principles anchor a healthy Christian spirituality of sexuality?

Four fundamental principles need special mentioning:

a. For a Christian, sex is something sacred. Hence it can never be simply a casual, unimportant, neutral thing. If its proper nature is respected, it builds the soul as a sacrament, and brings God's physical touch to us. Conversely, though, if its proper nature is not respected, it becomes a perverse thing that works at disintegrating the soul.

In a committed, loving, covenantal relationship sex is sacramental, part of a couple's Eucharist. It is then a privileged vehicle of grace, an extraordinary source of integration for the soul, a deep well of gratitude, and something that will through its own inner dynamics open both persons (in a way that perhaps nothing else can) to becoming life-giving, gracious, and blessing adults. Conversely, sex that is devoid of those conditions will normally bring about the opposite effect. It will harden the soul, trivialize it, and work at disintegrating its unity. It will, as well, not open those engaging in it to real community, graciousness, and blessing, but instead help alienate them from real community.

Our culture today, of course, resists that notion and protests that sex can be casual and neutral, that it need not be a big deal. The irony is, however, that just as our culture is affirming that sex can be casual and spiritually and psychologically neutral, it is recognizing for the first time the incredible devastation of soul that occurs when someone is sexually violated. This is progress. Unfortunately, this deepening of insight has not yet extended itself to the recognition of how destructive of true community, and often of the individual soul as well, casual sex can be.

Sex is not just like anything else, despite our culture's protest. Its fire is so powerful, so precious, so close to the heart and soul of a person, and so godly, that it either gives life or it takes it away. It can never be casual, but is either a sacrament or a destructive act.

b. For a Christian, sex by its very nature must be linked to marriage, monogamy, and a covenantal commitment that is, by definition, all-embracing and permanent. What is wrong with sex outside of marriage, for a Christian, is not so much that it breaks a commandment (although it does) but that, ultimately, it is a schizophrenic act. How so?

By its very nature, sex speaks of total giving, total trust, and total commitment. There is an unconditionality inherent in so intimate a sharing of one's soul. Thus, if real trust, commitment, permanency, and unconditionality are not present within the wider relationship, sex is partly a lie. It pretends to give a gift that it does not really give and it asks for a gift that it cannot respectfully reciprocate. When one says, as does an old song, "Let the devil take tomorrow, tonight I need a friend," the devil indeed does take tomorrow and the friend usually disappears as well.

Again, our culture protests against this, but it can do little to mend the terrible heartaches, family breakups, violence, and occasional suicides that result from fractured sexual relationships. I once read a rather punishing critique of Christianity's insistence that sex be linked to marriage. Its author ended his criticism by asking: "Why is Christianity so hung up on this? Who has ever been hurt by sex anyway?" In trying courageously to answer the latter of his two questions, we will more clearly see the wisdom of Christianity's traditional teaching.

c. Sex has an inner dynamic that, if followed faithfully, will lead its partners to sanctity. Sexuality is God's energy within us. Hence, ideally, sex should lead persons to sanctity and when its principles are respected it does precisely that. How? What are its inner dynamics that can lead one to sanctity? Let us look at a typical example:

A young man, nursing more than his share of selfishness, hurt, and personal ambition, sets out to make his mark in life when his sexuality intercepts him. Initially, given the adolescent stage of his development, what he wants is sex, with or without love and intimacy. But he meets a young woman with whom he falls in love. He still wants sex, but now the very inner dynamics of sex help mature his desire. Being in love, his sexuality now demands not just sex but intimacy, exclusivity, and commitment as well. He marries and, for a while, he is satisfied with sex and intimacy. However, as he and his relationship to his wife mature, there naturally comes a day when he wants children. They begin to have children and even though he had wanted them he is surprised at himself by how much he loves his children and how much they have changed him and his whole outlook on life. Whole new dimensions of desire (of which he was previously unaware) are triggered within him and he finds that he can, without resentment, put his own needs aside so as to give more of himself to his children and, of course, to his wife as well.

And then the children start growing up, mixing with other children, going to school, and demanding lessons of every kind. His house starts filling with other children and their parents and their concerns—and he finds himself busy each evening discussing concerns with other parents, attending parent-teacher meetings, coaching kids' football, and driving kids to every kind of class and tournament in the area. His world keeps widening and he, and his desires and maturity, keep widening with it. Slowly, imperceptibly, through the years he grows, widens, mellows out, becomes more unselfish, and a gracious, blessing, adult father.

Sex, followed in fidelity, leads to sanctity. This man's story is one kind of scenario. There are many, many others that work in the same way, including the dynamics of a healthy celibate sexuality. Desire, working through us, if followed faithfully, keeps opening us up further and further to gracious adulthood.[3]

d. For a Christian, sex always needs the protection of a healthy chastity. In the Christian view of things, chastity is one of the keys to a healthy sexuality. This, however, needs to be correctly understood.

First, there is the concept of chastity itself: Chastity is not the same thing as celibacy. To be chaste does not mean that one does not have sex. Nor does it mean that one is a prude. My parents were two of the most chaste persons I ever met, yet they obviously enjoyed sex—as a large family and a warm, vivacious bond between them gave more than ample evidence of. Chastity is, first of all, not even primarily a sexual concept, though, given the power and urgency of sex, faults in chastity are often within the area of sexuality.

Chastity has to do with all experiencing. It is about the ap-

propriateness of any experience. Ultimately, chastity is reverence—and sin, all sin, is irreverence. To be chaste is to experience
people, things, places, entertainment, the phases of our lives, and
sex in a way that does not violate them or ourselves. To be chaste
is to experience things reverently, in such a way that the experience leaves both them and ourselves more, not less, integrated.

Thus, we are chaste when we relate to others in a way that
does not transgress their moral, psychological, emotional, aesthetic, and sexual boundaries. That is an abstract way of saying
that we are chaste when we do not let impatience, irreverence, or
selfishness ruin what is a gift by somehow violating it. Conversely, we lack chastity when we cross boundaries prematurely
or irreverently, when we violate anything and somehow reduce
what it is. Chastity is respect, reverence, and patience. Its fruits
are integration, gratitude, and joy. Lack of chastity is impatience, irreverence, and violation. Its fruits are disintegration of
soul, bitterness, and cynicism.

Whenever there is violence, disrespect, emotional chaos, lack
of community, bitterness, cynicism, and sexual irresponsibility,
there is a lack of chastity. Those are its infallible indicators.

Sex, precisely because it is such a powerful fire, always needs
the protection of chastity. As Karl Jung suggests, we should
never be naive about the imperialistic power of energy. All energy, especially sexual energy, is not always friendly and it often
seeks to take us across borders prematurely or irreverently.
There is more than a little wisdom in some of the classical sexual
taboos. Fire that is so powerful and sacred, sexual fire, needs to
be disciplined and contained by more things than just our emotional state on a given day. The wisdom of the ages, some codified in the commandments and some buried archetypally in our
instincts, tells us that, before the fire of sex, we should stand in a
certain reverence and holy awe, knowing that divine fire demands that we have our shoes off.[4] Before anything as powerful
as sex there need to be some taboos.

Again, of course, our culture objects. Few things are as subject to cynicism today as is the concept of sexual chastity. Contemporary culture considers the overcoming of chastity a moral victory, one that has finally helped set us free sexually. Christians could perhaps take that claim more seriously if this supposed sexual liberation had in fact translated into more respect between the sexes and into sex that actually relieves loneliness, builds lasting community, builds more stable souls, results in less sexual exploitation of others, and helps create a society of less lonely, more loving, more gracious, and happier adults. Sadly, that is not the case and one is reminded of Albert Camus' lament that there is a time when moving beyond chastity is considered a victory, but this soon turns into a defeat.[5]

A final comment regarding chastity: Someone once said that Christianity does not understand sexual passion while the world does not understand chastity. That is an oversimplification, given that there are important individual voices on both sides that do not fit the description, but the statement is true as a generalization and says something very important. Christianity has struggled, and still does, to healthily and fully celebrate sexual passion. The world, for its part, has struggled, and still does, to honestly and courageously look at what happens to our innocence and our happiness when we denigrate chastity. Both need to learn from each other. Passion and chastity, sex and purity, must be brought together.

Christianity must have the courage to let go of some of its fears and timidities and learn to celebrate the goodness of sexual passion, of sex. Indeed it must be the moral force that challenges the culture to celebrate the goodness of sex. As long as it hesitates to do this, it will, at this level at least, remain the enemy of legitimate delight and creativity. Chastity outside of the goodness of sex is frigidity. On the other hand, our culture must relearn the value of chastity and purity. It must admit how much of its emotional pain and chaos is the result of trivializing sex and ignoring the value of chastity and purity. As long as the world continues to see chastity as naivete, fear, and Victorian morality, it will remain its own enemy. Sexual passion is only something of depth when it is related to chastity and purity. It is archetypal, not incidental, that we want to get married in white.[6]

Living in Inconsummation—Some Christian Perspectives

1. The Frustration of a Lifelong Unfinished Symphony

Karl Rahner once said that in the torment of the insufficiency of everything attainable we eventually realize that, here in this life, all symphonies remain unfinished. He is right. In this world there is no such a thing as a fully consummate joy. We are always in some way frustrated, in some way sleeping alone, whether we are having sex or not.

This is true especially of our sexuality. Ultimately, as Freud suggested, everyone is sexually frustrated in that we all have sexual needs that can never be met, regardless of how much sex we have. Our sexual hungers are simply too wide and all-encompassing to ever be fulfilled and they are of such a complex nature that sometimes having sex does little to fulfill them.

What are we to do with this? How are we to live with that frustration so as not to unconsciously take it out on life and on our loved ones? How do we live in an incomplete world without demanding that our lives, our spouses, our friends, our homes, our vocations, and our jobs give us something that they cannot ultimately give, namely, the final symphony, full consummation?

2. Some Christian Perspectives—What to Do Until the Messiah Returns

What perspectives can Christian spirituality bring to bear on this question? What does one ultimately do with this sexual inconsummation that offers no exemptions?

Five interrelated things that can be helpful to us as Christians in living with this frustration.

a. UNDERSTAND THE TIME WE ARE LIVING IN

Henri Nouwen once suggested that we would all live happier lives if we accepted this, unalterable, truth: "Our life is a short time in expectation, a time in which sadness and joy kiss each other at every moment. There is a quality of sadness that pervades all the moments of our life. It seems that there is no such thing as a clear-cut pure joy, but that even in the most happy moments of our existence we sense a tinge of sadness. In every satisfaction, there is an awareness of limitations. In every success, there is the fear of jealousy. Behind every smile, there is a tear. In every embrace, there is loneliness. In every friendship, distance. And in all forms of light, there is the knowledge of surrounding darkness. . . . But this intimate experience in which every bit of life is touched by a bit of death can point us beyond the limits of our existence. It can do so by making us look forward in expectation to the day when our hearts will be filled with perfect joy, a joy that no one shall take away from us."[7]

What Nouwen affirms here, in simple language, is what Christian theology means when it tells that we are living in the interim eschatological age. We are living in that time between Christ's resurrection (the initial triumph of God's promise to give us fulfillment) and the final consummation of that promise, the end of time (when all tears will be wiped away).

During that time, and it is an interim time, we will always live in tension, waiting for the final consummation of history and our lives. Our happiness depends not on overcoming this, which we cannot do in any case, but in making our peace with it. And that peace is not made by a stoic acceptance that we cannot have it all in this life. It is made by living our incompleteness in face of a future promise.

To live in the interim eschatological age is to be like a couple waiting to get married who, for a good reason (for example, the death of parent), have chosen to postpone their marriage for a period of time. There is a certain frustration in that, but that frustration is offset by the clear knowledge that this is only a temporary delay, soon to be overcome. Our essential inconsummation in life must be understood in this way. The frustration is real, but it is, as Nouwen so well puts it, something we will one day overcome, albeit that day will not meet us in this life.

To understand the time we live in, is to be less frustrated with the fact that it cannot offer us the final symphony.

b. UNDERSTAND HOW WIDE IS SEXUALITY'S HUNGER

Janis Joplin was once asked what it was like being a rock star. She replied: "It's pretty hard sometimes. You go on stage, make love to fifteen thousand people, then you go home and sleep alone."

Jesus was once asked, as a test: If a woman marries seven times and all her husbands die before she dies, whose wife will she be after the resurrection? He answered that, after the resurrection, we will no longer marry or be given in marriage.[8]

These two answers, Janis Joplin's and Jesus', are not unconnected. Each, in its own way, says something about the all-embracing intent of our sexuality. What Janis Joplin is saying is that, in our sexuality and our creativity, we are ultimately trying to make love to everyone. What Jesus is saying is not that we will be celibate in heaven, but rather that, in heaven, all will be married to all. In heaven, unlike life here on earth where that is not possible, our sexuality will finally be able to embrace everyone. In heaven, everyone will make love to everyone else and, already now, we hunger for that within every cell of our being. Sexually our hungers are very wide. We are built to ultimately embrace the universe and everything in it.

To understand our sexuality and to live with its unfulfilled tensions, it can be most helpful simply to understand this. In loving, the ultimate wound is not to be able to marry everyone. The greatest human hunger, felt in every cell in our being, is that we cannot be completely united with everyone and everything. This should not surprise us. As Sidney Callahan says: "We are united through all matter with all creation, and we are united as a species destined to come together in an ultimate unity in a new creation. We are destined to end up as members of one body in Christ. Is it surprising, then, that we hunger for this along the way?"[9]

It is important to understand this, but it is also important not to misunderstand it. Because our sexuality is ultimately geared to embrace everyone does not mean that we can be promiscuous and, already here in this life, try to live that out. In fact, paradoxically, it means the opposite. Only God can sleep with everyone and, thus, only in God can we sleep with everyone. In this life, even though our sexuality has us geared up for universal embrace, we only have two options that are life-giving: Either we embrace the many through the one (by sleeping with one person within a monogamous marriage) or we embrace the one through the many (by sleeping with no one, in celibacy). Both of these are ways that will eventually open our sexuality up so as to embrace everyone. If we go the route of promiscuity, eventually, we will embrace no one.

c. Turn Our Inconsummation into Solitude

The pain of sexual inconsummation drives us outward, as is its function, to seek union with persons and things beyond ourselves. Up to a point, this is good. All of us, like Augustine, can thank God for giving us restless hearts. Our restlessness is the source of all of our energies. But it is also what keeps us from restfulness, from prayer, from being centered, and from being happy.

There comes a point in our restlessness when its purpose is no longer to direct us outward, but inward. When instead of letting our restlessness drive us outward to try to satisfy our incompleteness by yet more activity, friendship, sex, work, entertainment, or distraction, we must enter it in such a way as to turn it into solitude.

Solitude, as we know, is not the same thing as loneliness. It is being alone, but it is being alone in such a way that our very incompleteness is a source of quiet strength and not of anxious dissipation. Few spiritual writers have written with as much insight on this question as has Henri Nouwen.[10] For him, the movement to turn our restless incompleteness into a restful solitude has four steps:

1. Own your pain and incompleteness. Like an alcoholic cannot be helped until he or she admits helplessness, we too cannot move toward solitude until we acknowledge honestly our pathological restlessness and fundamental sexual unwholeness. Hence, the first step toward solitude is precisely to accept that, here in this life, we will find no final symphony and we may not give our congenital hungers for full consummation free reign but must direct them toward something else.

2. Give up false messianic expectations. Once we have accepted that we are fundamentally dis-eased in that nothing in this life will ever fully complete us, we need then give up our messianic expectations and demands. Hence, we must stop expecting that somewhere, sometime, in some place, we will meet just the right person, the right situation, or the right combination of circumstances so that we can be completely happy. We will stop demanding that our spouses, families, friends, and jobs give us what only God can give us, clear-cut pure joy.

3. Go inward. When we are restless, everything in us screams to move outward, to seek some activity that will soothe the ache. However, to find solitude we must move inward, away from all activity. Ultimately, what turns our restless aching into inner quiet and peace is not more activity, but sitting still long enough for restlessness to turn to restfulness, compulsion to freedom, impatience to patience, self-absorption to altruism, and heartache to empathy.

4. It is a movement that is never made once and for all. Turning restlessness into restfulness, aching inconsummation into peaceful solitude, is not something that is ever accomplished once and for all. The world is not divided up between two kinds of persons, restless ones and ones who have found solitude. Rather our own lives are divided between two different modes of

feeling: Some days we are more restless and other days we are more restful, sometimes our congenital sexual aching is one huge heartache and at other times it is a deep well of empathy, and some days we find being alone almost too painful to bear and other days we bask in quiet solitude. Coming to grips with unfulfilled sexual hunger is to, more and more, find the latter.

d. Sexual Incompleteness as Solidarity with the Poor

As we struggle with the pain of inconsummation, it is valuable too for us as Christians to look at Jesus and the way he incarnated his sexuality to see what might be learned from that.

Jesus, as we know, never married. However, the proper question to ask is not: "Why did Christ remain celibate?" Why? Because, asked in this way, the very question suggests that somehow celibacy is a higher state than marriage. Moreover, if the focus is on celibacy then married persons cannot imitate Jesus in this important part of his life, his sexual stance.

The question ideally should be asked this way: "What did Christ try to reveal through the way he incarnated himself as a sexual being?" If asked this way, the answer to the question will have the same meaning for both married people and celibates.

So why did Christ incarnate his sexuality in this manner? What was he trying to teach us? Among many other things, through his celibacy, Christ was trying to tell us that love and sex are not always the same thing, that chastity, waiting, and inconsummation have an important role to play within the interim eschatological age we live in, and that, ultimately, in our sexuality we are meant to embrace everyone. But his celibacy had another purpose too. It was a key part of his solidarity with the poor.

How so? Simply put, when Christ went to bed alone at night he was in real solidarity with the many persons who, not by choice but by circumstance, sleep alone. And there is a real poverty, a painful searing one, in this kind of aloneness. The poor are not just those who are more manifestly victimized by poverty, violence, war, and unjust economic systems. There are other less obvious manifestations of poverty, violence, and injustice. Celibacy by conscription is one of them.

Anyone who because of unwanted circumstance (physical unattractiveness, emotional instability, advanced age, geographical separation, frigidity or uptightness, bad history, or simple bad luck) is effectively blocked from enjoying sexual consummation is a victim of a most painful poverty. This is particularly true today in a culture that so idealizes sexual intimacy and the right sexual relationship. The universe works in pairs, from the birds through to humanity. To sleep alone is to be poor. To sleep alone is to be stigmatized. To sleep alone is to be outside the norm for human intimacy and to acutely feel the sting of that. To sleep alone, as Thomas Merton once put it, is to live in a loneliness that God himself condemned.

When Jesus went to bed alone he was in solidarity with that pain, in solidarity with the poor. Sexual inconsummation, whatever its negatives, does this for us, it puts us into a privileged solidarity with a special kind of poverty, the loneliness of those who sleep alone, not because they want to, but because circumstance denies them from enjoying perhaps the deepest human experience that there is, sexual consummation.

And all of us, married and celibate, have more than ample opportunity to be in this kind of solidarity with the poor. If we are married, even if we are enjoying a healthy sexual relationship, nonetheless there will still remain, always, certain painful areas of inconsummation, places in our life and in our soul where we sleep alone. Those places of loneliness, rather than being places for bitterness and anger, can become those places where we are most in solidarity with the poor. If we are celibate, or married but somewhat or deeply frustrated with our sexual relationship there, we should know that, like Jesus, when we sleep alone we are in solidarity with the poor.

e. ACCEPT THE INADEQUACY OF OUR LOVE SO THAT ITS REAL POWER
CAN SHOW THROUGH

In a number of her novels, Anita Brookner suggests the first task
of a man and a woman in marriage, or in any deep relationship,
is to console each other for the fact that they cannot not disappoint each other. Human beings are not gods and thus what we
offer to each other will always be less than what we need and
look for from each other.

Thus, for example, in her recent novel, *Altered States,* her
main character, Alan, whose wife has committed suicide, is reflecting back on what went wrong in their marriage. He realizes
that it was not so much that something positively went wrong
but that they were not able to get the essential thing right in the
first place: "The tragedy was that we could not console each
other. Our woes were never acknowledged and so remained unknown. To me she had always appeared transparent; I foolishly
had not seen that there was more for me to discover. And what
she had wanted, I now saw, was some kind of confessor, to
whom she could reveal secrets over which she had kept silent for
far too long, since childhood, perhaps . . ."[11]

Brookner is right. At the end of the day, given the scope and
power inherent in our sexuality, what we really need from each
other in deep relationships is precisely a confessor, someone before whom we can stop having to lie, someone before whom we
do not have to try to measure up, and someone who can console
us for the fact that we cannot not disappoint him or her because,
even at its best, the love we give each other is not enough. We are
not gods and parts of us will always remain untouched, incon-
summate, bursting with secrets kept silent for far too long.

However, as Thomas Merton once said, to acknowledge this
tragedy, that our love cannot be enough for each other, is, at the
same time, to reveal its real nobility and life-giving power. By
acknowledging its limit, we rise above ourselves and let go of
those imaginings and unrealistic expectations that prevent us
from seeing and enjoying the powerful goodness that is in fact

there. It is false romanticism, the unrealistic and imperialistic belief that we can have the full symphony that serves to hide the real tragedy, real meaning, and real nobility of human love and sexuality, as these express themselves in either marriage or in celibate friendship. A loneliness will always exist. We cannot be enough for each other and will always remain painfully sexed, separate, and somewhat alone.

But if this is recognized and accepted, its very absurdity becomes the center of peace where, finally, things begin to make sense and marriage and celibacy become both possible and beautiful.[12]

10

Sustaining Ourselves
in the Spiritual Life

To pray, I think, does not mean to think about God in contrast to thinking about other things, or to spend time with God instead of spending time with other people. Rather, it means to think and live in the presence of God. All our actions must have their origin in prayer. Praying is not an isolated activity; it takes place in the midst of all the things and affairs that keep us active. In prayer a "self-centred monologue" becomes a "God-centred dialogue."[1]

The Need for Sustenance, Not Just Clarity of Truth

Knowledge alone cannot save us. When St. Augustine coined that phrase nearly seventeen hundred years ago he meant it as a principle of truth, but he was also writing a commentary on his own life. Augustine, as we know, had two conversions, one in his head and the other in his heart. At age twenty-five, he converted to Christianity, intellectually. After years of experimenting with various pagan philosophies and ways of living, he was now convinced in his head that Christianity was correct. The rest of him, however, was not as willing a convert. For nine more years, until he was thirty-four years old, he was unable to bring his moral life into harmony with his intellectual faith. It was during these years that he not infrequently prayed his infamous prayer: "Lord, make me a good and chaste Christian, but not yet."

We see from that example that it is not enough just to know the truth, to have clarity of conviction, and to know where ideally our lives should be heading, though that can be a valuable start. There is also the question of heart, of energy, of willpower, of sustaining ourselves on the road. The spiritual life is not a quick sprint to a well-marked finish line, but a marathon, an arduous lifelong journey into an ever-widening horizon. To sustain ourselves on that road, even after we have some assurance that we are on the right road, requires that along the way we continually find what metaphorically might be termed "Elijah's jug,"[2] namely, the sustenance that God promised to provide to those who are walking the long road toward the divine mountain.

The previous chapters of this book focused mainly on the question of clarifying principles, on trying to lay out a positive vision of Christian spirituality. Obviously, Augustine's dictum notwithstanding, that is important, without vision we perish. Bernard Lonergan, one of the great intellectuals of our century, and a pious Christian, insisted that all genuine conversion must involve an intellectual conversion. He is right, the heart needs guidance from the head, but his statement tells only part of the story. Morris West, the novelist, also a very committed Christian, insists that genuine conversion is ultimately a question of falling in love. He too is right, as anyone of us who has ever known the truth but felt too tired, lonely, lazy, bitter, or addicted to old habits to move toward it can testify to. We need knowledge and heart. Spirituality is about both.

How do we develop the heart to sustain ourselves on the long road? How do we move beyond our fatigue, loneliness, laziness, bitterness, and bad habits so as to become gracious, happy, self-sacrificing, generative, adult Christians? What do we do during those times when, as Henri Nouwen puts it, we are "too tired to read the Gospels, too restless to have spiritual thoughts, too depressed to find words for God, or too exhausted to do anything."[3]

What practices and exercises (analogous to keeping our bodies physically healthy) are helpful for us as we struggle as Christians to live healthy spiritual lives?

There are many time-honored, canonized, spiritual practices, as outlined in classical spiritual writings from scripture down to our own day. Generally, the following practices formed the core of a healthy Christian spirituality: Regular prayer (both private and communal), the practice of charity and self-sacrifice (both at home and in the wider world), some concrete involvement with the poor, involvement within some church community, and a willingness to be vulnerable for love (as Christ was vulnerable). From the Bible, through the early church fathers, through the medieval theologians, through the great reformers, through the great mystics, through the founders of the various religious orders, down to Henri Nouwen, these are the spiritual practices you see everywhere emphasized.

Nothing has changed. These are still the core practices for a healthy spiritual life. Hopefully everything that has been said so far in this book endorses that. The task of this final chapter, however, is not so much to elaborate on these essentials as to take them healthily for granted and then to push things a little farther.

Given the particular struggles of our own time, what are the signs of the times for today? What is unique to us and what particular exercises and practices do we need today in order to sustain ourselves, given our own peculiar struggles?

The signs of the times seem to dictate several complementary directions.

Commandments for the Long Haul

1. Be a Mystic . . .

"The time is fast approaching when one will either be a mystic or an unbeliever."[4]

a. THE NEED FOR A PERSONAL ACT OF FAITH

Karl Rahner is credited with making the statement that today one is either a mystic or a nonbeliever. He is right. None of us can rely any longer on the fact that we live in a culture that was once Christian, that we are seemingly surrounded by other Christians, or that we once had faith. None of these alone is enough today to sustain a Christian faith in an age which is as agnostic, pluralistic, secular, seductive, and distracting as our own. We live in a post-Christian situation within which the culture no longer carries the faith for us.

Thus, to be a believer today is to live in a certain moral loneliness. To sustain faith today is not to vote with the majority, but rather to be what sociologists term a cognitive minority, that is, to stand outside of the dominant consciousness. One can no longer simply roll with the flow of one's own particular community, even one's faith community, if one wishes to have a living faith.

Twenty-five years ago, while teaching at Yale, Henri Nouwen had already made the statement that, even among seminarians, the dominant consciousness was agnostic. God essentially had no place, even among people talking about religion and preparing for Christian ministry.[5]

That is basically true for most of us today. It is no longer enough to have been born into a Christian family, to have been baptized, or even to be part of a worshiping community. None of these, alone, will necessarily give us real faith. This is evident, not just because so many people (including many of our own children) are drifting away from Christianity, but because, even within our churches, it is easier to have faith in Christianity, in a code of ethics, in Jesus' moral teaching, in God's call for justice, and in the human value of gathering as community, than it is to have personal faith in a living God. Too often what we have, in fact, is not Christianity but an ideology of Christianity.

Thus there is a important challenge in Rahner's comment. To have a living faith today one must at some point in his or her life make a deep, private act of faith. That act, which he equates with becoming a mystic, is unfortunately itself very difficult because the very forces that have helped erode our cultural, communal faith also work against us making this private act of faith.

What are these antifaith forces? They are not the product of some conscious conspiracy by godlessness. They are, instead, all those things, good and bad, within us and around us that tempt us away from prayer, from self-sacrifice, from being more communal, from being willing to sweat blood in a garden in order to keep our integrity and commitments, and from mustering up the time and courage to enter deeply into our own souls. Hence they are not abstract, foreign forces. They live in the house with us and are as comfortable to us as a well-worn shoe. What blocks faith is that myriad of innocent things within our ordinary, normal lives which precisely make our lives comfortable: our laziness, our self-indulgence, our ambition, our restlessness, our envy, our refusal to live in tension, our consumerism, our greed for things and experience, our need to have a certain lifestyle, our busyness and overextension, our perpetual tiredness, our obsession with celebrities, and our perpetual distraction with sports, sit-coms, and talk shows. These are the antimystical forces of our time.

b. Personal Faith Depends upon Prayer

So how do we become mystics in the midst of all of this? Virtually all classical spiritual writers, from every tradition, suggest one road beyond all of this, private prayer. Among classical spiritual writers, there is this leitmotif: In order to sustain yourself in faith you must regularly (most would say daily) spend an extended period of time in private prayer. Failure to do so, they warn, results in a certain dissipation of the soul, even when our sincerity remains intact. There is no way to stay in touch with one's soul and to keep a balance there, outside of regular private prayer.

Christianity has always taught this. Interestingly, today many other traditions and philosophies teach this as well. Sometimes other words are used instead of the word prayer (meditation, contemplation, inner work, soul work, active imagination, contact with our inner King and Queen, and so on), but the essential idea is the same. To stay in contact with one's soul and to keep some health and balance there, we must have some conscious dialogue with a God, a higher power, a daimon, an inner King and Queen, a guiding angel, or whatever we conceive of as that ultimate something or somebody within which we live and move and breathe and have our being.[6]

Few have written on this question, our need for prayer, with more depth and eloquence than has Robert Moore, a psychologist and philosopher of religion from the University of Chicago. Moore addresses both secular and Christian audiences, but his message is ultimately the same for both: If you don't pray you will inevitably become either depressed or inflated—or bounce back and forth between the two. Only prayer can provide for you that fine line (spiritual, psychological, and emotional) between depression and inflation. If you don't believe in God and the value of religious prayer, then practice some form of active imagination or meditation and, through them, get into conscious contact with the King and Queen inside of you because only prayer can ground a soul—and only it can save you from being either a depressive or an asinine personality. If you do not pray, you will either be habitually depressed or obsessed with your own ego. This, according to Moore, is true, irrespective of whether you are religious or not.[7]

Hence, both from what is best in Christian and secular tradition, we hear the truth that sustaining a life of faith, and a balanced life in general, depends upon developing a habit of private prayer. Moreover, as these same sources assure us, we should not expect this to be easy. All the things that work against our faith also work against us developing the habit of private prayer. We must, however, continue to try, continue to consistently set a time to spend apart with God. As Henri Nouwen assures us, that time apart will keep us centered, even when it does not feel as if we are praying or making any headway:

[My time apart is not a time] . . . *of deep prayer, nor a time in which I experience a special closeness to God; it is not a period of serious attentiveness to the divine mysteries. I wish it were! On the contrary, it is full of distractions, inner restlessness, sleepiness, confusion, and boredom. It seldom, if ever, pleases my senses. But the simple fact of being for one hour in the presence of the Lord and of showing him all that I feel, think, sense, and experience, without trying to hide anything, must please him. Somehow, somewhere, I know that he loves me, even though I do not feel that love as I can feel a human embrace, even though I do not hear a voice as I hear human words of consolation, even though I do not see a smile, as I can see in a human face. Still God speaks to me, looks at me, and embraces me there, where I am still unable to notice it.*[8]

c. A Mysticism for Our Age—Prayer as Pondering, Carrying Tension

But prayer is more than just saying prayers, just as mysticism is more than a question of merely seeking God through formal prayer. Ultimately, mysticism and prayer are something we must do within all the activities of our lives and not just in certain formal moments set aside for them. "Pray always," scripture tells us.[9] But how does one do this?

There are many answers one might give to that question and, depending upon how one reads the signs of the times, different things might be emphasized for different generations. For our generation, given our own particular, spiritual Achilles' heel, the brand of mysticism that we most need is that of pondering in the biblical sense.

What, according to scripture, does it mean to ponder? Pondering, in the Gospels, does not mean what it meant for the Greek philosophers like Socrates, Plato, and Aristotle. For them, to ponder meant taking seriously the dictum that the unexamined life is not worth living. It meant to reflect more consciously about things as opposed to simply rolling with the flow and leaving life to circumstance and chance. For the Greek mind, to ponder meant to intellectually contemplate life's great mysteries.

Scripture, however, does not reflect this Greek mind-set. In the Gospels, which exhibit more the Hebrew way of understanding things, to ponder is less a question of intellectually contemplating something as it is of patiently holding it inside of one's soul, complete with all the tension that brings. Thus, when Mary stands under the cross of Jesus and watches him die—and there is absolutely nothing she can do to save him or even to protest his innocence and goodness—she is pondering in the biblical sense. She is carrying a great tension that she is helpless to resolve and must simply live with. That is what scripture refers to when it tells us that Mary "kept these things in her heart and pondered them."[10]

Thus, to ponder, biblically, is to stand before life's great mysteries the way Mary stood before the various events of Jesus' life, including the way she stood under the cross. There is great joy in that but there can also be incredible tension. The type of mysticism that we most need today to revitalize our faith is precisely this kind of pondering, a willingness to carry tension as Mary did.

I would like to illustrate this with a rather earthy example (which I apologize for, but use nonetheless because of its clarity): When I was in graduate school, in class one day the professor was lecturing on sexuality and morality. The issue of masturbation was raised and a student stopped him dead in his tracks with the question: "Do you masturbate?"

The professor's first reaction was one of anger at the impertinence of the question. He turned away from the class toward the blackboard and his body language said what his words did not: "You are out of order with that question!"

However, he recovered himself soon enough and turned and faced his questioner and the class with these words: "My first reaction is to tell you that you're out of order and that you've no business asking a question like that in this class, or anywhere else. However, since this is a class in moral theology and in the end your question has some value, I will in fact answer you: Yes, sometimes I do—and I'm not proud of it. I don't think it's very wrong and I don't think it's very right either. I do know this though . . . I'm a better person when I don't because then I am carrying more of the tension that we, all of us, should carry in this life. I'm a better person when I carry that tension."

Whatever its merits or lack of them in moral theology, that answer says something about mysticism and what ultimately helps sustain faith. We are better persons when we carry tension, as opposed to always looking for its easy resolution. To carry tension, especially great tension, is to ponder in the biblical sense.

We see examples of this in great literature. What makes for a great hero or heroine? What constitutes what we call nobility of soul? Usually we ascribe that quality to the person who, mindless of his or her own comfort, need, and pain, is willing for a higher reason to carry a great tension for a long period of time, not acquiescing to the temptation to prematurely resolve things.

Thus, for instance, we have already seen in the heroine of Jane Austen's *Sense and Sensibility* a certain greatness of soul. Why? Because she puts other people's needs and the proper order of things above her own need to have her tension resolved. We see too in that story, as well as in many others of its kind, what makes for sublimity—namely, the fact that first there has been some sublimation. Generally, the more prior sublimation there is the more sublime the experience. Great joy depends upon first having carried great tension.

And this is true for every area of life, not just for sexuality.

Nobility of soul is connected to carrying tension. The great illustration of this is, of course, Jesus sweating blood in the Garden of Gethsemane.[11] There we see the necessary connection between suffering and faith, the necessary connection between sweating blood in a garden and keeping our commitments and our integrity. Nobody will ever remain faithful in a marriage, a vocation, a friendship, a family, a job, or just to his or her own integrity without sometimes sweating blood in a garden. To offer just one, but very illustrative, example:

Some years ago there was an American television series entitled "Thirty Something," which focused on a number of couples in their thirties as they struggled with the tensions of their lives in general and their marriages in particular. One episode ran this way: The men had gathered at a downtown hotel for an all-male party while their wives met in one of the homes for an all-female party. At the men's party, one of the men (several years married and away from his wife) found himself very attracted to one of the hotel managers, a young woman, whom he had to deal with, off and on, during the course of the evening with regards to arranging food, drinks, music, and the like. She too was attracted to him and before the evening was over, despite the fact that nothing had really been said between them, they both sensed that timeless old magic between them. That romantic charge increased as the evening wore on.

So, when the evening was ending, they both did what comes naturally. They both lingered as the others left, not really sure what they would say to each other, but knowing that something special had passed between them and something further was demanding to happen. They covered up their nervousness by making practical talk about cleaning up the room and when the bills would be paid and so on. Finally, the moment came to part. Both had tarried as long as they decently could, but now it was time to go home. As the man stalled a little longer by thanking her yet another time for helping with the arrangements, she, not wanting to lose the moment, said to him: "I very much appreciated meeting you. Would you like to get together again sometime?"

The man, fingering his wedding ring and feeling somewhat guilty for not being more upfront about his marital status earlier, did what too few of us have the moral courage to do today. He smiled graciously, but said: "Thank you, but I don't think that would be a good idea. I'm sorry, I'm a married man . . . and I guess I should have been clearer about that earlier. I'm sorry. I'd best be getting home. It was nice meeting you." And, like Jesus sweating blood in the garden, he left and went home to his wife.

After his resurrection, on the road to Emmaus, in trying to explain to his disciples (who had slept through the lesson in Gethsemane) the connection between carrying tension and remaining true to who we are and what is asked of us, Jesus asks them this question: "Wasn't it necessary?" Isn't there a necessary connection between carrying tension, sweating blood in a garden, and fidelity?[12] Looking at the incident from "Thirty Something" (which so typifies the struggle of fidelity in general) it becomes clear that obviously there is.

In Jesus' message there is a strong motif of waiting, of pondering, of chastity, of having to carry tension without giving in to premature resolution. The idea is that the resurrection follows only after there has been an agony in the garden. That is also true for faith. When Karl Rahner says that today we will either be mystics or nonbelievers, that can also be translated to say that unless we are willing at times to sweat blood in a garden so as to remain true to our commitments, personal integrity, and the things that faith asks of us—as did the heroine of Jane Austen's *Sense and Sensibility,* as did the man in "Thirty Something," and as did Jesus and Mary—we will not sustain a real faith.

But why? What is the value in carrying tension?

At a more obvious level, it is good to carry tension and not resolve it prematurely because, ultimately, that is what respect means. By not demanding that our tensions be resolved we let others be themselves, we let God be God, and gift be gift. This can best be understood by looking at its opposite. When we refuse to carry tension, and instead approach others and the world with the attitude that what we want should be ours, regardless of the consequences, our lives will always be more destructive than life-giving. We will also be constantly failing in respect and chastity. Only someone who can live with the tension of an unfinished symphony will truly respect others.

More deeply, however, the real value in carrying tension for the sake of love is that it is a gestation process. By pondering as Mary did, as she stood helplessly beneath the cross, and by enduring suffering as Jesus did in the garden at Gethsemane, we have the opportunity to turn hurt into forgiveness, anger into compassion, and hatred into love. We see an illustration of this in Jesus' life:

He was hated, but he hated no one; he was met by anger, but he did not respond in anger; and he was killed by jealousy, but he was jealous of and hurt no one. He was on the receiving end of murderous anger, jealousy, and hatred, but he never passed them on to others. Instead he carried hatred, anger, jealousy, and wound long enough until he was able to transform them into forgiveness, compassion, and love. Only someone who has already sweated real blood to remain true to what is highest and best will be able to look at his or her own murderers and say: "Forgive them, for they know not what they are doing."[13] This is what constitutes true nobility of soul.

Accepting to carry tension for the sake of God, love, truth, and principle, is the mysticism that is most needed in our day. Almost everything within our culture invites us to avoid tension and to resolve it whenever possible, even at the cost of some of our more noble instincts. This is true for virtually every aspect of contemporary life, save those areas where we can be fiercely ascetical and sweat blood for purposes of our careers or the health and slimness of our bodies. Waiting in frustration and inconsummation is not our strong point. From minor frustrations, like waiting in a queue at the bank or the bus, to more major frustrations with interpersonal tensions and our unresolved sexual needs, we find it difficult to stay inside of unresolved tension.

Jacques Maritain, the great Catholic philosopher, once

stated that one of the great spiritual tragedies is that so many people of good will would become persons of noble soul, if only they would not panic and resolve the painful tensions within their lives too prematurely, but rather stay with them long enough, as one does in a dark night of the soul, until those tensions are transformed and help give birth to what is most noble inside of us—compassion, forgiveness, and love.

2. Sin Bravely . . .

"You are as sick as your sickest secret!"[14]

a. HONESTY WITHIN OUR WEAKNESSES

Martin Luther is credited with coining the phrase "Sin boldly!" Understood correctly, there is more than a little spiritual wisdom in that saying. It is a recipe for a certain confederate, rudimentary mysticism. It does not, as a superficial understanding might interpret, invite us to sin, but rather it invites us always to be in that space where God can help us after we have sinned, namely, in a state where we honestly admit our sin.

The English mystic, Ruth Burrows, in one of her earlier books,[15] sheds some light on what Luther meant. She tells the story of two nuns with whom she once lived. Both, as contemplative nuns, were thoroughly mediocre in that they had left the active world to seek God in prayer and now, in a monastery, they were not praying very much. However, as Burrows tells the story, their individual cases were quite different. The first nun, later on in life, was diagnosed with a terminal illness and the threat of imminent death inspired her to try harder. But old habits die hard and she died before she could get her prayer-life in order. She died, though, comments Burrows, a happy death—the death of a sinner, asking God to forgive her for a life of weakness. The second nun also died, but she did not die nearly as happily. As Burrows puts it, until the very end she tried to pretend to herself and to others that she was not what she was—a weak human being. After sharing this story, Burrows makes this comment about the place of honesty and contrition within our lives.

Only a saint, she says, can afford to die a saint's death. The rest of us have to go out of this world in our own eyes and in the eyes of our entourage, for what we really are, sinners asking God for mercy. Moreover, comments Burrows, what is most spiritually troubling is not our weaknesses and our sin, but our lack of searing contrition. In Luther's terms, the problem is not so much that we sin but that we do not sin boldly.

What Luther and Burrows point out is what the Gospels emphasize continually, that it is not weakness that is problematic within our relationship to God, but rationalization, denial, lying, and the hardening of our hearts in the face of truth. In the teachings of Jesus there is only one sin that God cannot deal with, the sin against the Holy Spirit.

b. THE UNFORGIVABLE SIN AGAINST THE HOLY SPIRIT

At one point in his ministry, Jesus makes the statement that all human sins and blasphemies will be forgiven, except if one blasphemes against the Holy Spirit. Should one do that, he or she is guilty of an eternal sin, one that can never be forgiven.[16] What is this blasphemy against the Holy Spirit and why is it an eternal sin that can never be forgiven?

To understand what Jesus is teaching here, it is necessary to put his statement about this unforgivable sin within the context in which it was spoken. He had just performed a miracle, the exorcism of a demon. In the Jewish theology of the time, to which the scribes and pharisees and everyone else adhered, the belief was that only someone who came from God could perform that type of miracle. The scribes and pharisees had just witnessed this miracle and all evidence, therefore, pointed to the fact that Jesus was from God. But in their jealousy of him the scribes and pharisees could not admit the truth that they had just seen. They chose to lie. Hence, instead of admitting what they had just witnessed, they deny what they know and accuse Jesus of working miracles by the power of Satan. At first, Jesus tries to reason with them, pointing out that it would not make much strategic sense for Satan to be working against himself, but they remain obstinate, choosing to deny the obvious rather than admit their weakness. Finally, Jesus issues a warning (for that is what this is, merely a warning, not a statement that they have committed an unforgivable sin), which, unpackaged and paraphrased, might sound like this:

Be careful not to lie, not to distort the truth, because the real danger is that, by lying, you begin to distort and warp your own hearts. If you lie to yourself long enough, eventually you will lose sight of the truth and believe the lie and become unable any longer to tell the difference between truth and lies. What becomes unforgivable about that is not that God does not want to forgive, but that you no longer want to be forgiven. God easily forgives all of your weaknesses and will always forgive anyone who wants to be forgiven, but you can so warp your own conscience that you see God's truth and forgiveness itself as a lie, as Satan, and see your own lie as truth and forgiveness. That is the only sin that truly puts us outside of God's mercy, not because God refuses to extend mercy further, but because you can look mercy in the eye and call it a lie.

It is always presumptuous to suggest what Jesus was trying to say, as opposed to what he actually did say, but scripture scholars generally agree that Jesus' admonition to not blaspheme against the Holy Spirit is a warning against sustained dishonesty and rationalization. Luther's one-line commentary, "sin boldly," captures the heart of that warning.

An interesting commentary too on this text comes from the gospel of John, wherein Jesus does not speak about the sin against the Holy Spirit. Instead the same lesson, do not lie, is taught through a positive illustration of it, in the story of the man born blind.[17] John tells that story this way:

One day, as Jesus is walking he comes upon a man who has been blind from birth. Jesus makes a paste out of mud, puts it on the man's eyes, and the man's sight is restored. But his friends and neighbors, who had not witnessed the event, ask him how it is that he can now see. The man, in a rather simple innocence, answers that it was Jesus who put mud into his eyes and restored his sight. So they take him to the pharisees, who ask him the same question. When the man again responds that it was Jesus who cured his blindness, the pharisees (in their hatred and jealousy) try to deflect him from the truth, telling him that it is impossible that Jesus had done this since only someone who comes from God could do this and Jesus, for reasons they outline, has not come from God. The man, however, holds his ground, refusing to lie, even though he feels somewhat overwhelmed by what the pharisees are telling him. This scene, them questioning him and his refusal to lie, repeats itself a number of times. Finally, the pharisees insult him, tell him that he is stupid, a sinner, and that he should not be contradicting them. The man, for his part, humbly sticks to the truth as he knows it. He does not deny either his stupidity or his sin, but he does not deny the truth either, even though it means that he is expelled from the Jewish religious community. Later on, Jesus finds him and he, the man, makes a profession of faith in Jesus.

What happens in this story is, in a manner of speaking, the opposite of the sin against the Holy Spirit. The blind man is presented by John as not being particularly bright, as not being very religiously keen, and as being essentially disprivileged in terms of opportunity to recognize Christ. Yet, in John's gospel, he is one of the first persons to clearly recognize Jesus for who he is and make a profession of faith. And he moves toward that faith through one singular virtue, he refuses to lie. Simply through his honesty, he is led to God. That simple honesty is a rudimentary mysticism that brings about faith. It, alone, can take one to God.

That insight, the singular value of honesty for a healthy soul, is verified today in virtually all therapeutic programs that are in any way effective in dealing with addictions. Hence, for example, in all so-called twelve-step programs (such as those used by Alcoholics Anonymous, Sexual Anonymous, Eaters Anonymous, and the like), there is always one step in the program, a very critical one, where the person must make a searing face-to-face confession to another human being and accept the truth about his or her own weakness without lying. The program is clear; without this type of honesty there can be no help. It is the literature of these programs that coined the expression: "You are as sick as your sickest secret and you will remain sick as long as it remains a secret." In all effective addiction programs, health and sobriety are essentially synonymous with honesty. As one pamphlet puts it: Sobriety is only 10 percent about alcohol; it's 90 percent about honesty.

The Gospels would essentially agree with that assessment, spiritual health is 90 percent about honesty. What is best within the secular world would also agree with that; despite our moral and emotional struggles, we still identify integrity with honesty.

Some years ago, a young filmmaker, working with a very small budget, made a remarkable film. Entitled *Sex, Lies, and Videotape,* it told the story of a young man who was in fact quite damaged emotionally and sexually. However, at one point in his life, he made a simple vow that he would never again tell a lie, even about the most trivial thing. He keeps his vow and, slowly, he begins to gain more and more health. Moreover, he sets up a video camera and invites others to come and do the same, that is, to simply tell their stories in honesty. This secular confessional box works a remarkable spiritual magic. All those who do tell the truth get better. Conversely, everyone who lies, who refuses to face the truth of his or her own life, becomes progressively more dishonest, bitter, and hard in soul and attitude. Like the story of the man born blind in the Gospels, this too is a story of how one does the opposite of the sin against the Holy Spirit.

c. Honesty as Letting Us See Colors Again

Some years ago, at a retreat, a man shared a story with me. He had recently undergone a major conversion, but one which he described as not strictly a religious one, nor, in a certain manner of speaking, even a moral one. It was an aesthetic conversion of sorts, though ultimately it was also profoundly religious and moral. What had happened to him?

He was a man in early middle-age, unmarried, gay, and even though his religious life was essentially in order, he suffered from two interrelated addictions, masturbation and alcohol. But even here, on the surface at least, these were relatively under control. They never, at least so it seemed, interfered with his work, his relationships, or his religious life. He was highly respected and no one who knew him would have guessed that he had a problem. Except . . . except he knew he had one and as he matured, through his prayer life and through the respect that others entrusted him with, he began to see his own inconsistencies and sought help.

His counselor advised him to enter a separate twelve-step program for each addiction, alcohol and sex. At first, he resisted, thinking: "I'm not an alcoholic! My sexual issues aren't that serious!" Eventually, however, he entered the programs and they, to use his own words, "wrought a great transformation" inside of him: "It wasn't like I was that bad or anything before I entered those programs. My life was essentially in order. So what happened to me? As best as I can put it, now that I go regularly to Alcoholics and Sexual Anonymous meetings, is that I see colors again. Before that, I wasn't a bad person, but I was always so taken up with my own needs and yearnings that, most of the time, I wasn't really seeing what was in front of me. Now, I see colors again and my life is rich in a way that it never was before."

What kind of conversion is this? Is the challenge of the gospel about seeing colors? It would seem so and the way to clear our eyesight is precisely through radical honesty, through courageously facing the truth of our own weaknesses.

To be healthy today in one's soul, there can be no more important prescription than that given us by the Gospels and by what is still highest within our conscience: Do not lie, be weak if you must, but sin boldly!

If we are honest, eventually God, truth, and love will find us.

3. Gather Ritually Around the Word
and Break the Bread . . .

"For where two or three gather in my name, I am there among them."[18]

a. In Every Circumstance of Life, Gather Ritually in Prayer

Jesus promised that whenever a group of people gather in prayer, he will be there with them. The early church took that promise literally. The first disciples had been used to having Jesus physically among them and then, after his ascension, they often struggled to know what Jesus would want them to do. However, they had a simple formula for every occasion and difficulty, Jesus' invitation to gather in his name: They would gather around the word and the breaking of the bread and, there, let Jesus make his presence felt and effect through them what they could not otherwise accomplish themselves.

As Christians today we still need to take that same promise literally. Christian life is not sustained only by private acts of prayer, justice, and virtue. It is sustained in a community, by gathering ritually around the word of God and through the breaking of the bread. However, it is important to understand that this kind of gathering is not simply a social one, capable only of doing what social gatherings can do. To gather around the word of God and the breaking of the bread is a ritual gathering and ritual brings something that normal social gathering does not, namely, transformative power beyond what can be understood and explained through the physical, psychological, and social dynamics that are present. This, I suspect, sounds abstract and more than a little esoteric, hence it needs some careful explanation.

b. The Meaning of Ritual and Our Current Struggle with It

Ritual is something that, for the most part, we no longer understand. Former cultures did and they utilized conscious ritual a lot more than we do. We, the adult children of the Enlightenment, tend to be ritually tone-deaf in that we distrust basically everything that we cannot rationally explain. Hence, for us, all ritual is suspect and smacks of superstition or magic.

However, slowly that notion is changing. Curiously, the change is not happening, as yet, as much in the churches as within the secular culture, especially within feminist, New Age, and men's circles. Here ritual is being rediscovered and powerfully utilized. Thus, for example, in some feminist circles, they will look at a woman who has been the victim of a rape or of some other sexual abuse and will see that counseling can go only so far in helping her, that she needs something which psychological therapy alone cannot provide. She needs ritual healing. Hence, they will devise various rituals of cleansing or rebirth and celebrate them with her. In many cases, as a result of those rituals, she gets better.

How does this work? We do not know, and that is the point. We cannot give ritual a rational explanation, extrapolate its transformative principle, and duplicate its effects psychodynamically. It just works! Ritual works in the way a kiss, the most primal of all rituals, works. Kisses do things that words do not and there is no metaphysics that needs to be written about them.

Men's groups do similar things. Sometimes they will look at man who has not been loved or blessed by his own father and whose life is now scarred by that fact. Like women's groups they also see that psychological counseling cannot go the full distance in terms of providing that man with what he really needs. Such a man needs more than counseling. He needs to be blessed. He needs ritual. Again, when this ritual is performed often the man gets better. How does it work? How does a kiss work? There is a power in it that is, precisely, beyond the rational. Only an older, premodern language—with words that speak of angels and demons, blessings and exorcisms, and of sacred rivers beyond time—can give some help to the imagination here; because, indeed, something real happens in ritual.

Good ritual carries a power beyond what we can rationally

explain. Rituals can help bring about group unity, healing, and other kinds of transformation, for which we cannot lay out a strict phenomenology. As Christians we have always had such rituals. We simply had them under other names—baptism, christening, blessings, gatherings around the word of God, breaking the bread together. If these were major rituals, such as baptism, most Christians called them sacraments and intuitively understood that something occurred in them for which there was no full rational explanation. If they were minor, such as a simple gathering to share scripture, we often did not realize that they were rituals at all, but we still often felt their special power.

I would like to offer two personal examples here. They come from my own experience and from my own denominational background, that of being a Roman Catholic, but they could be anyone's experience within any religious denomination. Both examples speak of the transformative power of ritual.

During the six years that I spent studying theology and preparing for ordination to the priesthood, I lived in a large seminary community. During some of those years we would be about seventy students, all living within the same building. We came from different backgrounds, had different temperaments, and had our various faults. There was more natural incompatibility than temperamental harmony among us. We had not picked each other and were, at a psychological level, purely an accidental collection of individuals. Yet, somehow, we were able to form harmonious community with each other.

There were many reasons why community formed among us; after all, we lived in the same building and did a lot of things together. We ate together, studied together, and recreated together and, given the regulations of seminary life at the time, were rarely apart from each other. Moreover, we all too had the same essential motivation and faith focus. Interestingly though, among all the things we did as a group which pulled us together, one stands out. Twice each day for a half hour, we would, all seventy of us, sit in chapel, in silent prayer, in Quaker silence. *Oraison,* we called this. We started and ended each of these sessions with a short common prayer but for the rest of the time we just sat together in silence.

What was happening when we did this? Prayer, yes. But something more. As we sat together in silence, each of us trying to focus on God rather than on self, we would achieve, at least for that short period of time, some real community and intimacy with each other. Our temperamental and ideological differences, our jealousies, and our angers would dissolve for a while. For that half hour (and often for a time afterward) we were a little more together as a community. Why? Was it just that we were all a bit more centered and focused on why we were there? Yes, surely. But there was more. That half hour together, that *Oraison,* was also a ritual that, like a kiss, in silence, helped create a unity that we could not otherwise achieve through a more rational, discursive process.

My second example, also taken from my own experience as a Roman Catholic, focuses on another ritual, daily Eucharist. I have been a Roman Catholic priest for more than twenty-five years and one of the privileges of that has been the opportunity to preside daily at what Roman Catholics call the Eucharist or the mass. Through the years, I have met an interesting variety of persons at this daily gathering. I say "variety" because there is not just one type of person who comes to daily mass.

Who does come to daily mass? In my experience no single category does justice here. On the surface at least, it appears that there is little in common among those who attend daily mass. It is a strange mixture of people: some nuns, some unemployed people, a lot of retired women, some retired men, a few young persons, some housewives, and a motley collection of nurses, businessmen, secretaries, and other such professionals on their lunch break.

There is no similarity in character among them, but there is something among them (and I am speaking here only of those who truly have the habit of attending daily mass) that is held in common, namely, in the end, they are all there for the same reason. What is that reason? It is something that is deeper and less obvious than is immediately evident. Simply put, people who go to mass daily are there in order to not fall apart. They go to mass because they know that, without mass, they would either inflate or become depressed and be unable to handle their own lives.

I doubt that most people who attend mass daily would tell you that. More likely they would tell you something to the effect that they go to mass to pray to God, or to be nurtured and sustained by God, or to touch God and to receive God's blessing upon their day, or because they feel it is only right that they should offer some of their day back to God. On the surface, those are their reasons. But for anyone who sustains the habit of daily mass for a long period of time there is a deeper reason, always. Daily mass is a ritual, a deep powerful one that sustains a person in the same way that the habit of attending an Alcoholics Anonymous meeting sustains a man or a woman seeking sobriety.

A recovering alcoholic friend once explained to me why he goes regularly to Alcoholics Anonymous meetings: "I know, and know for sure, that if I don't go to meetings regularly, I'll begin to drink again. It's funny, the meetings are always the same, the same things get said over and over again. Everything is totally predictable; I know everything that will be said. Everyone coming there knows it too. Also I don't go to those meetings to be a nice person. I go there to stay alive. I go there because, if I don't, I will eventually destroy myself!"

What is true about Alcoholics Anonymous meetings is also true for those who go to daily Eucharist. Granted, it is a prayer, a coming together of Christians mandated by Jesus himself. Eucharist is these things, but it is more: It is also a ritual, a container, a sustainer, a coming together which keeps us, in ways that we cannot explain rationally, from falling apart.

Significant too is a second thing that is common among those who attend daily mass, they do not want a service that is too long or too creative. They want a clear ritual, a predictable one, and a short one. Because of this they are often at the mercy of critics who look at this and, simplistically, see nothing other than empty ritual, rote prayer, and people going through the mechanics of worship seemingly without heart. Nothing could be further from the truth and this type of accusation betrays the misunderstanding not just of an outsider but also of somebody who is ritually tone-deaf.

There are rituals, especially initiation rituals, that one undergoes only once, where the transformative power works partly by overstimulating the psyche and by heating the emotions to a new fever. But the rituals that are meant to sustain our daily lives do not work that way. In fact, they work the opposite way. They are not meant to be an experience of high energy and creativity, but are meant precisely to be predictable, repetitive, simple, straightforward, and brief. Any community or family that has sustained a daily life of common prayer, common meals, and common fellowship for any length of time knows this—as do all monks. The rituals that sustain our daily lives do not work through novelty or by seeking to raise our psychic temperature. What they try to effect is not novelty, but rhythm; not the current, but the timeless; and not the emotional, but the archetypal.

Our ordinary church gatherings, our gatherings for prayer and faith-sharing, and our times of prayer as a couple or within a family, are meant to be this type of ritual gathering. When we gather communally in prayer, we need not look for novelty, excitement, brilliance, or family therapy. The words that we do use (a scriptural text, a psalm, the Lord's Prayer, formula prayers out of a prayerbook, or a hymn) are, in the end, intended to create among us a certain Quaker silence within which something happens between God and ourselves and among ourselves that novelty, excitement, brilliance, and various discursive therapies precisely have been unable to achieve. When we gather ritually around the word of God and the breaking of the bread which Jesus left us, we are coming together not to have a family or community meeting, or to discuss our emotions and problems, or to seek some communal therapy, or even to rally our faltering faith in a pagan world. We gather to communally worship God and to let God do in us what we cannot do within ourselves, namely, give us faith and shape us into a community beyond our conflicting emotional pulls and all the things we need therapy for.

Christianity has sustained itself for two thousand years. How has it accomplished that? In trying to answer that question, we can uncover a secret worth knowing. Faith sustains itself through ritual gathering around the word of God and the breaking of the bread. Like a marriage or a family that keeps itself from falling apart by saying: We will all be home at regular times, we will all eat two meals a day together, and we will all be together in the living room at least once a day . . . even if it is not exciting, even if no real feelings get discussed, even if everyone is bored, and even if half the family is constantly protesting that it is not worthwhile. We will do this because if we don't, we will eventually fall apart and die as a family. As a human family needs to sustain itself by set, straightforward, repetitive, predictable, unexciting rituals, so too the Christian family. Without ritual gathering we will, like any family, soon fall apart.

In an age when it is so difficult to sustain faith and to sustain community, there can be no better advice to us than that of Jesus himself: Gather around the word of God and break the bread together. We do not have to even understand what we are doing and we do not have to be brilliant, imaginative, or stimulating. We just have to gather in his name around the simple, clear rituals he gave us. He promised to do the rest.

4. Worship and Serve the Right God . . .

A pattern that others have made may prevail in the world and following the wrong god home we may both miss our star.[19]

a. SUSTAINING OURSELVES BY KEEPING THE FIRST COMMANDMENT

In trying to sustain ourselves as Christians, few things are as important as worshiping and serving the right God. To have a distorted concept of God, no matter how sincere that misconception, is to worship an idol and break the first commandment.

What does God look like? What kind of God did Jesus reveal?

One of the great Christian mystics, Julian of Norwich, once described God this way: "Completely relaxed and courteous, he was himself the happiness and peace of his dear friends, his beautiful face, radiating measureless love, like a marvellous symphony; and it was that wonderful face shining with the beauty of God that filled that heavenly place with joy and light."[20]

God, as Julian describes him, is both smiling and relaxed. Jesus would agree with that description. Unfortunately, too few Christians, past and present, agree with it.

In the past, our concept of God was often too much a projection of our own anger and incapacity to forgive each other. Hence, we tended to paint God as a punishing God, a God with a great recording book within which every one of our sins was written and who subsequently demanded some kind of payment for every one of those sins. He was a God who had drawn up some very strict criteria ("the narrow way") for salvation. Hellfire awaited those who could not morally vault over that rather lofty high-jump bar. We lived in fear of that God.

Today that God has fallen on hard times, both inside and outside the churches. There is no preacher, secular or religious, who does not make it his or her mission to dethrone that punishing, exacting God. Sadly, however, we have not replaced Him with anything much better.

In conservative religious circles, the old punishing God has been replaced by the God of orthodoxy. He is still a God whose primary facial expression is a frown. He (and in conservative circles God is always a He) is looking at the world and seeing there a confused, morally lax, lazy, and sexually promiscuous rabble. He cheers up once in a while when we pull ourselves together a bit, but his first mode of reaction to us is still displeasure.

Liberal circles are different, but no closer to what is prescribed by the first commandment. Their God tends to be the God of liberal ideology and is a very anxious, worried, hypersensitive, politically correct, workaholic, and generally whining God. This God still wears a frown and when he or she looks at the world the spontaneous reaction is not one of blessing, but of disapproval at the world's stupidity and lack of social conscience. The liberal God sees a Yuppie rabble down here.

The God whom Jesus calls his Father does not see the world as rabble. When we read the first pages of the Bible, we see that, immediately upon creating each item within creation, God looks at it and says: "It is good!" Then, after all of creation is finished, God looks at everything, the world and all its people, and says: "It is very good!"[21] That original blessing, that gaze of appreciation, has never changed, despite the existence of evil and sin. God's first gaze upon us is still that of appreciation.

We see a reiteration of that at the beginning of the Gospels, when Jesus is baptized. As the Gospels describe it, at his baptism, as Jesus' head came out of the water after John the Baptist had immersed him, the heavens opened and a voice from heaven, God's voice, said: "This is my beloved child in whom I am well-pleased."[22] Again, as at the original creation, God is looking down upon the earth, his child, and seeing it as good.

Awareness of that, God's smile upon the planet, was very much part of the consciousness of Jesus. To understand Jesus' attitude and his teachings, it can be helpful to imagine that through his entire lifetime, God, his Father, kept whispering into his ears that blessing from his baptism: "You are my beloved, my blessed one, my son, and in you I am well-pleased." Those words, in fact, form the consciousness of Jesus, especially in Luke's gospel. Thus, when Jesus looks at the poor, the hungry, and the weeping and sees them as blessed, it is because first of all he is hearing God's voice inside of himself, telling him that God is seeing him and the world in that way.

There is a contemporary Buddhist parable that can help us to understand what is being said here:

One day the Buddha, badly overweight, was sitting under a

tree. A young soldier, trim and handsome, came along, looked at the Buddha, and said: "You look like a pig!" The Buddha replied: "Well, you look like God!" "Why would you say that?" asked the rather surprised young soldier. "Well," replied the Buddha, "we see what's inside us. I think about God all day and when I look out that is what I see. You, obviously, must think about other things . . ."

What we see outside of ourselves is very much colored by what is, first of all, inside of us. Thus, Jesus had within him a concept of a God who was relaxed, smiling, and blessing the earth. Hence, Jesus too looked out at us and saw, in us, something worth smiling at and blessing.

A couple of years before he died, Henri Nouwen, perhaps the best spiritual writer of our generation, wrote a book that many consider to be a spiritual masterpiece. It is entitled *The Return of the Prodigal Son,*[23] and is both a commentary on Rembrandt's famous painting by that same title and a long spiritual reflection on the Fatherhood and Motherhood of God.

Nouwen points out that, in Rembrandt's painting of the *Father of the Prodigal Son,* the figure painted there, representing God, has a number of interesting features: First of all, he is depicted as blind. His eyes are shut and he sees the prodigal son not with his eyes but with his heart (to which he is tenderly holding the son's head). The implication is obvious, God sees with the heart. Moreover, the figure representing God has one male hand (which is pulling the wayward son to himself) and one female hand (which is caressing the son's back). Thus God is presented here as both mother and father, loving as does a woman and as does a man.

Moreover, the scene, as depicted by Rembrandt, highlights three characters: the prodigal son, his older brother, and the all-compassionate father/mother figure who is offering the embrace of compassion and forgiveness. What the painting invites us to do is to see ourselves in each of these characters, that is, in the weakness of the wayward son, in the bitterness of the older brother, and in the compassion of the father/mother, God.

The first two identifications are more obvious for us. We know that, like the younger son, we are often away from God's house because of our weaknesses; just as we know too that, like the older brother, we are often absent from the Father's love and celebration through our bitterness and anger. As we get older, we begin to realize that we are really both sons; the younger one, weak and sinful, and the older one, bitter and angry.

However, what Jesus' revelation in this parable really invites us to (which is so powerfully evident in Rembrandt's painting) is to identify with the Father and his/her all-embracing, all-forgiving, caressing compassion. At the end of the day, that is what we are called to in the spiritual life. Ultimately, we are meant to radiate both God's masculine, fatherly, embrace of the wayward and God's feminine, motherly, caress of the bitter.

To do that, however, we need first to have experienced that ourselves and part of accepting God's forgiving embrace is to conceive of God correctly. To have the courage to let ourselves be embraced when we are sinful and bitter is to, first of all, know a God who—as Jesus, Julian of Norwich, Rembrandt, and Henri Nouwen assure us—is both a blessing Father and a caressing Mother, who sees with the eyes of the heart, and who, despite our weaknesses and angers, sits completely relaxed, smiling, with a face like a marvelous symphony.

That symphony, which is always evident in God's face, is the future to which all of us, and our earth itself, can look forward. Thus, given that we live under a smiling, relaxed, all-forgiving, and all-powerful God, we too should relax and smile, at least once in a while, because, irrespective of anything that has ever happened or will ever happen, in the end, "all shall be well, and all shall be well, and every manner of being shall be well."[24]

Notes

Chapter One

1. "The Holy Longing," Johann Wolfgang von Goethe, translated by Robert Bly, in *The Rag and Bone Shop of the Heart: A Poetry Anthology*, edited by Robert Bly, Michael Meade, and James Hillman (New York: HarperPerennial, 1993), p. 382.

2. Paraphrase of a phrase attributed to Plato.

3. St. Augustine, *The Confessions of St. Augustine*, translated by Frank Sheed (New York: Sheed & Ward, 1943), p. 1.

4. The classical books under this rubric were of course titles such as Thomas à Kempis, *The Imitation of Christ*; Francis de Sales, *An Introduction to the Devout Life*; and the seminary manual by A. Tanquerey, *The Spiritual Life*.

5. Note that the word "discipleship" takes its root and meaning in the word "discipline." To be a disciple is to be under a certain discipline. This can be an explicitly religious discipline, so that we speak of disciples of Jesus as being under the discipline of Jesus, but it can also be another kind of discipline; e.g., an ideology, a philosophy, an ambition, a bitterness, etc.

6. From the poem "The Dark Night of the Soul," stanza one, by John of the Cross. The entire stanza reads as follows:

> One dark night
> Fired by love's urgent longings
> Ah, the sheer grace
> I went out unseen
> My house being now all stilled.

See *The Collected Works of John of the Cross* (Washington, D.C.: ICS Publications, 1989), p. 113.

7. I use the word "soul" here in its classical sense, at least in how it was classically used in most ancient, medieval, and modern philosophy in the West. As you know, in those places not influenced by Greek philosophy, and this includes good parts of Scripture, the word is used differently. Today, for example, there is a school of thought (e.g., James Hillman, Thomas Moore, Richard Rohr) that is distinguishing *soul* from *spirit*. That distinction, valid and valuable in itself, will not be employed here. *Soul,* the way it will be used in this chapter and in this book, will include the idea of *spirit*.

8. For an excellent survey of some of these legends, including an explication of Plato's famous one, see James Hillman, *The Soul's Code—In Search of Character and Calling* (New York: Random House, 1996), pp. 41–62.

9. A few more technical definitions of spirituality are in order:

a. Sandra Schneiders, in an article in *Theological Studies,* Volume 50, pp. 198, 676–97, gives two valuable, and complementary, definitions:

In defining spirituality as a generic notion (i.e., and not as an explicitly Christian endeavor) Schneiders notes the fluidity of the term but suggests it might be defined along these essential lines: As the conscious and deliberate striving to integrate one's life, not just in terms of self-integration and self-development, but in terms of self-transcendence toward the horizon of the ultimate concern.

In defining it as an academic discipline, she suggests the following: Spirituality is the field of study which attempts to investigate in an interdisciplinary way spiritual experience as such. Spiritual experience here is used to indicate not only religious experience in the technical sense but those analogous experiences of ultimate meaning and value which have transcendent and life-integrating power for individuals and groups.

b. Hans Urs von Balthasar defines spirituality as the way a person understands his or her own ethically and religiously committed existence, and the way he or she acts and reacts habitually to this understanding.

c. John of the Cross, one of the great masters of the spiritual life, could, in a paraphrase, be said to define spirituality as follows: Spirituality is the attempt by an individual or a group to meet and undergo the presence of God, others, and the cosmic world in such a way so as to come into a community of life and celebration with them. The generic and specific patterns and habits of interaction that develop from this then form the basis of a spirituality.

Chapter Two

1. Theodore Roethke, "In A Dark Time," in *The Rag and Bone Shop of the Heart,* edited by Bly, Meade, and Hillman (New York: HarperPerennial, 1993).

2. Ivan Klima, *My First Loves* (New York: Harper & Row, 1986).

3. For an analysis of the subtle new forms of religiously grounded violence, I recommend two excellent sources: Gil Bailie, *Violence Unveiled, Humanity at the Crossroads* (New York: Crossroad Publishing, 1997), and René Girard, *Things Hidden Since the Foundation of the World* (Stanford, Calif.: Stanford University Press, 1987).

4. For a brilliant secular comment on how our society is naive about energy—where it comes from and what role it plays in our lives— I recommend the works of James Hillman, especially his book *The Soul's Code, In Search of Character and Calling* (New York: Random House, 1996).

5. Albert Camus has some insightful comments on this. For example, in his *Carnets* he comments frequently on the necessity, and beauty, of asceticism. At one stage, commenting on sexuality, he writes: "Sexuality leads to nothing: it isn't immoral, but it's unproductive. One can abandon oneself to it when one does not want to produce anything. But only chastity is linked to personal progress. There is a time when sexuality is a victory—when one separates it from moral imperatives—but then it quickly becomes a defeat, and in turn, the only victory which is won over it is chastity."

A few days later, writing in his *Carnets,* he added to this comment: "Uncontrolled sexuality leads to a philosophy of the world's insignificance. In contrast, chastity gives back meaning to the world." Albert Camus, *Carnets,* quoted by Olivier Todd, *Albert Camus, A Life* (New York: Knopf, 1997), p. 157.

6. Exodus 33:18–23.

7. Exodus 3:1–6.

8. Annie Dillard, *Holy the Firm* (New York: HarperCollins, 1977), p. 59.

9. From a private conversation. However, some of that conversation is written up in a short article. (See Ronald Rolheiser, "Just Too Busy to Bow Down," in *Forgotten Among the Lilies* (London: Hodder & Stoughton, 1990), pp. 112–14.

10. See Ronald Rolheiser, *The Shattered Lantern, Rediscovering the Felt Presence of God* (London: Hodder & Stoughton, 1994); and (New York: Crossroads, 1996).

11. For a detailed analysis of narcissism, pragmatism, and unbridled restlessness as reducing spiritual awareness see Rolheiser, *The Shattered Lantern*, pp. 24–43.

12. Quoted in Rolheiser, *The Shattered Lantern*, p. 34.

13. Neil Postman, *Amusing Ourselves to Death, Public Discourse in the Age of Show Business* (New York: Penguin Books, 1985).

14. Henri Nouwen, *Reaching Out, The Three Movements of the Spiritual Life* (New York: Doubleday, 1975).

15. Many people are trying to bridge this gap by turning sexuality itself into either a quasi or a full-blown religion. Thus, for example, you see this at a very popular level in a writer like Tom Robbins *(Skinny Legs and All, The Wayside Attraction),* and at a more deliberate religious level in somebody like Jalaja Bonheim *(Aphrodite's Daughters,* [New York: Fireside, Simon & Schuster, 1997]).

16. Sam Keen, *Hymns to an Unknown God*, 1994.

17. John 15:13.

18. Alice Miller, *The Drama of the Gifted Child* (New York: Basic Books, 1994).

19. Jesus makes it clear that he is not a victim. He gives his life over, it is not taken from him. This is everywhere present in the four gospels, though especially in the accounts of him agonizing in the Garden of Gethsemane and, eventually, giving himself over, in a free act, to the will of his Father. Thus, he can stand before Pilate and say: "You have no power over me", i.e., "How can you kill me, if I have already given my life away?"

20. See Michael Meade, *Stories of Spirit, Descent, and Healing,* Oral Traditions Archives, LIMBUS, P.O. Box 364, Vashon Island, WA 98070.

21. René Girard, quoted in Bailie, *op. cit.,* p. 191.

22. St. Augustine, *De Trinitate,* 1, 3.

Chapter Three

1. Up until quite recently this was a very defining phrase with Roman Catholicism, i.e., a "practicing Catholic" (as opposed to someone who, while baptized a Roman Catholic, was not considered to be practicing his or her faith). What made one a practicing Catholic? Three things (beyond full initiation into the church—baptism, confirmation, Eucharist): a) Regular churchgoing—every Sunday—and participation in the Eucharist; b) private prayer and private morality, especially as it pertained to the commandments regarding sexuality and marriage; and

c) respect of public forum, i.e., nothing publicly in one's life that gave major scandal.

2. There are some most curious anomalies here. It is no accident that things like Mardi Gras and Carnival arose in Roman Catholic cultures (where there is precisely an emphasis on asceticism) and that Roman Catholics have never tried to ban alcohol or tobacco. Conversely, it is also no accident, though it seems things should be in reverse, that Protestantism, which has always looked askance at the Roman Catholic emphasis on asceticism, has struggled more with wine drinking, especially with Jesus as a wine drinker.

3. Looking at the many ways that our supposed secular activity is, in fact, religious, one is reminded of Jung's statement that we are doomed to act out unconsciously all the archetypal configurations which we do not access and control through conscious ritual. Small wonder that antireligious activity is so indistinguishable, phenomenologically, from religious activity.

4. The word "accidental" here is used in its technical, philosophical sense (as opposed to its commonsense usage), i.e., as Aristotle defined "accident" (as opposed to "substance"). Accident refers to those qualities of something or somebody which, while part of the makeup, can (and do) change. Thus, for example, Aristotle would say that in the case of a living organism (e.g., a rabbit) what remains the same throughout its lifetime is the substance, but what changes (color, hair, shape, size, bone texture, etc.) are its accidents. In this view of things, accidents take their being inside the substance and have no value outside of that.

5. Matthew 6.

6. T. S. Eliot, *Beckett* (New York: Harcourt Brace, 1935), p. 44.

7. A paraphrase interpretation of John 21:18.

8. Matthew 6:5–6.

9. John 14–15; 23.

10. Henri Nouwen, *The Inner Voice of Love, A Journey Through Anguish to Freedom* (New York: Doubleday, 1996), p. xiv.

11. Matthew 25:31–46.

12. Luke 14:12–14.

13. See, for example: Gustavo Gutiérrez, *We Drink from Our Own Wells* (Maryknoll, N.Y.: Orbis, 1984).

14. See Henri Nouwen's discussion of Gutiérrez's view on this in *Gracias! A Latin American Journal* (San Francisco: Harper and Row, 1983).

15. See Henri Nouwen's brilliant discussion of this in *The Return of the Prodigal Son: A Meditation on Fathers, Brothers, and Sons* (New York: Doubleday, 1992).

16. William Stafford, "A Ritual to Read to Each Other," in *The Rag and Bone Shop of the Heart*, edited by Bly, Meade, and Hillman, p. 233.

17. Julian of Norwich, *Enfolded in Love, Daily Readings with Julian of Norwich* (London: Darton, Longmann & Todd, 1980), p. 10. The actual quote runs this way: "Completely relaxed and courteous, he [God] was himself the happiness and peace of his dear friends, his beautiful face radiating measureless love like a marvellous symphony."

18. Albert Camus, quoted by Oliver Todd in *Albert Camus, A Life* (New York: Knopf, 1997), p. 419.

19. For a good, short summary of Lonergan's views on this see Edward Braxton, *The Wisdom Community* (New York: Paulist Press, 1980), especially Chapter 3: "The Turn to Interiority: Conversion—The Process of Self-Transcendence," pp. 71–100.

20. John 6. See Chapter 5 of this book, "Consequences of the Incarnation for Spirituality," for an explanation of this.

Chapter Four

1. John Shea, *The Hour of the Unexpected* (Allan, Tex.: Argus Communications, 1977), p. 68.

2. A prayer attributed to St. Teresa of Avila.

3. John Shea, *Stories of Faith* (Chicago: Thomas More Press, 1980). The comment quoted here is the entire thesis of this and his earlier, 1978, book, *Stories of God—An Unauthorized Biography* (Chicago, Thomas More Press). However, for a precise comment on the way of *undergoing* as opposed to the way of *admiration* and *imitation*, see the first section of *Stories of Faith*.

4. John 1:14. I have put the verb "dwells" deliberately in the present tense, even though it is normally translated as past tense. While linguistically although not technically accurate here, the present tense does, however, more accurately convey what John is saying—given that he is using the inceptive aorist, which connotes an action which started at a clear point in the past and continues into the present. Hence the phrase might be translated: *And the word started to become flesh.*

5. Nikos Kazantzakis, *The Last Temptation of Jesus* (New York: Simon & Schuster, 1960), pp. 189ff.

6. For a brilliant description of how the physical, earthiness of the incarnation shocks, I recommend a description given by a Graham Greene character, Sarah Miles, in Greene's novel, *The End of the Affair* (London: Penguin Books, 1951), pp. 109–12.

7. Pius II, upon releasing his encyclical Letter on the Body of Christ,

Mystici Corporis Christi, in 1943, is reported to have said: "When explaining the mystery of the Body of Christ, don't be afraid to exaggerate because it is impossible to exaggerate so great a mystery." I am unable to track down the written reference. However, suffice it here to say that this entire encyclical, in effect, says as much.

8. 1 Corinthians 12:27 and 1 Corinthians 6:15 are explicit texts, but the idea is everywhere present in Jesus' teaching and in the teaching of the New Testament as a whole.

9. A lengthy footnote is in order here: There is no consensus among scholars on precisely how literally Paul, and the New Testament in general, understands this.

John A. T. Robinson, for example, understands Paul as meaning this very literally, i.e., as "something not corporate but corporeal. . . . to say that the church is the body of Christ is no more of a metaphor than to say that the flesh of the incarnate Jesus or the bread of the Eucharist is the body of Christ. None of them is "like" His body (Paul never says this): each of them *is* the body of Christ, in that each is the physical complement and extension of the one and same Person and Life. They are all expressions of a single Christology. It is almost impossible to exaggerate the materialism and crudity of Paul's doctrine of the church as literally now the resurrection body of Christ. . . . The body that he has in mind is as concrete and as singular as the body of the Incarnation. His underlying conception is not of a supra-personal collective, but of a specific personal organism." *(The Body, A Study in Pauline Theology* (London: SCM Press, 1966), pp. 50–51.

Some scholars, however, would see this view by Robinson as interpreting things in a too-crass, physical way. Robert Gundry, *Soma in Biblical Theology—with Emphasis on Pauline Anthropology* (London: Cambridge University Press, 1976) concedes Robinson's central point, that this is not just a metaphor, but sees Robinson as taking things too far. He then gives a good, critical survey of all the opinions.

10. As a balanced theological position on this, I recommend Jerome Murphy-O'Connor, *Becoming Human Together* (Wilmington, Del.: Michael Glazier Press, 1977). Murphy-O'Connor walks through the various positions and concludes by saying, irrespective of precise theological nuance, what is being taught by Paul is that Christ and the community of believers perform the same functions (see pp. 202–3).

11. Ibid., p. 203.

Chapter Five

1. Matthew 7:7–8.

2. For an excellent analysis of all of this, see Jerome Murphy-O'Connor, "Prayer of Petition and Community, in *What Is Religious Life?—Ask the Scriptures,* Supplement to Doctrine and Life, vol. 11 (Dublin: Dominican Publications, not dated), pp. 31–40.

3. Ibid., p. 36.

4. Not a direct quote, a paraphrase.

5. Mark 5:25–34.

6. St. Augustine has this idea several times in some of his homilies on the Eucharist; e.g., see *Sermo 272, In die Pentecostes Postremus (b)—Ad Infantes, de Sacramento,* vol. 38. Here, in explaining the order of the Eucharist, step by step, he says to the newly baptized: "Next the Lord's Prayer is said which you have already received and recited. Why is it said before receiving the body and blood of Christ? Because of our human fragility perhaps our minds imagined something which is not becoming, our eyes saw something which was not decent, our ears heard something exaggeratedly which was not fitting. If perhaps such things have been kept in because of temptation and the fragility of human life, *they are washed away by the Lord's Prayer at the moment we say 'Forgive us our trespasses' so that we can safely approach the sacrament."* (Translation by Johannes van Bavel—emphases my own.)

7. John 14:12.

8. Matthew 16:19.

9. John 20:23.

Another note is in order here: It is easier to accept the fact that God can ratify our forgiveness of each other, but it is not so easy to accept that God would ratify our grudges and nonforgiveness. Can we hold someone in sin just as we can forgive him or her? The answer, obviously, is no. The logic of grace works only one way—it can be overly generous but it cannot, on that account, be petty and arbitrary. God ratifies only what we do when we are acting as Jesus did. But this is a complex discussion and contains many rich minefields. For a fuller discussion, see Ronald Rolheiser, "Our Power to Bind and Loose," in *Western Catholic Reporter,* May 13, 1996, and in *Catholic Herald,* April 23, 1996.

10. Slightly redacted from a piece by G. K. Chesterton, *Everlasting Man.*

11. James 5:13–16.

12. A long, Roman Catholic, footnote is necessary here:

Many Roman Catholics will object at this point, claiming that the Council of Trent defined, dogmatically, that there can be no forgiveness of serious sin without private confession to a priest. Without entering into a full-blown discussion, four things need to be said:

a) Nobody seriously can teach, in the name of Christ, that serious sin in this world is not forgiven by God unless the person committing it confesses it to an ordained minister. In that belief, there are elements of legalism, chance, luck, and delimiting God's power and mercy that go directly against everything that Christ stood for. It also goes against everything the Catholic tradition has stood for—and lived.

b) Trent does not teach, dogmatically, that there can be no forgiveness of serious sin except through private confession. What it defines, dogmatically, for Roman Catholics, is the necessity of private confession. That is not the same thing as saying serious sin cannot be forgiven except through private confession.

c) Moreover, Trent, and Catholic practice afterward, stated that if one commits a serious sin he or she is obliged to go to confession before he or she can receive holy communion. However, it then went on to qualify this by defining that the obligation to go to confession before communion is not so much a radical obligation as an existential one. Thus, for instance, it taught that if you lived in a place where the priest would recognize you and his hearing a certain something from you in the confession would be, for whatever reason, detrimental to him, you could wait to make your confession until you had the opportunity to go to another priest . . . and in the meantime you could go to communion. In essence, without ever saying confession wasn't necessary, it allowed for a certain time lapse between the essential touch and the explicit exchange (just as was the case for the woman who touched the hem of Jesus' garment and as is the case for millions and millions of persons whose maturity is developmental and who have to be given time to make an explicit apology).

d) Finally, all of this posits an old question: Does this mean you can go to communion with a mortal sin on your soul? Again, a larger discussion would be needed, but, within this context, the following points need to be made:

Going to church and going to receive communion are not moral statements. There is never a question of worthiness. Christ came to save sinners. When we are in sin, any kind of sin, it is then, precisely, that we most need to touch God. There is more than a little hint of heresy (Donatism and Jansensism) in anyone who worries too much that somebody unworthy is receiving the Body of Christ. Any emphasis on worthiness too wreaks a terrible religious havoc (which we see today), i.e., invariably when we most need God and church, when our lives are messed up, we stay away—so that we can first, all on our own, get our lives in order and then we can return, church and Eucharist all cleaned up, tantamount to first doing the cleaning and then calling in the cleaners. The case of scandal, of course, adds a different dimension and needs to be treated differently.

13. Acts 9:1–19.

14. John of the Cross, *The Living Flame of Love*, commentary on stanza 1, no. 7.

15. John 6:41–71.

16. John 6:53.

17. John 6:60.

18. 1 John 4:20.

19. Nikos Kazantzakis, *The Last Temptation of Christ* (New York: Simon & Schuster, 1960).

20. 1 John 4:7–16.

21. The text quoted is a slightly redacted version of one written by Marie Livingston Roy in *Alive Now*, 1975, p. 44.

22. Matthew 28:29–30.

23. Ezekiel 3:1–3.

24. Mark 13:28.

25. John Shea, *The Challenge of Jesus* (Chicago: Thomas More, 1976), p. 11.

Chapter Six

1. Alan Jones, *Journey into Christ* (New York: Seabury Press, 1900), p. 53.

2. Sam Keen, *Hymns to an Unknown God* (New York: Bantam Books, 1994).

3. See, for example, the research on this that has been done in Canada by Reginald Bibby, *Fragmented Gods* (Toronto: Irwin Publishing, 1987).

4. *Idem.*

5. John 20:19 and Acts 2:1.

6. Henri Nouwen, *Making All Things New* (New York: Harper and Row, 1981), pp. 89–90.

7. See Paul's definition of the Holy Spirit in Galatians 5:22–25.

8. Roman Catholicism used to have a very simple distinction which was very helpful here. They spoke of the Body of Christ as having both

a *visible* aspect (the historical churches) and an *invisible* aspect (all people of sincere will, regardless of explicit religion).

9. Roman Catholics and Protestants agree on the central point here, namely, that we become church by being called together by the word of Christ and the Eucharist, but they disagree somewhat vis-à-vis which of these, word or Eucharist, has the priority. In Roman Catholic thought (including some Anglican, Episcopalian, and "high" Protestant churches), the Eucharist is the central reason for meeting, and the word feeds the Eucharist. In classical Protestant theology, it is, first and foremost, the word that calls us together, albeit there is also always, at a point, Eucharist.

10. For a very strong example, see the first chapters of the Acts of the Apostles, especially Chapter 2, where (perhaps idyllically) Luke describes how in the early church "all things were held in common."

11. John 21:18.

12. Acts 9:16.

13. Acts 9:8.

14. Genesis 7:16.

15. Carlo Carretto, *I Sought and I Found* (London: Darton, Longmann, Todd, 1984). This is a paraphrase, though fairly close to the original text, rather than an exact rendering.

16. John 14:2.

17. Shea, "The Indiscriminate Host," in *Stories of Faith*.

18. John 12:1–8, and parallel texts.

19. John Powell, *Unconditional Love* (Chicago: Argus Communications, 1976).

20. Ibid., pp. 112–14.

21. Job 1:21.

Chapter Seven

1. John 12:24.

2. See, for example, Philip Rieff's commentary in *The Triumph of the Therapeutic* (New York: Harper Torchbooks, 1996) for an excellent analysis of this.

3. See *Civilization and Its Discontents,* translated by James Strackey (New York: W. W. Norton, 1961).

4. Brian Moore, *The Lonely Passion of Judith Hearne* (Toronto: Little, Brown, 1964). There is also a major motion picture by the same title, starring Maggie Smith as Judith Hearne and quite faithful to the story given in the book.

5. With apologies to Brian Moore, this is a paraphrase, not direct quote, which tries, in caption, to summarize an essence.

6. See 1 Corinthians 12, especially verse 7, which speaks of (as the New Jerusalem Bible translates it) *"particular manifestations* of the spirit." However, all of Chapter 12 really teaches that, as does the general theology of the Holy Spirit in the New Testament.

7. Shea, *Stories of Faith.*

8. 2 Samuel 12:1–24.

9. John 12:24.

10. Judges 11:29–40.

11. See Luke 24:13–35 for Luke's description of how we can walk with God and not recognize that presence (because of how we formerly knew God) and how, in this situation, Jesus paschally restructures the disciples' imagination.

12. Abraham Heschel, *A Passion for Truth* (New York: Farrar, Straus & Giroux, 1973).

13. Henri Nouwen, "On Mourning and Dancing," in *The New Oxford Review,* June 1992.

14. Luke 15:11–32.

15. Miller, *op. cit.*

16. John 20:11–18.

17. Ronald Rolheiser, "Mary Magdala's Easter Prayer," in *Forgotten Among the Lilies,* p. 176.

Chapter Eight

1. A rather loose, but popular, translation of Micah 6:8.

2. Few books have ever explained the concept of social justice for a Christian more clearly, more concisely, and with more faith than does one of Jim Wallis' early works: Jim Wallis, *The Call to Conversion, Recovering the Gospel for Our Times* (San Francisco: Harper and Row, 1981).

3. David R. Weiss, "Putting the Rich on Notice," in *Sojourners,* January-February 1998, pp. 34–35.

4. Matthew 25:31–46.

5. *Idem.* Matthew 25 is clear on this—as are numerous other texts which invite us to make a preferential option for the poor; e.g., Luke 14:12–14.

6. See, for example, Luke 16:19–31 (the parable of the rich man and Lazarus); Luke 18:18–27 (the story of the rich young man and Jesus' admonition regarding how it is very difficult for anyone rich to enter the kingdom of heaven); and Luke 6:20–26 (the Beatitudes).

, Roman Catholics) have
even taken this principle further and have caught that if a person is in
extreme necessity he or she may take from the riches of others what he
or she needs (E.g. *Gaudium et Spes*, document of Vatican II, number
69).

8. Elizabeth A. Johnson, *The Search for the Living God,* John M.
Kelly Lecture of 1994, University of St. Michael's College, Toronto,
printed edition, p. Johnson goes on to say that she sees four develop-
ments within Christian theology and spirituality that hold promise for
the future: a) suffering based theology; b) feminist theology; c) interre-
ligious dialogue; and d) the new dialogue between science and religion.

9. Bailie, *op. cit.,* p. 89.

10. Jim Wallis is the founder of *Sojourners*—a Christian community,
a Christian justice and peace movement, and an international magazine.
The magazine is based in Washington, D.C., but the community and the
justice and peace movement are worldwide.

The principles enunciated here are a paraphrase taken from a set of
retreat talks ("On Peacemaking") that he gave in 1986. These talks, on
audiocassette, can be obtained through Sojourners: Sojourners, 2401
15th Street NW, Washington, D.C. 20009, USA.

11. Gil Bailie submits that this is the connection: "When moral con-
tempt for a form of violence inspires so explicit a replication of it, there
is only one conclusion to be drawn: The moral revulsion the initial
violence awakened proved weaker than the mimetic fascination it inspired." See Bailie, *op. cit.,* p. 89.

12. John 8:3–11.

13. Daniel 13.

14. G. K. Chesterton, *Orthodoxy* (New York: Doubleday, 1959),
p. 100.

15. Daniel Berrigan, in a talk given at the University of Notre Dame.
Available on audiocassette through Ave Maria Press, Notre Dame,
South Bend, Ind. 46556-0428.

16. Recounted by Jim Wallis—see note 10, above.

Chapter Nine

1. Ronald Rolheiser article, "How Children Raise Their Parents,"
in *Western Catholic Reporter,* March 27, 1995.

2. Genesis 2:18.

3. For a further development on this point, I heartily recommend
an article by Sidney Callahan, "Stages in Sexual Development, Adult
Phases," in *Chicago Studies,* vol. 20, Spring 1981, pp. 19–39.

4. Exodus 3:1–6.

5. Albert Camus, quoted by Olivier Todd, *op. cit.*, p. 157.

6. For more development on this see Ronald Rolheiser, "Passion and Purity," in *Against and Infinite Horizon* (London: Hodder & Stoughton, 1995), pp. 39ff.

7. Nouwen, *Making All Things New: An Invitation to the Spiritual Life* (San Francisco: Harper & Row, 1981), pp. 51–53.

8. Luke 20:27–40.

9. Sidney Callahan, "Sex and the Single Catholic," in *Critic*, February 1968, pp. 50–59. (Emphases are my own.)

10. See "From Loneliness to Solitude," in Nouwen, *Reaching Out, The Three Movements of the Spiritual Life*. The starting point for any theology of sexuality is that "it is not good to be alone," that marriage and sexual union are what God intended as the norm.

11. Anita Brookner, *Altered States* (Toronto: Vintage Canada, Random House, 1996), p. 197. That same theme too is very strong in a number of her early books, especially *Brief Lives*.

12. For some of Merton's thoughts on this, see John Howard Griffin, *Follow the Ecstasy: Thomas Merton, The Hermitage Years, 1965–1968* (Fort Worth, Tex.: JGH Editions/Latitudes Press, 1983).

Chapter Ten

1. Henri Nouwen, *Clowning in Rome: Reflections on Solitude, Celibacy, Prayer, and Contemplation* (New York: Doubleday, 1979), pp. 70–71.

2. 1 Kings 19:1–8.

3. Henri Nouwen, *Behold the Beauty of the Lord: Praying with Icons* (Notre Dame, South Bend, Ind.: Ave Maria Press, 1987), p. 11.

4. Attributed to Karl Rahner, a German theologian who died in 1984.

5. Henri Nouwen, early chapters of his book *Intimacy: Essays in Pastoral Psychology* (San Francisco: Harper and Row, 1969).

6. Acts 17:28.

7. Robert Moore is an internationally recognized Jungian psychoanalyst, lecturer, and author. As well, he is an authority on cross-cultural studies, comparative religion, and human spirituality. He is also one of the major architects of masculine spirituality. He is presently at the University of Chicago.

Vis-à-vis the question of the necessity of prayer for the soul, I recommend his series of books on archetypal potentials within the human person (e.g., *King, Warrior, Magician, Lover* (with Douglas Gillette)

(New York: Harper and Row, 1990); but especially a series of talks entitled: *Jungian Psychology and Human Spirituality: Liberation from Tribalism in Religious Life,* available through LIMBUS, P.O. Box 364, Vashon Island, WA 98070.

8. Nouwen, *Gracias! A Latin American Journal* (San Francisco: Harper & Row, 1983), p. 69. (Emphases are my own.)

9. 1 Thessalonians 5:17.

10. Luke 2:51.

11. Luke 22:39–46 and parallel texts.

12. Luke 24:26.

13. Luke 23:34.

14. An axiom of challenge within the language of twelve-step programs.

15. Ruth Burrows, *Guidelines for Mystical Prayer* (Danville, N.J.: Dimension Books, 1980).

16. Mark 3:22–30.

17. John 9:1–40.

18. Matthew 18:20.

19. William Stafford, "A Ritual to Read to Each Other," in *The Rag and Bone Shop of the Heart,* edited by Bly, Meade, and Hillman, p. 233.

20. Julian of Norwich, *op. cit.,* p. 10.

21. Genesis 1.

22. Matthew 3:13–17; Mark 1:9–11; and Luke 3:21–22.

23. Nouwen, *The Return of the Prodigal Son.*

24. Julian of Norwich, *op. cit.,* p. 13.